Official
Cambridge
Exam
Preparation

IELTS
Vocabulary

Up to Band
6.0

D1615102

Pauline Cullen

532 510 88 X

Cambridge University Press
www.cambridge.org/elt

Cambridge Assessment English
www.cambridgeenglish.org

Information on this title: www.cambridge.org/9781108900607

© Cambridge University Press and UCLES 2021

First published 2008

20 19 18 17 16 15 14 13 12 11 10 9 8 7 6 5 4 3 2 1

Printed in Dubai by Oriental Press

A catalogue record for this publication is available from the British Library

The publishers have no responsibility for the persistence or accuracy of URLs
for external or third-party internet websites referred to in this publication, and
do not guarantee that any content on such websites is, or will remain, accurate
or appropriate. Information regarding prices and travel timetables and other
factual information given in this work is correct at the time of first printing but
the publishers do not guarantee the accuracy of such information thereafter.

Contents

Map of the book

Unit number	Title	Topics	Test practice
Unit 1	Growing up	Relationships, families and early learning	Listening Part 1
Unit 2	Mental and physical development	The body, the mind	Speaking Part 2 General Training Writing Task 1
Unit 3	Keeping fit	Diet, health and exercise	General Training Reading Section 1
Unit 4	Lifestyles	Life, leisure	Listening Part 2
Unit 5	Student life	Study, education, research	General Training Reading Section 2
Unit 6	Effective communication	Language, linguistics	Academic Reading
Unit 7	On the move	Tourism, travel	General Training Reading Section 1
Unit 8	Through the ages	Time, history	Listening Part 4
Unit 9	The natural world	Flora and fauna, agriculture	Academic Reading Section 3
Unit 10	Reaching for the skies	Space, the planets	Listening Part 3
Unit 11	Design and innovation	Building, engineering	Academic Reading
Unit 12	Information technology	Telecommunications, computers and technology	Speaking Parts 1, 2, 3
Unit 13	The modern world	Globalisation, changing attitudes and trends	Academic Writing Task 1 (describing a chart)
Unit 14	Urbanisation	Problems and solutions, big city life	Academic Reading Section 3
Unit 15	The green revolution	The environment, climate change and pollution	Academic Writing Task 1 (describing a process)

Unit number	Title	Topics	Test practice
Unit 16	The energy crisis	Natural resources, alternative fuels	Academic Reading
Unit 17	Talking business	Employment, management and marketing	General Training Writing Task 1 Academic Writing Task 2
Unit 18	The law	Crime, punishment	General Training Writing Task 2
Unit 19	The media	The news, fame	General Training Writing Task 1 Academic Writing Task 2
Unit 20	The arts	Art appreciation, the performing arts	Academic Reading

Reference section		
Unit 21	Language building 1	Using a dictionary, word families
Unit 22	Language building 2	Learning vocabulary, collocation
Unit 23	Academic Writing Task 1	Data, graphs and tables, diagrams and processes
Unit 24	Academic Writing Task 2	Linking words, opinion words, register
Unit 25	General Training Writing	Vocabulary for Writing Tasks 1 and 2

Introduction

What does this book aim to do?

This book aims to extend and improve the accuracy of your vocabulary and help you prepare for the IELTS test. Broadening your vocabulary will help in every part of the IELTS test. Each unit introduces vocabulary through listening and reading texts that reflect the materials used in the IELTS test. Learning new words in context can help you to remember them and also helps you to understand their meaning. The book also gives you opportunities to practise new words in IELTS Writing and Speaking, so that they can become part of your active vocabulary.

Who is it aimed at?

The book is designed for students working alone who want to revise and extend their vocabulary, but it can also be used as part of an IELTS preparation course in the classroom, or set as homework by a teacher. It is suitable for both the General Training and the Academic module, and for students from Bands 5 onwards.

What order should I do the units in?

Units 21 to 25 give helpful tips on learning new vocabulary and how to use a dictionary, as well as important information about the writing test that will help you as you study, so it may be a good idea to look at these first. You can work through the vocabulary teaching units (1–20) in any order, but you should study all of the units if you want to broaden your vocabulary and prepare thoroughly for the test.

How do I use the book?

It is best to work through a unit from beginning to end as one exercise may revise the vocabulary from a previous exercise. The test practice sections provide further opportunities to extend your vocabulary, as well as giving you practice in the different sections of the IELTS test.

How are the units organised?

There are 25 units. The first 20 units present and practise vocabulary based on general and academic topics. Each topic is divided into smaller sections. Each unit has three pages of vocabulary exercises based on listening, reading, writing and speaking materials that reflect those found in the IELTS test. In addition, each unit has a test practice activity. The test practice includes examples of all the different tasks in each part of the Academic Reading and General Training tests. These tasks resemble the level and task types found in the real test as closely as possible and can be used for timed test practice.

At the front of the book is a summary of each part of the IELTS test. The last five units of the book provide a general guide to learning and using new vocabulary as well as teaching you useful vocabulary for the different writing sections of the IELTS test. Units 23 and 24 focus on Task 1 and Task 2 of the Academic Module, and Unit 25 deals with Task 1 and Task 2 of the General Training Module. At the end of the book you will also find:

- an answer key for each unit including model answers for each writing task
- recording scripts
- wordlists for each unit

How do I use the wordlists?

There is a wordlist for each unit at the back of the book. Some of these words may be specific to one topic area, but many of them can be found and used in a wide variety of contexts. You may want to divide these wordlists up into groups of ten words to learn at a time. It may be a good idea to study the wordlist before you begin each unit. Alternatively your teacher might use the wordlist as a test or review at the end of each unit (or you could ask a friend to do this). You should be able to understand these words when you read or hear them, but you should also try to extend your active vocabulary by using them as often as possible in your writing and speaking practice. You should learn the correct spellings of these words as well as any words that collocate, or can be used together with them. Use Units 21 and 22 to help you develop good vocabulary learning strategies.

How do I do the writing test practice?

The writing test practice questions give an opportunity to use the vocabulary from the unit. There are model answers in the answer key. Try to write your own answers before looking at the model answer. These can be used as a guide to organising ideas and using vocabulary accurately and effectively. You will be penalised if you produce a learnt essay in the IELTS test, so you should not attempt to do this

How do I do the speaking test practice?

The speaking test practice questions give an opportunity to use the vocabulary from the unit. In part 2 of the speaking test you will be allowed to make notes, so think of any useful vocabulary you could use and write this down to help you as you talk. If possible, you should record your answers and play them back. Consider your pronunciation and intonation as well as the words you used. How could you improve your answer? Ask a friend or a teacher for their comments.

When should I do the vocabulary tests?

There are five tests. Each one tests the vocabulary in five units (Test 1: Units 1–5, Test 2: Units 6–10, Test 3: Units 11–15, Test 4: Units 16–20, Test 5: Units 21–25). When you have finished five units, do the relevant test and mark it. Highlight the questions you got wrong and go back to the units you need to look at again. If you are an advanced student then you may want to do the vocabulary test before you begin the units to see how much you already know. This may help to pinpoint your weak areas so that you can focus on these in the main units (1–20).

When should I use a dictionary?

The aim of the listening and reading activities in each unit is to give you practice in guessing the meaning from context, so you should try to do each exercise without a dictionary first, unless you are instructed to do so. When you have finished, use the *Cambridge Advanced Learner's Dictionary* or another suitable monolingual dictionary to look up any words you don't know. You can also check your answers in the answer key, but you may want to use your dictionary as a further check. Try to be aware of words that you need to look up more than once as these are likely to be key words for you to learn. Write them down with their meanings, together with any example sentences used in the dictionary. A good dictionary will also tell you words that collocate or can be used together with them, it is a good idea to make a note of these as well. Remember that some words have more than one meaning, so check what the unit or exercise is about to make sure you find the correct meaning. Look at Unit 21 if you need more help on how to use a dictionary.

How do I learn and revise vocabulary?

Some of the vocabulary in a unit will be new to you and some will be words you are familiar with, but cannot yet use accurately. Even if you feel you know a word, you may be making collocation mistakes and using the incorrect preposition or verb, for example. You might like to use a notebook and organise your vocabulary under the following categories:

- New words to learn
- Words I need to use more often
- Words I often make mistakes with
- Topic words (e.g. The Environment; Fuel; Energy; Work)

Alternatively, you could simply highlight these words using a different colour highlighter for each category: for example, a blue highlighter for topic words, a red highlighter for words you often make mistakes with, and so on.

Units 21 and 22 will help you to develop good vocabulary learning techniques.

IELTS test summary

Academic module

Academic Reading (1 hour)

This includes the time needed to transfer your answers, there is no extra time given for this

There are three reading passages and 40 questions. The texts are taken from books, journals, magazines and newspapers. They are written for a non-specialist audience but are appropriate for people entering university courses or seeking professional registration. Examples can be found in units 6, 9, 11, 14, 16, 20. Visit the following website for a detailed description of each of the different question types: www.ielts.org

Academic Writing (1 hour)

There are two writing tasks, writing task 1 and writing task 2. You must complete both tasks. Task 2 contributes twice as much as task 1 to your overall writing score.

Task	Timing	Length	What do I have to do?	Assessment	Example units
Task 1	20 minutes	150 words	Describe visual information, e.g. a diagram, chart, graph or table.	• Task achievement • Coherence and cohesion • Lexical resource • Grammatical range and accuracy	7, 13, 15, 23
Task 2	40 minutes	250 words	Write a discursive essay. You may be asked to: discuss and evaluate one opinion and say to what extent you agree with this opinion; discuss and evaluate two differing opinions and give your own opinion; discuss and evaluate the advantages and disadvantages of something; discuss whether a development is positive or negative; evaluate a problem and suggest possible solutions.	• Task response • Coherence and cohesion • Lexical resource • Grammatical range and accuracy	7, 10, 13,1 7, 18, 19, 24

Listening (approximately 30 minutes)

plus 10 minutes to transfer your answers to the answer sheet

There are four parts and 40 questions. In the IELTS listening test you will hear the recording ONCE ONLY. Each section is a little more difficult than the one before. The test is divided up as follows:

Part	What will I hear?	Example units
1	A conversation between two people: e.g. finding out information about travel.	1
2	A monologue or prompted monologue on a general topic, e.g. a radio broadcast.	4
3	A dialogue between two or three people in an academic context, e.g. discussing an essay.	10
4	A monologue in an academic context, e.g. a lecture.	8

There are ten questions for each part. Visit the following website for a detailed description of each of the different question types: www.ielts.org

Speaking (11 to 14 minutes)

In the IELTS speaking test you will be interviewed on your own by one examiner. The interview has three separate parts and is divided up as follows:

Part	Timing	What do I have to do?	Example units	Assessment
1	4–5 mins	Answer questions on familiar topics, e.g. hobbies, daily routine.	12	• Fluency and coherence
2	3–4 mins	You are given a card with a topic (e.g. describe a good friend) and some suggestions for what to say on it. You have one minute to make notes. You then talk about the topic for one to two minutes.	2, 12, 15	• Lexical resource • Grammatical range and accuracy
3	4–5 mins	Answer more abstract questions about the topic, e.g. **How important is friendship?**	12	• Pronunciation

General Training module

Candidates for the General Training module take the same listening and speaking test as the Academic module. Only the reading and writing papers are different.

General Training Reading (1 hour)

This includes the time needed to transfer your answers, there is no extra time given for this

The General Training reading paper has three sections each of increasing difficulty. The sections are organised as follows:
Visit the following website for a detailed description of each of the different question types: www.ielts.org

Section	Reading texts	Example units
1	Two or three short texts or several shorter texts, e.g. advertisements.	3, 7
2	Two texts giving work-related information, e.g. information about how to apply for a job.	5
3	One long text.	9, 14

General Training Writing (1 hour)

There are two writing tasks, writing task 1 and writing task 2. You must answer both tasks. Task 2 contributes twice as much as task 1 to your overall writing score.

Task	Timing	Length	What do I have to do?	Assessment	Example units
Task 1	20 minutes	150 words	Write a letter in response to a given situation.	• Task achievement • Coherence and cohesion • Lexical resource • Grammatical range and accuracy	2, 17, 25
Task 2	40 minutes	250 words	Write a discursive essay. You may be asked to: discuss an opinion and say whether you agree or disagree with this opinion; discuss and evaluate two differing opinions and give your own opinion; discuss and evaluate the advantages and disadvantages of something; discuss whether a development is positive or negative; evaluate a problem and suggest possible solutions.	• Task response • Coherence and cohesion • Lexical resource • Grammatical range and accuracy	7,10, 13, 17, 18, 19, 25

1 Growing up

Relationships, families and early learning

Relationships

1.1 Look at the following topics and decide whether you would discuss them with

A   your family   B   your friends   C   a teacher

1   a study problem   3   buying something expensive

2   your favourite music   4   the last film you saw

1.2 **1a** Listen to four people talking about the topics above. Write the number of the topic (1–4) from the list above and the person/ people the speakers say they would talk to about this. Write the words that helped you decide.

Speaker	Topic (1–4)	Words that helped you	Person/people they would talk to
A	4	movies, latest releases	classmates
B			
C			
D			

> ### Vocabulary note
>
> Group together words that are similar in meaning or form, e.g. *adulthood, brotherhood, fatherhood*. NB -hood is used to form a noun and shows something belongs to a particular group or has reached a particular stage (*adulthood* = the stage of being an adult).

1.3 **1a** Listen again and decide which of the speakers (A–D) the sentences apply to.

1   The relationship between my brother and me is very close. .....C.....

2   I have a lot more in common with my friends than with my family. ....

3   I have established a close connection with an older member of my family. ....

4   The relationship between my parents and me has broken down. ....

1.4 COLLOCATION Learn words that go together naturally. Complete the sentences using words and phrases from the recording and the statements in 1.3.

1   My sister and I have totally different tastes. In fact we don't <u>have</u> much .... at all.

2   There is a very <u>close</u> .... <u>between</u> a mother and a newborn baby.

3   It is important to .... <u>a</u> good working <u>relationship</u> .... your work colleagues.

4   A relationship can easily .... if you don't work at it.

5   I really admire the <u>relationship</u> .... my mother and my grandmother.

6   There can be a lot of .... <u>between</u> teenagers and their parents.

Families and early learning

2.1 Scan the text below and underline these words:

rewarding   sibling   relate   accommodating   adolescence   interaction   nurture

Study links early friendships with high-quality sibling relationships

Children who experience a rewarding friendship before the birth of a sibling are likely to have a better relationship with that brother or sister that endures throughout their childhood, said Laurie Kramer in a University of Illinois study published in December's *Journal of Family Psychology*.

'When early friendships are successful, young children get the chance to master sophisticated social and emotional skills, even more than they do with a parent. When parents relate to a child, they do a lot of the work, figuring out what the child needs and then accommodating those needs,' says Kramer. However, this is not usually the case when two children are interacting.

The research showed that the benefits of early friends are long-lasting. 'Children who had a positive relationship with a best friend before the birth of a sibling ultimately had a good relationship with their sibling that lasted throughout adolescence,' Kramer said. 'And children who as preschoolers were able to coordinate play with a friend, manage conflicts, and keep an interaction positive in tone were most likely as teenagers to avoid the negative sibling interaction that can sometimes launch children on a path of anti-social behavior,' she added. 'From birth, parents can nurture and help develop these social competencies (or skills) by making eye contact with their babies, offering toys and playing with them,' she said.

2.2 Read the text and match the words you have underlined to the following definitions.

1 help someone/something develop and grow ....

2 agreeing to a demand ....

3 brother or sister ....

4 respond to somebody ....

5 the stage between childhood and adulthood ....

6 giving a lot of pleasure ....

7 communication ....

> **Vocabulary note**
>
> Look for familiar words in longer words to work out their meaning, e.g. cor**relation** (one thing is linked with another); inter**related** (the relationship between two or more things). NB The prefix co-, (**co**rrelation or **co**operate) often means *with* or *together*. The prefix inter- (**inter**act or **inter**city) often means *between*.

2.3 Read the text again and say whether these sentences are true (T) or false (F). Underline the part of the text that gave you your answer.

1 If young children have good friends then they will have a good relationship with their brother or sister. ....

2 Parents help their children develop more social and emotional skills than friends do. ....

3 Friends will give you what you want more often than your parents do. ....

4 Teenagers who fight with their brothers or sisters may behave in a way that is socially unacceptable. ....

5 If parents play with their children more then they will learn how to be more sociable. ....

2.4 A lot of words connected with families and relationships can also be used in a different context. Complete the sentences with a word from the box.

adopt	nurture	relationship
conflict	related	relative
family	relation	

1 The wolf is a member of the dog ....

2 The company decided to .... a new approach to staff recruitment.

3 The study found a strong .... between a lack of friends and sibling rivalry.

4 Whether you think the price of goods is high is .... to the amount of money you earn.

5 Studies have shown that stress in adulthood can be .... to an unhappy childhood.

6 Good teachers identify the talents of their students and .... them.

7 This evidence seems to .... with the findings from previous studies.

8 I am writing in .... to the job advertisement in yesterday's paper.

3.1 COMPOUND NOUNS Match the words in box A with the words in box B to make 10 compound nouns. You will need to use some words more than once.

A	active	family	maternal	sibling	stable
	extended	immediate	physical	striking	

B	family	instinct	rivalry	upbringing
	gatherings	resemblance	role	

3.2 🔊 1b Think about your answers to these questions. Then listen to a student's answers and tick the phrases you hear in 3.1.

1 Tell me about your family.

2 Who are you most similar to in your family?

3 What do you think it takes to be a good parent?

3.3 🔊 1b Listen again and find the words that match these definitions.

1 caring and supportive ....

2 the emotional connection between people or places ....

3 similar ....

4 a person's nature or character ....

5 determined to an unreasonable degree ....

6 received (a characteristic) from a parent or grandparent ....

3.4 Now practise answering the questions fully. Record your answers, if possible.

Error warning

Note the following common errors: I am writing **in relation to** your job advertisement. NOT in relation of ... . My **relationship with** my parents is very strong. NOT My relation with my parents ...

Vocabulary note

Note these collocations with the word *relationship*.
Verbs: **build** a relationship, **develop** a relationship, **establish** a relationship, **form** a relationship, **have** a relationship
Adjectives: a **close** relationship, a **long-standing** relationship, a **working** relationship, a **successful** relationship
Prepositions: a relationship **with** someone, a relationship **between** two things or people (NOT relationship to someone)

Test practice

Test tip

You may not hear exactly the same words as you see on the question paper, so you need to listen for paraphrases. If you miss an answer, go on to the next one. Remember that the questions are in the same order as the information in the recording. For notes completion items make sure you stick to the word limit given and check your spelling at the end.

Listening Part 1

 1c

Questions 1–10

Complete the form below using NO MORE THAN TWO WORDS AND/OR A NUMBER for each answer.

Ascot Child-Care Centre
Enrolment form

Personal details

Family name: .... *Cullen* ....

Child's first name: (1) ....

Age: (2) ....

Birthday: (3) ....

Other children in the family: a brother aged (4) ....

Address: (5) ...., Maidstone

Emergency contact number: 3467 8890

Relationship to child: (6) ....

Development

- Has difficulty (7) .... during the day
- Is able to (8) .... herself

Child-care arrangements

Days required: (9) .... and ....

Pick-up time: (10) ....

---

2 Mental and physical development

The body, the mind

The body

1.1 **How old were you when you first learned to**

A crawl ....

B walk ....

C talk ....

D ride a bike ....

E read ....

F tie a shoelace? ....

1.2 **2a** You will hear a talk about early development in children. Listen and complete the table below.
Write NO MORE THAN TWO WORDS for each answer.

Stage	Social and emotional milestones	Physical milestones	Cognitive and communicative milestones
Infant	• likes to mimic • tries to see how parents react to their (1)	• can sit and stand without help	• can use basic words and (2) .... • uses objects for their intended purpose
(3)	• is more (4) .... • takes turns	is able to • run • (5) .... things • ride a tricycle	• greater understanding of language • uses (6) .... in play
Middle childhood	• the (7) .... has a greater impact on development • some children appear grown up, others are (8)	• growth is not as (9) .... as in earlier stages • (10) .... and (11) .... are the same size as in adulthood	• good reading and writing (12) ....

1.3 **2a** Listen to the talk again and find words that mean the same as the following.

1 learned (a skill) ....

2 copying people ....

3 without help ....

4 in a natural, unforced way ....

5 developed a skill to a high level ....

6 phase (2 words) ....

1.4 WORD BUILDING Complete the table.

Verb	Noun	Adjective
develop		
grow		fully-
		mature

2.1 **Read this text about development in adolescence. Then complete the following sentences with words from the text.**

The final stage before adulthood is adolescence. This is a period of transition for teenagers and there are many crucial milestones. Socially and emotionally, teens worry that they may not be developing at the same rate as their peers. They become extremely self-conscious and may be overly sensitive about their appearance. Teens may rebel against their parents but are also more able to accept the consequences of their actions.

This is also a period of enormous physical change and adolescents experience changes in their physical development at a rate unparalleled since infancy. These changes include significant gains in height and weight. Within a year, boys and girls can gain an average of 4.1 inches and 3.5 inches in height respectively. This growth spurt typically occurs two years earlier for girls than for boys and can tend to make both sexes go through a clumsy phase. In terms of their cognitive development, adolescents have greater reasoning skills and have developed the ability to think logically and hypothetically. They are also able to discuss more abstract concepts. They should also have developed strategies to help them study.

1   First-year students often struggle with the ......*transition*...... from high school to university.

2   The .... at which a change occurs can cause problems for both the very young and the elderly.

3   It can be less stressful to make a presentation to your .... than to your teachers.

4   The increase in violence among young people may be a .... of watching too much violence on TV and in video games.

5   Petrol prices are increasing at a speed that is ....

6   Teenagers .... rebel against their parents between the ages of 14 and 16.

7   In part three of the speaking test you are expected to be able to talk about more .... topics.

8   Infinity is a very difficult .... for children to grasp.

2.2 **What stage would you associate the following words and phrases with? Write the words in the correct column below.**

crawling	immature
irresponsible	nurturing
overindulgent	overprotective
patient	rebellious
throw a tantrum	tolerant
unsteady	

Childhood	Parenthood
clumsy	mature

Vocabulary note

The prefix *im-* is often in front of adjectives beginning with *b*, *m* or *p* to form the opposite or to show that something is lacking: **im**mature, **im**possible. Similarly, *ir-* often comes in front of words beginning with *r*, *il-* often comes in front of words beginning with *l* and *in-* in front of other words: **ir**responsible, **il**legal, **in**sensitive. However, there are exceptions: *unbelievable, displeased, unlikely, unpopular* etc. The prefix *over-* can also be negative, meaning too much: *overdeveloped, overdue, overcrowded, oversensitive.*

Error warning

Grow can be used with plants: *We could grow flowers and trees here.* Or with things: *The business is growing rapidly.* But *grow up* can only be used with people or cities: *The city grew up from a small group of houses near the river. Grow up* is intransitive, which means you can't use it with an object. NOT ~~*The government grew up the city.*~~

2.3 Many words used to talk about human growth can also be used to talk about data and statistics. Complete the sentences with a suitable word from the text in 2.1. You may need to change the form of the words.

1 The p............................... of greatest stability occurred between 1985 and 1990.

2 The greatest period of g............................... was in 2014.

3 The figures g............................... from 2,500 to 6,000 in 2017.

4 The company g............................... an extra 2,000 employees in 2015.

5 Sales increased at a significant r............................... between 2010 and 2015.

6 The number of migrants rose s............................... from 1990 to 2010.

The mind

3 Match the phrases in A with the definitions in B.

A

1 keep an open mind

2 bear in mind

3 have something in mind

4 have something on your mind

5 my mind went blank

6 it slipped my mind

7 put your mind at ease

8 broaden the mind

B

A increase your knowledge

B I forgot

C I couldn't remember a thing

D remember

E try not to judge before you know the facts

F be worried about something

G have an idea

H stop you from worrying

4.1 Think about your answers to these questions.

1 What do you remember about your early childhood?

2 Do you think you have a good memory or a poor memory?

4.2 🔊 2b Now listen to a student answering the questions in 4.1 and make a note of all of the words and phrases connected with memory.

remember, memories,

....

....

....

Error warning

Remember = to have a memory in your mind. *I **remember** my first day at school.*
Remind = to help someone or something to remember something. *Remind* is not usually used with the subject *I*. *It reminds me of when I lived in Egypt.* NOT *I remind of when.* *You remind me of my sister.* NOT *I remind me of.*

4.3 Correct the vocabulary mistakes in these sentences.

1 I will always ~~memory~~ how beautiful the sunset was on that day. ....remember.......

2 I have very fond reminders of my school days. ....

3 Could you remember me to buy some bread on the way home? ....

4 At school we always had to memory long lists of vocabulary. ....

5 I remind how happy our childhood was. ....

Test practice

Speaking Part 2

> Describe a memorable period or event from your childhood.
>
> **You should say:**
> * **what the event or period was**
> * **what happened during this event or time**
> * **why it was memorable and what you learned from this experience.**
>
> **You will have to talk about the topic for 1–2 minutes. You have 1 minute to think about what you are going to say. You can make notes if you wish.**

....
....
....
....
....
....

General Training Writing Task 1

You should spend about 20 minutes on this task.

You are travelling on an important business trip and realise you have left something important behind in one of the hotels you stayed in.

Write a letter to the manager of the hotel. In your letter
* **explain what has happened**
* **say why the thing you left behind is important**
* **tell the manager what you would like him / her to do about this**

Write at least 150 words.

You do **NOT** need to write any addresses.

Begin your letter as follows:

Dear ...

3 Keeping fit

Diet, health and exercise

Diet

1.1 **Answer these questions.**

1 How healthy are you? A very healthy B moderately healthy C unhealthy?

2 Tick the appropriate column below to show how often you eat the different foods.

I eat ...	at least once a day	a few times a week	once a week	rarely / never
cakes or chocolate				
fried fast foods				
fish				
fruit				
meat				
vegetables				

1.2 **Complete the gaps in the text below using words from the box.**

factors   ingredients   maintain   nutrients   overeating   overweight   servings   variety

How to improve your diet

- Make sure that you eat a (1).. of foods. It is important to eat from all five food groups.
- Eat plenty of fruit and vegetables. These contain vital (2).. and leading dietitians recommend eating at least two (3).. of fruit and three of vegetables every day.
- Try to (4).. a healthy weight. Being too thin can cause as many health problems as being (5).. Remember, the correct weight for you depends on many different (6).., including your age, height and sex.
- Eat moderate portions and don't be tempted to order a larger size when eating out. Skipping meals can lead to (7).. as you will be much hungrier later, so be sure to eat regularly if you want to curb your appetite.
- You don't need to eliminate all of your favourite foods but do check the (8).. on food labels and make sure that you reduce your intake of foods that are high in fats, sugar and salt.
- If you have a food allergy, make sure you avoid any of the ingredients that can trigger an attack.

1.3 **Match these words and phrases with words from the advice in 1.2.**

1 very important ....

2 food scientists ....

3 neither small nor large ....

4 servings ....

5 missing out on ....

6 limit ....

7 desire to eat ....

8 totally remove ....

9 a condition that causes illness if you eat certain foods ....

10 activate ....

Health and exercise

2.1 🎧 **3a** **You will hear part of a health talk. Listen and complete the summary below. Write NO MORE THAN TWO WORDS.**

The heart is a (1).. . A diet high in (2).. can slow down the (3).. and lead to heart problems. A heart attack is caused when an artery that (4).. to the heart becomes (5).. . Patients must be given (6).. immediately. A stroke is caused when there is a blockage in an artery that leads to the (7).. . A stroke can have a major effect on your body and as yet there is no (8).. . A healthy diet will keep your arteries (9).. and can lower the (10).. of a stroke or heart attack.

> ### 🔖 Vocabulary note
>
> The following words are often used with the word *health*.
> Nouns: *health* **benefits**, *health* **risks**, *health* **problems**, *health* **care**, *health* **education**, *health* **system**
> Adjectives: **in good** *health*, **in poor** *health*, **in excellent** *health*
> We can use *healthy* to describe things other than your body: *a healthy* **appetite**, *a healthy* **diet**, *a healthy* **economy**, *a healthy* **disrespect for authority**

2.2 🎧 **3b** **Now listen to part 2 of the talk and answer the questions.**

1 Write down three types of aerobic exercise that are mentioned: ....

2 Listen again and find words that mean the same as the following:

A in a fixed pattern ....*regular*........

B quickly ....

C little by little ....

D a strong suggestion ....

E speed ....

F doing something to excess ....

G get better ....

H do one thing then another thing and then the first thing again, etc ....

> ### ⚠️ Error warning
>
> Note that *health* is a noun and *healthy* is the adjective. We write or talk about *education and* **health** or *mental* **health**. NOT ~~education and healthy~~ or ~~mental healthy~~. We say someone is *strong and* **healthy** NOT ~~strong and health~~.

> ### 🔖 Vocabulary note
>
> *-tion* at the end of a word usually indicates that the word is a noun: ac*tion*, repeti*tion*.
> *-tious* indicates an adjective: repeti*tious*.

3 **WORD BUILDING Complete the table below. You do not need to write anything in the shaded areas. Write the opposites too, where indicated (*opp.*).**

Noun	Verb	Adjective
allergy		
benefit		
harm		
		opp. =
health		
		opp. =
infection		
	opp. =	

Noun	Verb	Adjective
nutrition		
		obese
	prevent	
		recommended
variety		

4.1 PRONUNCIATION 🔊 3c **Put the words into the correct box according to their sound, then practise saying the words. Listen and check your answers.**

b̶a̶t̶h̶, b̶a̶t̶h̶e̶, birth, breath, breathe, death, growth, health, mouth (v), mouth (n), teeth, teethe, writhe

θ *(an unvoiced sound as in **th**ink)*	ð *(a voiced sound as in **th**is)*
bath	*bathe*

4.2 🔊 3d **Complete the sentences with words from 4.1. Then listen to the recording to check your answers. Practise saying the sentences.**

1   I took a deep .... before diving into the water.

2   The baby is crying because he's .... He got two new .... only yesterday.

3   Old people should take care of their ....

4   He's been so happy since the .... of his son.

5   The pain was so bad she was .... in agony.

6   He can't .... You need to get him to hospital.

5   **Improve this essay by replacing the words in *italics* with ONE OR TWO words from this unit.**

In the future we won't have to worry about what we eat. We'll just take a tablet to give us all that our body needs and cooking will become a thing of the past.

In our modern world we often look for quick solutions to our problems. We expect to be able to achieve a great deal with little effort. But I don't believe we can apply this notion to our diet and still remain healthy. Preparing a healthy meal can take a lot of time. First you need to have fresh ingredients. Pre-packaged foods can contain a lot of unhealthy additives and so they are not as [1] *good for your body* as fresh food. You also need to make sure to include a [2] *lot of different* foods to make sure that you receive all of the vitamins and minerals that are [3] *very, very important* to a healthy diet. It is not surprising, then, that some people want to find a simple solution to this in the form of a pill. Fast foods are very high in fat, sugar and salt and so we should eat them in small amounts. For some people, however, these foods have become their staple diet and as a result they are [4] *fat*. If we want to [5] *stop* this from becoming an even bigger problem in the future then we need to address this situation now. While vitamin tablets may be of some benefit, they are unlikely to be effective in the fight against [6] *people getting too fat.*

Health authorities need to increase public awareness of these issues, but we also need to be realistic. Fast food is popular not only because it is convenient but also because it is tasty. Perhaps we should [7] *strongly advise* that people who eat fast food every day should at least [8] *swap* fast food with fresh food *on every second day*. Finally, we eat for pleasure as well as nutrition and for this reason I believe that pills will never replace freshly-cooked food.

1   ....*nutritious*........   3   5   7   ....

2   4   6   8   ....

6   **Answer the questions. Write one or two sentences.**

1   Do you think young people are more or less fit than 50 years ago? (Why? / Why not?)

....

2   In what way is your diet different from when you were a young child?

....

3   What changes do you think will occur in our diet in the future?

....

Test practice

General Training Reading Section 1

Questions 1–9

The text below has five sections, A–E.

For which home exercise equipment are the following true?

Write the correct letter, A–E, next to questions 1–9.

***NB** You may use any letter more than once.*

Home exercise equipment

If you like the idea of working out in the comfort of your own home, our latest review looks at what's new in home exercise equipment.

A **The Ellipsis 45** works with an up-and-down motion which feels a bit like skiing or climbing stairs. The machine provides a great workout that the joints. You can alter the resistance manually, however, the highest setting doesn't require a lot of effort, so you'll need to use it longer to get a good workout if you are used to something more demanding.

B The **Rower 2000** works the muscles in the back, arms, and legs simultaneously, this is as close to a complete workout as possible from one machine. Unless you're an avid rower, the motions of rowing can feel strange, and some people may find it hard on the back. However, if you love rowing, you'll love using this machine because the pulley system offers a very realistic rowing experience.

C **The Stepper 360**. These machines offer a lower-impact workout that's a little like climbing stairs, but beginners may struggle and find this stepper machine exhausting. Also, if you suffer from painful joints, you should probably avoid this one as the motion can put stress on the knees. The best versions are equipped with handrails and wide pedals for your feet, but sadly this one doesn't and feels a little unstable and flimsy.

D The **Rayley Pro** is a nice looking exercise bike. The great benefit of these is that there's no special training needed to operate it, just be warned that it's not ideal for longer training sessions. While riding isn't as effective in preventing bone weakening diseases like osteoporosis as weight-bearing exercise, it's a great example of excellent cardio workout. This model has a fairly hard seat, but if you prefer, there's a softer cushioned version you can buy separately.

E The **Roadstar** is a traditional treadmill that enables you to walk or run in the comfort of your own home. The basic models don't seem to run very smoothly, so, although it's quite a lot more expensive, it's best to go for the motorized version. All models have an emergency stop device so there are no worries there, and the speed and grade are adjustable, so you can set it to a more suitable pace for you.

1   It is best to use it for a short period of time.

2   Some people may think it is not challenging enough.

3   It is not good for those with certain joint problems.

4   You can exercise all parts of the body at the same time.

5   The electric model is best.

6   It can be hard work if you are not used to exercise.

7   You can buy an extra part to make it more comfortable.

8   At first, the movement may feel unusual for some people.

9   This machine does not feel very safe.

A Guide to Using the Medical Services in the District of Hightown

When to go to the hospital emergency department (A&E)

Many hospitals have an Accident and Emergency Department, also known as A&E. These departments deal with genuine emergencies only. Less severe injuries can be treated in an Urgent Care Centre. It's important to remember that A&E departments are not an alternative to visiting your doctor's surgery. If your local surgery is closed, you can phone 100 for medical advice. Alternatively, you can visit one of our Walk-in Centres, which can treat minor illnesses, be aware that there can be a wait during busy periods. Visit our website to find the nearest centre to you.

What happens at A&E?

If you arrive at hospital by ambulance, the ambulance crew will provide the relevant details to reception and hand you over to the clinical staff. If you're seriously ill, the staff will already know because the ambulance crew will have alerted them on the way in. If you're not in a serious condition, you'll be prioritised by the A&E hospital team along with other patients waiting to be seen. It is important to note that arriving by ambulance does not necessarily mean you'll be seen sooner than patients who take themselves to A&E.

If you go to A&E by yourself, you'll need to register at the reception first, then you'll be asked to wait until you're called for assessment by a nurse or doctor. This process is called triage and ensures people with the most serious conditions are seen first. What happens next depends on the results of your assessment. If the nurse or doctor feels your situation is not a serious accident or emergency, you may be sent to an Urgent Care centre, sent home and advised to see your usual doctor, or you may be given a prescription and sent home. In all cases, the hospital will inform your doctor that you have been to A&E.

Test tip

True / False / Not Given questions – False means that the information in the question is factually wrong. *Not Given* means that the information in the statement is impossible to check because it is not mentioned in the text. Use the questions to help guide you through the reading passage. Look for clues in the questions to find the correct part of the passage then read this section carefully.

Questions 10–14

Do the following statements agree with the information given in the text?

Next to question 10 – 14, write

TRUE	*if the statement agrees with the information*
FALSE	*is the statement contradicts the information*
NOT GIVEN	*if there is no information on this*

10 An Urgent Care Centre handles the most serious accidents.

11 It is best to phone ahead to check if the Walk-in Centre is busy.

12 Patients arriving at A&E by ambulance are always treated first.

13 Some patients at A&E may be transferred to another location for treatment.

14 You need to tell your doctor if you are seen by medical staff in a hospital.

4 Lifestyles

Life, leisure

Life

1.1 Think about how you would answer the following questions.

1 Do you think people work too much nowadays?

2 What do you like to do to relax?

3 What is your idea of a perfect day?

4 How would you describe your attitude to life?

1.2 🎧 4a Now listen to four people answering these questions and decide which of the words in the box best describes each speaker.

pessimist   realist   optimist   risk-taker

Speaker 1 ....   Speaker 3 ....

Speaker 2 ....   Speaker 4 ....

1.3 🎧 4a Listen to the speakers again and complete the following phrases.

Speaker 1	work hard for .... ; .... anything in your life; life has its ....
Speaker 2	live life on .... ; feel .... ; your quality ....
Speaker 3	have a .... attitude; life is full of ....
Speaker 4	have a positive........................... ; live life to .... ; .... a happy life

1.4 Make a note of any of these words and phrases that apply to you and then answer the questions in 1.1 again.

....

....

....

2 COLLOCATION **Complete the words or phrases in the sentences with** *life* **or** *living*. **Which answers are written as one word?**

1 Going to Egypt and seeing the pyramids was a *once in a* ....*time* opportunity for me.

2 The *standard of* .... in my country is very good; there are not many poor people there.

3 In my job as a nurse I get to meet people from *all walks of* ....

4 For me, being a vegetarian is not just about diet, it has become *a way of* ....

5 Many people only think about bills they need to pay and forget to allow for everyday .... *expenses* when they calculate a budget.

6 It was a ....*long* ambition of mine to travel to the Arctic Circle and see the Northern Lights.

7 A rise in petrol prices inevitably leads to a rise in the *cost of* ....

8 The happiest people are those who have found a way to *make a* .... from their hobby.

Leisure

3.1 **Read the text and decide whether the sentences below are true or false. Match the words in bold in the sentences with one of the underlined words or phrases in the text.**

'Leisure activity isn't just for fun,' says a University of Florida psychologist who has developed a scale that classifies hobbies based on needs they satisfy in people. The scale can help people find more personal fulfilment by giving them insight into what they really like. 'The surprising thing is that activities you might think are very different have similar effects on people,' said Howard E.A. Tinsley, the UF psychology professor who developed the measurement. 'Probably no one would consider acting to have the same characteristics as roller-skating or playing baseball, but men and women who act as a hobby report feeling an intense sense of belonging to a group, much the same way others do in playing sports.'

And activities providing the strongest sense of competition are not sports, but card, arcade and computer games, he found. Participating in soccer satisfies people's desire for a sense of 'belonging' and coin collecting and baking fulfil their need for 'creativity'. 'With so many people in jobs they don't care for, leisure is a prized aspect of people's lives,' Tinsley said. 'Yet it's not something psychologists really study. Economists tell us how much money people spend skiing, but nobody explains why skiing really appeals to people; or how one activity relates to another, perhaps in unexpected ways,' Tinsley said. 'Fishing, generally considered more of an outdoor recreational activity, for example, is a form of self-expression like quilting or stamp collecting, because it gives people the opportunity to express some aspect of their personality by doing something completely different from their daily routine,' he said.

1 Both acting and roller-skating give people a **strong feeling** of being part of a team. *True – intense sense*

2 **Taking part in** sports gives you the strongest **desire to win**. ....

3 Collecting things **satisfies people's desire** for **making things**. ....

4 Researchers already know why a hobby **attracts** a person. ....

5 Fishing allows you to show the **type of person you are**. ....

3.2 Now look at the remaining words and phrases that have been underlined in the text and match them to these definitions.

1 a feeling of doing what you have always wanted to do ....

2 a deep understanding ....

3 a feature ....

4 something that is done for enjoyment in your free time. (x3) ....

5 things you do every day ....

4.1 COLLOCATION Match the verbs with nouns from the box. You may use the words more than once.

achieve < *a goal* / *a balance*

make < *a living* / .... / .... / ....

meet ....

miss < ....

play ....

put ....

set ....

take < .... / ....

a need	a goal
a balance	a living
a choice	a role
a change	an opportunity
a chance	pressure (on)
a decision	

4.2 Correct the 14 vocabulary mistakes in the text.

Although we have a better standard of living nowadays, in many ways our quality of life is not as good as in the past because we are always too busy to enjoy what we have.

Everyday life today is much more complicated than in the past. Even in our leisure time we have to ~~take~~ so many choices about what to do or even what to watch on TV. We are often spoilt for choice and this can leave us feeling confused and dissatisfied. We all know that it is important to get a balance between work and play, but many of us do not succeed. Instead, we make extra pressure for ourselves by trying to be as successful in our work life as in our personal life.

Life in the past was much simpler as many people worked to get their basic needs. Today, for many of us, our job is not just a way of making a life. For many, work is an important role in our everyday life and gives us a strong sense of personal fulfilment. What is more, we have become much more materialistic. Many people get themselves goals such as buying a new house or car and so we measure our success by the material things we own. Desiring these luxuries is what motivates us to work much harder than in the past, so in many ways we choice this way of life.

We have worked hard to improve our standard of living, but it may have come at a very high price. We need to take some changes in our priorities so that family occasions are as important as business meetings. We should also make every possible opportunity to relax and enjoy our leisure time. Once you have given the decision to do this, you should find that your quality of life also improves. My ultimate aim is to have a happy family life. If I get this goal then I know I will not regret any chances I have lost to stay longer at the office.

1 *make*   6 ....   11 ....

2 ....   7 ....   12 ....

3 ....   8 ....   13 ....

4 ....   9 ....   14 ....

5 ....   10 ....

Test practice

Listening Part 2

 4b

Questions 1–3

Choose the correct letter, **A**, **B** or **C**.

School holiday activities

1   What does Julie say about the start of the school holidays?
  A   Children may be missing their friends.
  B   This is when children need the most rest.
  C   It is the best time to plan for going back to school.

2   What advice does Julie give about visiting the zoo?
  A   arrive as early as you can
  B   buy tickets before you go
  C   plan your route around the zoo.

3   Julie says that libraries are ideal for
  A   visiting once a week.
  B   accessing computers.
  C   finishing school projects.

Questions 4–10

What comment does the speaker make about each of the following suggested activities?

Choose **SEVEN** answers from the box and write the correct letter, **A–J**, next to questions 4–10.

Comments

  A   it can be messy
  B   takes a while to see results
  C   not suitable for young children
  D   older children may get bored
  E   it's educational
  F   a nice relaxing activity
  G   needs quite a bit of preparation
  H   will suit people with the right skills
  I   requires some technology
  J   children can work alone

Suggested activities

  4   Crafty kids
  5   Making a lava lamp
  6   Treasure hunt
  7   Story time
  8   Kitchen time
  9   Sport and fitness day
  10   Gardening

5 Student life

Study, education, research

Study

1.1 **Before you read the text, answer these questions.**

1 Do you prefer to study
  A at school or college   B in a library   C at home?

2 Do you study best
  A early in the morning   B during the day   C at night?

3 Do you prefer to work
  A with friends   B with background music   C in silence?

1.2 **Now complete the text with the correct form of the verbs in the box. There may be more than one possible answer so try to use each verb once only.**

concentrate   do   learn   overcome   organise   study   take   teach   review   revise

Even the most studious among you will probably have difficulty studying at some stage in your academic career. If or when this happens, the only way to (1)........................ this problem is to go back to basics. First, make sure you have a comfortable environment to (2)........................ in. Some students need to have a quiet space to themselves and can't (3)........................ if there are too many distractions. Others need some sort of background noise, such as music or the company of friends. Whatever your personal preference is, you need to (4)........................ this first of all. Next, make sure you have all of the equipment or tools that you need. For example, if you are (5)........................ a geography course and you have to (6)........................ about countries and their capital cities then you will need to have your atlas to hand. If you're (7)........................ your maths homework then be sure to find your calculator, ruler, protractor and compass before you start. Perhaps you're not preparing a homework assignment or project, but are trying to (8)........................ for an exam. If so, you need to know exactly what is on your curriculum. You should also (9)........................ your notes and make sure that you have a clear understanding of what your lecturers have (10)........................ you. Of course, people with a learning disorder such as dyslexia may need to work harder than others at their studies as they often struggle to read even relatively simple texts.

1.3 **Now read the text again and find a word or phrase to match these definitions.**

1 describes someone who studies a lot   ....

2 things that stop you from working   ....

3 a sound you can hear, but do not actively listen to   ....

4 two different types of homework or school task   .... and ....

5 to study for an exam   ....

6 another word for *syllabus*   ....

7 to check your work   ....

8 to do something with great difficulty   ....

1.4 Underline the correct words in each sentence.

1 I would really like to <u>learn about</u> / study about the ancient Egyptians.

2 We need to find out / know where to buy the tickets for the concert.

3 I got into trouble at school because I didn't know / find out my multiplication tables.

4 I did well in the test because I had known / learned how to spell all of the words on the list.

5 Excuse me, do you find out / know where the nearest post office is?

6 It was difficult for me to learn / study at home, because we didn't have a lot of space.

7 I want to learn how / study how to drive a car.

8 I think you can only really learn from / learn with experience.

> **Error warning**
>
> *Know* = already have the information; *find out* = get the information.
>
> *Study* = learn about a subject through books / a course: *I'm studying law; I'm studying for my exams*. We don't use any other prepositions after *study*. NOT ~~I am studying about law.~~
>
> *Learn* = get new knowledge or skills: *I'm learning English; I'm learning to knit*. Note that we say you are *taking a course*, NOT ~~learning a course.~~
>
> NB Prepositions after *learn*: learn about, learn from, learn to: *I learned a lot from this course*. NOT ~~I learned a lot with this course.~~

Education

2.1 🅖 5a Replace the words in *italics* below with ONE word. Then listen to the recording and check your answers.

Teacher Can you tell me about your early education?

Student Well, I went to ¹ *a school for very young children* from the age of four and I remember that I didn't enjoy it very much at all. My ² *from the age of 5 to 11* school was a little better, especially because my mum was a teacher in the school. She taught in the ³ *younger part of the* school and she was actually my teacher in first ⁴ *level*, but when I went up to the ⁵ *older part of the* school I didn't see very much of her. After that I was lucky enough to

receive a ⁶ *chance to go to school without paying fees* for a very good ⁷ *from age 11 to 18* school. My parents couldn't have afforded to send me to a ⁸ *not free* school so it was a really great opportunity for me. It was a ⁹ *only for one sex* school, so there were no boys. I'm glad I didn't go to a ¹⁰ *for boys and girls* school because I think there are fewer distractions so everyone can just concentrate on their studies.

1 ....kindergarten.... 6 ....

2 .... 7 ....

3 .... 8 ....

4 .... 9 ....

5 .... 10 ....

> **Vocabulary note**
>
> Words ending in *-ist* are usually used to describe a person who studies a particular subject or who holds a particular set of beliefs: *economist, scientist, feminist, Marxist*.

2.2 **WORD BUILDING** Complete the table.

Subject	Person	Adjective
architecture		
		archaeological
biology		
economics		
geology		
	geographer	
	journalist	
languages		
	lawyer	
		mathematical
science		

2.3 Complete the sentences with suitable words from the table.

1 I've always wanted to go on an ___archaeological___ dig to try to find fossils and ancient artefacts.

2 Have you seen a copy of the a............................... plan for the new building?

3 My daughter is a l...............................; she speaks six different languages.

4 The government has a good e............................... policy. I'm sure the recession will be over soon.

5 I'm studying j..............................., I've always wanted to be a political writer.

6 I'm not very familiar with the g............................... of that part of the world.

Research

3.1 🎧 **5b** You will hear part of a talk for students. Listen and complete the notes below. Write NO MORE THAN TWO WORDS for each answer.

> **Continuing your studies *after graduation*
> Writing your *dissertation***
>
> Important considerations:
> - Many students struggle to find a research (1)............................... .
> - Writing a (2)............................... is *easier* if you make the right choice.
>
> You need to:
> - study the (3)............................... .
> - have a *wide* (4)............................... of your *field of study*.
> - *establish* what is (5)............................... in your field.
> - have a clear idea of the (6)............................... of your study.
> - *consider* whether there are any (7)............................... in existing research.
> - *think about* your (8)............................... carefully.
> - ask about (9)............................... from outside sources.
> - ask your (10)............................... to check your *results*.

3.2 🎧 **5b** Listen to the talk again and write synonyms for the words in italics in 3.1.

after graduation = postgraduate,

....

....

....

....

....

....

....

4 **PRONUNCIATION** 🎧 **5c** Mark the stress on these words. Then listen and check to see if you were correct. Practise saying the words.

acad<u>e</u>mic	assignment	consideration
concentrate	controversy	conduct (v)
distraction	dissertation	economist
educational	educated	research (n)
thesis	theory	theoretical

Test practice

General Training Reading Section 2

Work experience and internship programmes

Through our student work experience programme, the education authority provides over 9,000 work experience placements for young people each year. Our programme is designed to offer employment opportunities for students that will enrich their academic studies and help them gain valuable work-related skills, thereby improving their chances of finding a good job after graduation. A placement can be unrelated to the student's field of study, and so participants may even discover areas of work they have never considered before.

All secondary and post-secondary school students in full-time education are eligible to apply for the work experience programme. Students will be assigned an individual case manager, who will inform students of the minimum level of academic achievement required for each job. During an academic term, a student may work part-time. During the summer holidays a student may work full-time or part-time. The education authority is responsible for the recruitment of all students under the work experience programme. Applicants apply in person to our office and we refer candidates to the appropriate department.

Our internship programme is designed specifically for post-secondary students, studying either part-time or full-time. Students on the programme are given an assignment related to their research area, thereby offering them the opportunity to use their academic knowledge in an actual work setting. Eligible students must be enrolled in a course of study at a university or equivalent institution, and should have completed at least one year of their course. Those who have already graduated may also be considered provided that they apply within six months after completion of their degree.

The academic institution where a student is enrolled plays an important role in the placement of students under the internship programme and they will determine the duration of a work assignment. These traditionally last four months but may vary from 4 to 18 months. Students in this programme normally work full-time.

Questions 1–6

Complete the sentences below.

Choose NO MORE THAN THREE WORDS AND/OR A NUMBER from the text for each answer.

1   A work experience programme does not need to be connected to a particular ....

2   Your .... will tell you what qualifications you need for your work experience job.

3   Students who would like to apply for the work experience should visit the ....

4   The internship programme is aimed at students at .... level.

5   Students may apply for an internship up to .... after graduation.

6   Your .... will decide how long your internship is.

> **Test tip**
>
> The information in the summary may not be in the same order as in the reading text.

Test One (Units 1–5)

Choose the correct letter A, B, C or D.

1   My company has .... a new approach to staff meetings. We now have them standing up!
    A adapted   **B** adopted   **C** addressed   **D** admitted

2   You can tell a lot by the way members of a family .... with each other.
    A identify   **B** interact   **C** relative   **D** understand

3   We were unable to reach an agreement because of the .... between the two groups.
    A contact   **B** concern   **C** connection   **D** conflict

4   If we don't .... the artistic skills of young children they are far less creative as adults.
    A nurture   **B** nature   **C** provide   **D** prevent

5   There is a very clear relationship .... education and academic success.
    A about   **B** between   **C** for   **D** in

6   I have a very close relationship .... my mother.
    A to   **B** with   **C** of   **D** for

7   The .... to make quick decisions is vital in an emergency.
    A ability   **B** knowledge   **C** skill   **D** talent

8   In my country people use their hands and .... a lot when they talk.
    A show   **B** tell   **C** gesture   **D** imitate

9   I have very fond .... of my time in Spain.
    A memorise   **B** minds   **C** souvenirs   **D** memories

10 Children need to learn to accept the consequences .... their actions.
    A of   **B** or   **C** in   **D** by

11 My older brother is very .... for his age. He still needs my parents to help him with everything.
    A mature   **B** maturity   **C** immature   **D** immaturity

12 Everyone should travel; it really .... the mind.
    A broadens   **B** develops   **C** opens   **D** widens

13 I can't eat peanuts because I'm .... to them.
    A allergy   **B** allergic   **C** appetite   **D** infection

14 Some forms of this disease are .... and can last for five years or more.
    A chronic   **B** acute   **C** moderate   **D** obese

15 Unfortunately, scientists have been unable to find a .... for this complaint.
   A prevention   B disorder   C therapy   D cure

16 The man was put into an isolation ward because the disease was highly ....
   A infected   B infectious   C harmful   D harmed

17 After several hours the doctor was finally able to give us his .... John had broken his ankle.
   A diagnosis   B disease   C symptoms   D signs

18 Eating fatty foods can damage your ....
   A healthy   B health   C harmful   D unhealthy

19 You can't always play it safe. Sometimes you need to .... a risk.
   A have   B make   C put   D take

20 It's important to set yourself clear .... so you know what you are aiming for.
   A ambitions   B goals   C decisions   D opportunities

21 She is very .... All she cares about is clothes and expensive cars.
   A realistic   B optimistic   C materialistic   D pessimistic

22 I like making things with my own hands. It gives me a lot of ....
   A satisfaction   B exhaustion   C fulfilment   D creation

23 I always try to keep a positive .... on life.
   A overview   B overlook   C outlook   D insight

24 The cost of .... has risen dramatically in the last few years.
   A life   B live   C lives   D living

25 The researchers .... many experiments to find the most effective materials.
   A confirmed   B conducted   C considered   D concerned

26 Children who do not learn to read before they finish .... school struggle throughout the rest of their education.
   A primary   B first   C nursery   D kindergarten

27 My tutor has some very interesting .... on how students learn.
   A topics   B thesis   C themes   D theories

28 We had to cancel the project due to lack of ....
   A findings   B funding   C limits   D controversy

29 We had to cover the rest of the .... ourselves while our teacher was ill.
   A contents   B current   C syllable   D syllabus

30 I can already speak three languages, but I'd really like to .... to speak Chinese.
   A know   B study   C learn   D teach

6 Effective communication

Language, linguistics

Language

1.1 Which of the following aspects of English do you find the most difficult?

A vocabulary   B grammar   C reading   D writing   E pronunciation
F speaking   G listening

1.2 🎧 6a Listen to somebody talking about learning a language and say which THREE things in 1.1 she had difficulty with. ....

1.3 🎧 6a Listen again and find words that match these definitions.

1 change words from one language to another ....

2 the ability to do something without making mistakes ....

3 something that prevents successful communication ....

4 a person who has spoken the language from birth ....

5 the ability to speak without hesitation ....

6 work or carry out daily tasks ....

2.1 idioms 📖 Use a dictionary to check the meaning of the phrases in the box. Then complete sentences 1–8 with the correct phrase.

There is something to be said for	You can say that again!	having said that	have a say
When all is said and done	Needless to say	That is to say	to say the least

1 **Bill** Hello, Sam, what a surprise meeting you here!
  Sam .... !

2 Nuclear power has its problems. However, ..., many people believe it is the energy source of the future.

3 .... switching to solar energy, although it is still too expensive for many people.

4 Life without a constant supply of water can be difficult, ...

5 ...., there is little we can do to save the environment without the full support of industry and the government.

6 The tanker spilled 5,000 megalitres of oil into the ocean. ...., this had a devastating effect on marine life in the area.

7 There is a clear link between humans and environmental problems. ...., wherever humans live, they damage the environment in some way.

8 I think it's important for everyone to .... in how the government is elected.

Error warning

Note the following common errors with *say, speak, talk, tell*.
I speak German. NOT ~~I talk German~~. *She's always **talking about** her dog.* NOT ~~tell about~~. *Can I **tell you** something?* NOT ~~tell something~~. NB *Tell* can be used to refer to a chart /graph: *The chart **tells** us how many students were enrolled.* However, it is better to use language that is more impersonal: *The chart **shows** how many students were enrolled.* NB You should not use *say* to talk about charts: ~~From the chart I can say how many students.~~

2.2 **Correct the mistakes in these sentences.**

1 The chart ~~talks~~ us how many students were studying in the college in 1990. ......*tells*......

2 I can't understand what he is speaking. He's almost incoherent. ....

3 Today I'm going to tell about my last holiday in America. ....

4 I can talk three languages fluently, but Italian is my mother tongue. ....

5 I learned English from a textbook, so I don't really understand it when it is said. ....

6 The table says the percentage of people moving into urban areas between 1960 and 1990. ....

2.3 **The words in column B should be similar in meaning to those in column A.**
Cross out the odd word in each group.

A	B			
communicate	*contact*	*correspond*	~~*indicate*~~	*interact*
1 *conclude*	*close*	*summarise*	*recap*	*recall*
2 *explain*	*clarify*	*define*	*express*	*illustrate*
3 *mean*	*indicate*	*intend*	*signify*	*stutter*
4 *meaning*	*conjecture*	*connotation*	*significance*	*sense*
5 *say*	*demonstrate*	*express*	*speak*	*verbalise*
6 *suggest*	*imply*	*intimate*	*propose*	*state*
7 *tell*	*gesture*	*narrate*	*recount*	*relate*
8 *understand*	*appreciate*	*comprehend*	*contradict*	*follow*

Linguistics

3.1 **Read the text.**

Signs of success
Deaf people are making a profound contribution to the study of language

Just as biologists rarely see a new species arise, **linguists** rarely get to discover an unknown **dialect** or, even better, to see a new language being born. But the past few decades have seen an exception. Academics have been able to follow the formation of a new language in Nicaragua. The catch is that it is not a spoken language but, rather, a sign language which arose **spontaneously** in deaf children.

The thing that makes language different from other **means** of communication is that it is made of units that can be combined in different ways to create different **meanings**. In a spoken language these units are words; in a sign language these units are **gestures**. Ann Senghas, of Columbia University, in New York, is one of the linguists who have been studying the way these have gradually **evolved** in Nicaraguan Sign Language (NSL).

The language **emerged** in the late 1970s, at a new school for deaf children. Initially, the children were instructed by teachers who could hear. No one taught them how to sign; they simply worked it out for themselves. By conducting experiments on people who attended the school at various points in its history, Dr Senghas has shown how NSL has become more **sophisticated** over time. For example, **concepts** that an older signer uses a single sign for, such as rolling and falling, have been unpacked into separate signs by youngsters. Early users, too, did not develop a way of **distinguishing** left from right. Dr Senghas showed this by asking signers of different ages to **converse** about a set of photographs that each could see. One signer had to pick a photograph and **describe** it. The other had to guess which photograph he was **referring** to.

When all the photographs contained the same elements, merely arranged differently, older people, who had learned the early form of the language, could neither signal which photo they meant, nor understand the signals of their younger partners. Nor could their younger partners teach them the signs that indicate left and right. The older people clearly understood the concept of left and right, they just could not **express** it. What intrigues the linguists is that, for a sign language to emerge spontaneously, deaf children must have some **inherent** tendency to link gestures to meaning.

3.2 Say whether the following statements are true or false. Give an explanation for each answer using words from the text. Then use your dictionary to check the meaning of any words in bold that you do not know.

1 Ann Senghas studies languages.

   True – she's a linguist.

2 Teachers taught the Nicaraguan deaf children how to use sign language.

   ....

3 The earliest form of the sign language was very basic.

   ....

4 The older signers were able to show the difference between left and right.

   ....

5 Linguists believe that deaf children are born with the ability to link gestures to meaning.

   ....

4.1 Think about your answers to these questions.

1 What do you need to do to be a good language learner?

2 What do you think makes a good language teacher?

3 What problems do people experience when they learn your language?

4.2 ⏺ 6b Look at these answers to the questions in 4.1 and complete them with a suitable word from this unit. Listen to the recording to check your answers.

1 Well, you need to be able to put down your textbooks from time to time and forget about (1)............................ . That's the only way to become more (2)............................ in a language. You also need to (3)............................ to (4)............................ speakers of the language as much as you can.

2 I think the best language teachers are those who can (5)............................ another language themselves. They also need to be able to (6)............................ things clearly and in a way that is easy to (7)............................ .

3 My (8)............................ language is very difficult to learn because of the (9)............................ . The individual sounds are very strange to other nationalities and difficult for them to (10)............................ .

Test practice

Academic Reading

First words
There are over 6,000 different languages today, but how did language evolve in the first place?

Pinpointing the origin of language might seem like idle speculation, because sound does not fossilise. However, music, chit-chat and even humour may have been driving forces in the evolution of language, and gossip possibly freed our ancestors from sitting around wondering what to say next.

There are over 6,000 different languages today, and the main language families are thought to have arisen as modern humans wandered about the globe in four great migrations beginning 100,000 years ago. But how did language evolve in the first place? Potential indicators of early language are written in our genetic code, behaviour and culture. The genetic evidence is a gene called FOXP2, in which mutations appear to be responsible for speech defects. FOXP2 in humans differs only slightly from the gene in chimpanzees, and may be about 200,000 years old, slightly older than the earliest modern humans. Such a recent origin for language seems at first rather silly. How could our speechless *Homo sapiens* ancestors colonise the ancient world, spreading from Africa to Asia, and perhaps making a short sea-crossing to Indonesia, without language? Well, language can have two meanings: the infinite variety of sentences that we string together, and the pointing and grunting communication that we share with other animals.

Marc Hauser (Harvard University) and colleagues argue that the study of animal behaviour and communication can teach us how the faculty of language in the narrow human sense evolved. Other animals don't come close to understanding our sophisticated thought processes. Nevertheless, the complexity of human expression may have started off as simple stages in animal 'thinking' or problem-solving – for example, number processing (how many lions are we up against?), navigation (time to fly south for the winter), or social relations (we need teamwork to build this shelter). In other words, we can potentially track language by looking at the behaviour of other animals.

William Noble and Iain Davidson (University of New England) look for the origin of language in early symbolic behaviour and the evolutionary selection in fine motor control. For example, throwing and making stone tools could have developed into simple gestures like pointing that eventually entailed a sense of self-awareness. They argue that language is a form of symbolic communication that has its roots in behavioural evolution. Even if archaic humans were physically capable of speech (a hyoid bone for supporting the larynx and tongue has been found in a Neanderthal skeleton), we cannot assume symbolic communication. They conclude that language is a feature of anatomically modern humans, and an essential precursor of the earliest symbolic pictures in rock art, ritual burial, major sea-crossings, structured shelters and hearths – all dating, they argue, to the last 100,000 years.

But the archaeological debate of when does not really help us with what was occurring in those first chats. Robin Dunbar (University of Liverpool) believes they were probably talking about each other – in other words, gossiping. He discovered a relationship between an animal's group size and its neocortex (the thinking part of the brain), and tried to reconstruct grooming times and group sizes for early humans based on overall size of fossil skulls. Dunbar argues that gossip provides the social glue permitting humans to live in cohesive groups up to the size of about 150, found in population studies among hunter-gatherers, personal networks and corporate organisations. Apes are reliant on grooming[1] to stick together, and that basically constrains their social complexity to groups of 50. Gelada baboons stroke and groom each other for several hours per day. Dunbar thus concludes that, if humans had no speech faculty, we would need to devote 40 per cent of the day to physical grooming, just to meet our social needs.

Humans manage large social networks by 'verbal grooming' or gossiping – chatting with friends over coffee, for example. So the 'audience' can be much bigger than for grooming or one-on-one massage. Giselle Bastion, who

[1]*Grooming: (in animals) cleaning the fur; (in humans) brushing the hair, making your appearance clean and neat*

recently completed her PhD at Flinders University, argues that gossip has acquired a bad name, being particularly associated with women and opposed by men who are defending their supposedly objective world. Yet it's no secret that men gossip too. We are all bent on keeping track of other people and maintaining alliances. But how did we graduate from grooming to gossip? Dunbar notes that just as grooming releases opiates that create a feeling of wellbeing in monkeys and apes, so do the smiles and laughter associated with human banter.

Dean Falk (Florida State University) suggests that before the first smattering of language there was *motherese*, that musical gurgling between a mother and her baby, along with a lot of eye contact and touching. Early human babies could not cling on to their mother as she walked on two feet, so *motherese* evolved to soothe and control infants. *Motherese* is a small social step up from the contact calls of primates, but at this stage grooming probably still did most of the bonding.

So when did archaic human groups get too big to groom each other? Dunbar suggests that nomadic expansion out of Africa, maybe 500,000 years ago, demanded larger group sizes and language sophistication to form the various alliances necessary for survival. Davidson and Noble, who reject Dunbar's gossip theory, suggest that there was a significant increase in brain size from about 400,000 years ago, and this may correlate with increasing infant dependence. Still, it probably took a long time before a mother delivered humanity's maiden speech. Nevertheless, once the words were out, and eventually put on paper, they acquired an existence of their own. Reading gossip magazines and newspapers today is essentially one-way communication with total strangers – a far cry from the roots of language.

Questions 1–5

Choose the correct answer, **A**, **B**, **C** or **D**.

1 In paragraph 1, the writer uses the term 'idle speculation' to refer to the study of
   A It cannot be separated from other forms of expression.
   B It may be impossible to identify with any certainty.
   C It shows that our need to talk is greater than any other.
   D It most likely occurred as a way to relieve boredom.

2 What does the writer tell us about FOXP2?
   A It is the main difference between chimpanzees and humans.
   B It explains why early man was unable to talk.
   C It was first discovered when diagnosing speech problems.
   D It may have first appeared just before modern humans did.

3 In the second paragraph, what notion does the writer refer to as being 'rather silly'?
   A that language began such a long time ago
   B that man could travel around the world unable to talk
   C that chimpanzees might ever be able to talk
   D that communication between chimpanzees pre-dates man

4 In the third paragraph, the writer refers to 'lions' in order to?
   A illustrate the type of communication needs faced by early man.
   B indicate how vulnerable early man was to predators.
   C provide evidence of other species existing at the same time.
   D show the relationship between early humans and other animals.

5 Gelada baboons are mentioned in order to show that
   A using grooming to form social bonds limits the size of a social group.
   B early humans would probably have lived in groups of up to 50.
   C baboons' social groups are larger than those of early humans.
   D baboons spend 40 per cent of their time grooming each other.

Test tip

For matching items, first locate all the people listed in the text. Read all the views they express and then find the statement which matches this. NB The ideas or statements in the questions will not be expressed in exactly the same words as in the text and they will not be in the same order as in the text. You may not need to use all of the people in the list.

Questions 6–14

Look at the following statements (questions 6–14) below and the list of people.
Match each statement with the correct person or people, **A–E**.
Write the correct letter, **A–E**, next to questions 6–14.
NB You may use any letter more than once.

6   There is physical evidence of increased human intelligence up to 400,000 years ago. ....

7   In the modern world, gossiping is seen in a negative way. ....

8   Language must have developed before art and travel. ....

9   The development of human language can be gauged by studying other species. ....

10   Gossiping makes humans feel good. ....

11   The actions of early humans could have evolved into a form of communication. ....

12   The first language emerged through a parent talking to an infant. ....

13   Gossip was the first purpose of human communication. ....

14   Early humans used language to help them live together. ....

List of people
A   Hauser
B   Noble and Davidson
C   Dunbar
D   Bastion
E   Falk

7 On the move
Tourism, travel

Tourism

1.1 Answer these questions about the place where you live.

1 What would you take a visitor to your hometown to see?

2 Which of the following best describes the place where you live?
   A coastal   B mountainous   C rural   D urban

1.2 🎧 7a Listen to four people describing where they live and complete the table below. Use the correct adjective from 1.1 for the 'Type of place' column. Write down any words that helped you decide.

Speaker	Type of place	Words that helped you decide
1		
2		
3		
4		

1.3 🎧 7a Listen again and decide which of the speakers' hometowns can be reached:

A by air ....   B by rail ....   C by road ....   D by sea ....

1.4 Complete the sentences using the correct form of the words in the box. You may use the words more than once.

at	low	of	peak	reach	trend	travel	trough

Harbour City Tourism

%
100
80
60
40
20
0
                1970   1985   2000

□ city hotel occupancy   ■ rail travel
□ coastal hotel occupancy   ■ air travel
■ adventure tourism

> **Ⓥ Vocabulary note**
>
> When talking about statistics we say that figures **reach a peak of** or **peak at**: *The number of visitors **reached a peak of** 10,000 / **peaked at** 10,000.* The opposite of *a peak* is *a low*. The word *trough* also has this meaning, but is usually used together with the word *peak*: *The number of visitors fell to **a low of** only 556 in 1978. The tourism industry has its **peaks and troughs**.*

1 The chart shows the .... in tourism in Harbour City in 1970, 1985 and 2000.

2 Adventure tourism rose from a low .... 20 per cent in 1970 to a peak .... 50 per cent in 2000.

3 The occupancy of coastal hotels .... at close to 90 per cent in 1985.

4 In 2000 the number of passengers .... by air .... a peak of 80 per cent.

5 The number of train passengers fell to a .... of approximately 25 per cent in 2000.

6 The two greatest .... occurred in adventure tourism in 1970 and coastal hotel occupancy in 2000.

7 The percentage of coastal hotel occupancy experienced the greatest .... and ....

8 City hotel occupancy peaked .... almost 80 per cent in 1985.

Travel

2.1 **Correct the seven vocabulary mistakes in the text.**

Thanks to modern transport people can now ~~journey~~ a lot more easily than in the past. However, modern-day trip also has its problems: airports can be very crowded and there are often long queues of people waiting to collect their luggages. One way to make this job easier is to tie a colourful ribbon around each of your luggage so they are easier to spot on the conveyor belt. If you are going away on a short journey of only a few days then you may be able to limit yourself to **hand** luggage and save even more time. For longer travels, make sure you take plenty of snacks and drinks, especially if you are trip with small children.

1 .....travel.....   5 ....

2 ....   6 ....

3 ....   7 ....

4 ....

Vocabulary note

Travel = a verb and an uncountable noun used to talk about travelling in a general way: *Air **travel** has become cheaper than rail **travel** in some places.*
Trip = short holiday or time away: *I have to go on a business **trip** to Japan. Trip can also be used to refer to a journey. The bus **trip** was really long.*
Journey = getting from A to B: *When driving a long way it is best to break your **journey** up into two-hour blocks.*
Tourism = the industry or business of providing holiday transport, accommodation and entertainment.

Error warning

Travel/Travelling = moving from one place to another: *I think **travel**/**travelling** helps to educate you about the world.* NOT *I think tourism helps to educate you*. NB *Travelling* = UK spelling, *Traveling* = US spelling.
Luggage is uncountable and refers to all of your bags: *Put your luggage/suitcases here.* Not *Put your luggages* …

2.2 **Think of a suitable word or words to complete the sentences. Then read the following travel advice and check your answers.**

1 I gave my parents a copy of my .... before I left so that they would know where I was.

2 It is difficult to get tickets at that time of year so we booked ours well ....

3 My bank has a lot of branches overseas so I could .... my own account easily.

4 Driving a car during .... periods can be horrendous.

5 Your passport, tickets and money are the only really .... items on any trip.

6 In the duty free shop they asked to see our tickets and some form of ....

7 The exchange rate can .... a great deal, so shop around for the best deal.

8 When we finally reached our .... we were very tired.

Travel advice

The price of holidays can **fluctuate** a great deal throughout the year so try to be flexible with your travel dates and avoid **peak** holiday times. It can also be cheaper if you book well **in advance**. Before your departure, make sure you do as much research about your **destination** as you can. Find out if you require any special visas or permits to travel there. Think about currency as well. Will you be able to **access** your own money easily enough or will you need to take cash with you? Think about eating larger lunches and smaller evening meals to help make your spending money go further, as lunch is generally cheaper. Make sure that you keep sufficient **identification** with you at all times. It may also help to email a copy of your passport details to yourself in case it is lost or stolen. Label your suitcases clearly so that they can be easily identified as yours. It can be useful to store a copy of your **itinerary** in a prominent place in your suitcase so that the airline will know where to find you if your luggage gets lost. Be sure to pack any medication or other **essential** items in your hand luggage. If your flight is delayed or your luggage is lost these can be difficult to obtain in an airport or foreign country.

2.3 Complete the essay below with suitable words from the box. Then, in your notebook, write a suitable introduction and conclusion for the essay.

holiday	affect	remote	transport	visitors	effects	tourism	ecotourism	tourists	peak

People who live in beautiful remote places do not always enjoy having tourists in their area. Do you think the advantages of tourism outweigh the disadvantages?

(1) .... certainly has its disadvantages for local people in pristine parts of the world. Firstly, the arrival of large groups of (2) .... can mean the end of peace and quiet. As the beaches and different forms of (3) .... all become overcrowded, local inhabitants may feel that they can no longer enjoy their own area. Furthermore, the development of hotels and (4) .... apartments may make the area too expensive for locals, who must surely resent the impact all of this has on the surrounding environment. Therefore, it is not surprising that some do not welcome these (5) ....

Nevertheless, tourism also has several positive (6) .... Firstly, there is a clear boost to the local economy. In (7) .... regions, young people are often forced to leave to find work, so the tourism industry provides much-needed employment opportunities and can help struggling communities to thrive. In addition, although tourism has been shown to negatively (8) .... the environment, the growing trend of (9) .... may help to reverse this. Furthermore, the invasion of tourists is relatively short-lived, and is mainly limited to the (10) .... tourist season; the rest of the year locals can relax and enjoy their beautiful surroundings. Thus, the benefits of tourism do appear to mitigate any problems it brings.

3 PRONUNCIATION (🎧 7b) All of these words contain the letters *ou*, but they are not all pronounced in the same way. Put these words into the correct box according to their pronunciation. Then listen and check.

boundary	bought	cough	course	country	double	doubt	drought	enough
journal	journey	nought	rough	south	southern	tourism	tourist	trouble	trough

ɜː (*as in* bird)	ʊə (*as in* pure)	ʌ (*as in* cup)
journey		
aʊ (*as in* cow)	ɒ (*as in* not)	ɔː (*as in* ball)

Test practice

General Training Reading Section 1

A

This summer we have a fabulous range of adventure holidays climbing up mountains or flying off them! With our unique all-inclusive formula and budget accommodation, we're sure you will not find better value elsewhere. Our holidays are ideal for young people travelling by themselves as there is no single person supplement and the group lessons included are a great way to meet new people. A minimum age applies to all activities.

B

Discover the hidden beauty of a Roman town and its 21st-century delights. Experience a sumptuous countryside welcome of fine food, admire our world-class heritage and the stunning scenery that surrounds our town. Enjoy the elegance and excitement of our five-star hotel. We offer exclusive couples-only accommodation and you are sure to leave us feeling pampered and relaxed.

C

We offer the widest choice of destinations, accommodation and activities throughout the Alps. We can provide accommodation only or a fully packaged activity holiday including flights and accommodation. As a specialist company we craft tailor-made holidays to your exact needs and specifications. Mountain biking, trekking, skiing and snowboarding are just some of the many activities on offer. We can provide top-quality chalets, hotels or apartments and any combination of the above activities.

D

This Icelandic wonderland never ceases to amaze – with its diverse scenery, wealth of activities and attractions including whale watching and the famous Blue Lagoon, this destination is, not surprisingly, addictive! One of the world's last genuine wilderness areas, this breathtaking, ice-covered landscape is more accessible in the summer than you might think. Forget about hiring a car – why not try rafting along a slow-moving river?

E

This is a captivating holiday destination. There are beautiful beaches, coastal villages, unspoilt coves and bays, clear turquoise waters, breathtaking scenery, mountains that appear to rise out of the sea, cities that sparkle with life, the brilliant sunshine – all contributing to a holiday paradise. There is plenty to see and do and families are particularly well-catered for.

Questions 1–8

Look at the five holiday advertisements, **A–E**.
For which holiday are the following statements true? Write the correct letter **A–E** next to questions 1–8.
NB You may use any letter more than once.

1 Offers both coast and mountains. ....

2 You can observe sea creatures. ....

3 Offers self-catering facilities. ....

4 Good for people travelling alone. ....

5 Offers winter sports. ....

6 Suitable for people with young children. ....

7 Suitable for people with not much money to spend. ....

8 Offers luxurious accommodation. ....

8 Through the ages
Time, history

Time

1.1 **Which of the statements are true for you?**

1 A I wear a digital watch. B I wear an analogue watch. C I don't wear a watch.

2 A I write important dates on my calendar. B I keep a diary. C I don't use either.

3 A I am very punctual. B I am often in a hurry. C I am always late.

1.2 🔊 8a **Listen to three people speaking about punctuality and decide whether they are**

A punctual B always in a hurry C always late

Speaker 1 .... Speaker 2 .... Speaker 3 ....

1.3 🔊 8a **Listen again and circle each of the phrases in the box as you hear them. Then complete the sentences below using the correct phrase.**

on time	in time	took so long	take my time
the right time	spend time	save time	
lose track of time	time-consuming		

1 When I surf the net I often .... Before I know it a few hours have gone by.

2 I try to make my lunch the night before to ....

3 At the weekend I try to .... with my family.

4 I find writing notes by hand very ....

5 We booked a taxi but it .... to arrive that we were 15 minutes late.

6 Excuse me, do you have ....? I have an appointment at 10 o'clock and I really want to get there ....

7 I ran for the bus, but I didn't get there ....

8 I got up very early so that I could .... getting ready.

Error warning

We use *take + time* in the following ways: *Take your time* (= don't hurry), *Take a long time / too much time*. NB We can say *It took a lot of time / so much time / too much time*, but be careful when you use *long: it took a long time / It took too long / It took so long*. NOT *It took too long time / It took so long time*. We can also say *I took three hours to get there* or *It took (me) three hours to get there*.

1.4 **Say whether the words in bold are closest in meaning to *before* or *after*.**

1 Twenty people were injured in the accident and the tower was **subsequently** demolished to prevent it from happening again.

2 **Prior to** the introduction of the steam engine, most people in the UK worked from home.

3 Three years **previously** the government had introduced a new law allowing women to vote for the first time.

4 There was a great deal of excitement in the days **preceding** the election.

5 This is the third year **in succession** that a female has been chosen to manage the club.

6 Istanbul was **formerly** known as Constantinople.

7 I had to pay $2,000 rent **in advance**.

8 The newspapers warned that a stock market crash was **imminent**.

History

2.1 Read the text and then answer the questions below.

> **Vocabulary note**
>
> *BC* is used in the Christian calendar to refer to the time before the birth of Jesus Christ. *AD* is used to refer to the time after Christ was born. *Circa* is used to mean *about* or *approximately* and is sometimes written simply *c*. NB We do not use an apostrophe to talk about decades: *the 1960s* NOT ~~*the 1960's*~~.

Stonehenge was built over a long period. If we consider only the ancient stones themselves, the work spanned 70 generations – some 1,600 years. However, the first construction at this site began in prehistoric times. True, these first artefacts were just wooden poles which have long gone, but these were raised by men in times so ancient that Britain was still recovering from the Ice Age. The timeline below shows this history, with a frenzy of activity from just before 3000 BC through to 1600 BC being responsible for most of what we now gaze upon in awe.

	postholes				Phase 1	Phase 2	Phase 3	
Ice Age ending								
8000 BC	7000 BC	6000 BC	5000 BC	4000 BC	3000 BC	2000 BC	1000 BC

Timeline of the building of Stonehenge

If we consider the structure chronologically, we can see that construction took place in several phases over more than a thousand years. Exact dates are not possible, since dates are inferred from minute changes in physical measurements, such as the radiocarbon dating method. Nevertheless, archaeologists have sketched out the following outline of events. First, the people of the Mesolithic period erected pine posts, known as the postholes, near Stonehenge. In the 1960s a car park was built over these. During the next stage, Phase 1 (c. 3100 to 2700 BC), a ditch was carved into the chalk less than 1 km from Stonehenge. This would have appeared brilliant white in the green of what had now become pastureland as the hunter-gatherers that erected the postholes gave way to farmers. Also during this time the 'henge' (the earthworks; ditch and bank) was constructed. Many visitors to Stonehenge fail to notice the 'henge' since the ditch and bank have been greatly eroded over the passing millennia. In Phase 2 of the construction (c. 2700 to c. 2500 BC), a large number of wooden posts were placed on the site. These may have served as markers for astronomical measurements. We do not know if there are more of them as excavation did not cover a large area. This was followed by Phase 3 (c. 2600 to 2500 BC). Stones began to arrive in this era and the circular shape and pattern of these enormous stones, which predate all other known structures, is still standing today. According to historians, there was no written mention of Stonehenge until 1100 AD.

1 Approximately when was the Mesolithic period? ....

2 What method was used to establish the dates of construction? ....

3 When did the earliest structures become permanently hidden from view? ....

4 What type of people lived at Stonehenge during the Mesolithic period? ....

5 Why do many visitors not see the 'henge'? ....

2.2 Read the text again and find a word or words that match these definitions.

1   an interval of time ....

2   very old ....

3   extended over ....

4   before people made written records of events

     ....

5   in the order in which they actually happened

     ....

6   stage of development ....

7   worn away over time ....

8   thousands of years ....

9   digging for artefacts ....

10   a period of history ....

11   to exist earlier than something else ....

2.3 Complete the sentences with suitable words from the box. You do not need to use all of the words. Use a dictionary and make a note of the different meanings in your notebook.

age   ancient   chronological   antique
antiquated   consecutive   era
the Middle Ages   middle-aged

> **Vocabulary note**
>
> *Age* = a particular period of history: *the Victorian* **age**, *the digital* **age**. *Era* = a period of time that is remembered for particular events: *The arrival of moving pictures marked the end of an* **era** *for live theatre*. *Middle-aged* = people in their middle years of life: *Most companies are run by* **middle-aged** *men*. *The Middle Ages* = a period of European history between 1000 and 1500 AD.

1   You should organise the dates into .... order, from the oldest to the most recent.

2   The museum has an excellent exhibition about life during ....

3   I much prefer studying .... history to modern history.

4   The first moon landing marked the beginning of an exciting .... in space exploration.

5   My grandparents are refusing to adapt to the computer ....

6   It would be better if the meetings were on .... days. We'd get more done that way.

3.1 Answer the questions in your notebook.

1   Do you often think back to the past or do you prefer to concentrate on the future?

2   Do you think it is important for children to study history? (Why? / Why not?)

3   If you could go back in time, which period of time would you like to visit? (Why?)

3.2 Correct the mistakes in *italics* in these answers to the questions in 3.1. Use a dictionary to help you.

1   Yes, I do think about the past almost all ~~times~~, in fact. I think I am a very *nostalgia* person, so I often *look backwards* at my life and remember good times as well as bad. I definitely think about it more than the future.

2   I didn't really enjoy studying history at school. I think teenagers are more interested in *the modern time* than in the past! But now that I'm older, I can see that actually it is very important. We need to know about important *history* events because hopefully they can stop us from making the same mistakes in the future.

3   The *stage* of history I'd most like to visit is ancient Egypt. I think it would be amazing to *go back in times* and watch how they lived and how they built the pyramids. I wouldn't want to stay long though – I think I would miss the digital *period* too much!

1   (of) the time ....
     ....
     ....

2   ....
     ....
     ....

3   ....
     ....
     ....

Test practice

Listening Part 4

 8b Questions 1–10

Complete the notes below using **NO MORE THAN TWO WORDS AND/OR A NUMBER.**

Early History

- 25,000 years ago – Cro-Magnon people showed signs of tooth decay and loss

- 7000 BC – Indus Valley – scientists believe that a **(1)** .... was used to deal with tooth decay

- 5000 BC – An ancient Sumerian text shows they thought tooth decay was caused by 'tooth **(2)** ....'

Natural Treatments and Remedies

- 1500 BC – Ancient Egypt

- The Ebers Papyrus mentions treatments for bad teeth, e.g. using **(3)** .... and **(4)** ....

- Garlic was put in the **(5)** .... to treat toothache

- In Ancient times, people would clean their teeth by **(6)** .... (some used fragrant sticks for this)

The Practice of Dentistry

- Egypt – 5th century – they had **(7)** .... in problems related to teeth

- The Middle Ages – Europe – poor people had bad teeth removed when in the **(8)** ....

- Pierre Fauchard – 'the father of modern dentistry' wrote *The Surgeon Dentist* in 1728

- He started training at 15 and learned a lot from working with **(9)** ....

- He identified **(10)** .... as a key cause of decay

---

9 The natural world
Flora and fauna, agriculture

Flora and fauna

1.1 How many plants and animals do you know? Can you name:

A five animals found in Africa?
....

D five animals found in Australia?
....

B five different types of flower?
....

E five different types of tree?
....

C five types of fruit?
....

F five types of vegetable?
....

1.2 Are these words associated with plants or animals? Put the words into the correct column. Which word can go in both columns?

| flora | fauna | vegetation | branch | twig | root | coat | predator | beak |
| trunk | fur | hide | scales | feathers | paw | claw | thorn | petal | horn |

Animals	Plants

Error warning

We say we must take care of **nature**. NOT ~~We must take care of the nature.~~ *Natural* is the adjective form: *It is a natural process.* NOT ~~It is a nature process.~~

Which five words in the animal column are connected to their skin or covering?

1.3 COMPOUND NOUNS Complete the sentences by adding one of these words *animal, human, nature, natural*.

1 It's *human* .... nature .... to want to find a solution to our problems.

2 Vegans do not use or eat any .... *products*.

3 I would rather be served by a .... *being* than by a computer.

4 I am constantly amazed by how beautiful and how destructive *mother* .... can be.

5 Man is said to be the most dangerous creature of all the .... *kingdom*.

6 Animals are much happier living in their .... *habitat*.

7 Manmade disasters such as chemical spills can destroy the .... *balance*.

8 In some countries prisoners are denied basic .... *rights*.

1.4 🎧 9a Listen to a description of an animal called a meerkat and complete the table.

Habitat	Diet
• Found in South Africa in (1).............................. areas. • Avoids woodland and thick (2).............................. . • It sleeps in (3).............................. . • If necessary, the meerkat will make a (4).............................. between rocks.	• Meerkats mostly eat (5).............................. , (6).............................. and (7).............................. . • They occasionally eat small rodents and the (8).............................. of certain plants.

Agriculture

2.1 Which is the odd one out? Circle the word which is different from the others and say why.

1 rose tulip daisy (weed) We want to grow the others.

2 plant grow cultivate soil ....

3 crop plant shrub bush ....

4 organic natural chemical biological ....

5 tropical subtropical humid arid ....

6 arid desert semi-arid tropical ....

7 endemic native introduced local ....

2.2 Read the text and then decide if the statements below are true or false. Find words in the text which mean the same or the opposite of the words in bold.

Introduced species

Since the birth of agriculture, farmers have tried to avoid using pesticides by employing various biological methods to control nature. The first method involved introducing a predator that would control pests by eating them. This was used successfully in 1925 to control the prickly pear population in Australia. The prickly pear had originally been used as a divider between paddocks. However, it eventually spread from a few farms to 4 million hectares of farming land, rendering them unusable. The *Cactoblastis* moth larva was introduced to help control the situation and within ten years, the prickly pear was virtually eradicated. Further attempts at biological control weren't so successful. When farmers tried to eliminate the cane beetle by introducing the South American cane toad, the results were catastrophic. The cane toad did not eat the cane beetle and the toad population spread rapidly, leading to the decline of native species of mammals and reptiles.

1 Farmers do not like using **chemicals to kill pests**. ....

2 The prickly pear was planted as a type of barrier between **fields**. ....

3 The *Cactoblastis* moth **killed off** nearly all prickly pear plants. ....

4 The cane toad was a **native** species to Australia. ....

5 Using the cane toad was **very successful**. ....

2.3 Now read the rest of the text and match the words in *italics* to the definitions below.

Other introduced species have proved similarly *disastrous* among native Australian animals. Since the introduction of the cat, the fox and the rabbit from Europe, 19 species of native animals have become *extinct* and a further 250 species are considered to be either *endangered* or *vulnerable*. The modern-day approach to the biological control of pests is through *genetically modified* crops. It remains to be seen whether this controversial method will have any long-term *repercussions*, particularly in regards to the *ecological balance* of the environment where they are grown. Some fear that insects may *become resistant* to these new crops and therefore become even more difficult to control.

1 at risk ....

2 negative effects ....

3 to stop being affected by something
....

4 at risk of dying out ....

5 no longer existing ....

6 crops whose genes have been scientifically changed
....

7 extremely bad or unsuccessful ....

8 the relationship between plants, animals, land, air, and water ....

2.4 WORD BUILDING Complete the table. You do not need to write anything in the shaded areas.

Noun	Adjective	Adverb	Verb
agriculture	agricultural		
ecology			
			evolve
	extinct		.... extinct
nature			
	genetic		

3 Improve the text by replacing the words in *italics* with a suitable word or phrase from this unit.

Some farmers believe that growing [1] *fruit and vegetables that have been* [2] *changed so that their genes are different* is a good way to [3] *totally stop* pests and improve the quality of their produce. However, this type of [4] *farming* has both advantages and disadvantages.

One of the advantages is that farmers can grow plants that produce a poison that is harmful to [5] *small animals like flies and caterpillars*. This means that farmers will not have to use [6] *chemicals to kill these animals* and so this should be better for the surrounding environment and the [7] *earth that plants grow in*. As a result, it could help to protect other [8] *plants* as well as the [9] *living space* of any animals in the area.

On the other hand, farmers usually only spray their fields once or twice per year but these new plants would be toxic all year round. Furthermore, it is possible that over time the pests may [10] *stop being killed by* the toxins and so the problem would be worse than ever. The toxins may also be poisonous to other plants and animals and this would upset the [11] *way plants and animals live and grow together* and may lead to more animals becoming [12] *at risk of extinction*.

4 PRONUNCIATION 🔊 9b Each of the words in the box below has a weak sound (ə) or *schwa*, e.g. *about*. Underline the schwa in each word, then listen and check your answers. Practise saying the words. There may be more than one schwa in each word.

adapt
agriculture
catastrophe
chemical
climate
disastrous
endangered
genetically
human
natural
vulnerable

Test practice

Academic Reading

A
About half the world's human population currently live in urban areas, which cover about 3% of the Earth's land surface. Both figures are increasing rapidly and, by 2050, it is estimated that two thirds of the world's population will live in an urban area. This growing trend of urbanisation represents the most extreme form of habitat loss for most plants and animals. As towns and cities grow, the natural habitats are removed and replaced with hard, impermeable structures such as roads and buildings. In a recent global study, researchers estimated that cities accommodate only 8% of the bird species and 25% of the plants that would have lived in those areas prior to urban development.

Test tip

This reading text is also good practice for General Training section 3.

B
Until recently, we knew relatively little about how many of the species that do live in towns and cities were coping. With a growing human population, it is now more important than ever for scientists and the public to work together to monitor wildlife and biodiversity effectively. When data is limited, it is difficult to understand the bigger picture: we can't know if animal populations are becoming more or less abundant and why; or whether conservation is needed.

C
One way that hundreds of ordinary people in the UK are helping to assess biodiversity is by setting up cameras in their gardens to record and then report any animal activity they capture on film. They are taking part in a project known as the MammalWeb database. Anyone with access to a camera can register to take part and become a 'spotter'. Using the general public in this way gives the ability to have far more cameras out in the field than any single researcher could manage, resulting in a much more comprehensive data set to analyse. The database has now amassed over 500,000 photographs of local wildlife, and recorded 34 species, ranging from the largest UK land mammal – the red deer – right down to some of the smallest, such as hedgehogs and bank voles.

D
Many of the participants have been surprised by what the animals were doing in their own back yard. At times the cameras have revealed an animal coexisting happily with one of its known predators. Another remarkable discovery was a North American raccoon, living wild in the north-east of England. It is not known how long the raccoon was roaming free and, without the aid of the public, it may never have been spotted, which highlights just how easy it is for urban wildlife to go unnoticed. Once discovered, the authorities were able to locate the animal and transfer it to a wildlife park, where it was given a more suitable home. The raccoon is not the only American visitor to have made itself at home in the UK. In fact, another – the American grey squirrel – is the most frequent sighting on MammalWeb, far outnumbering the native red squirrel.

E

In many European cities, the red squirrel appears well adapted to modern urban living, and they are abundant in countries such as Finland, France and Poland. They once thrived in the UK, too. However, since the grey squirrel was introduced in the 1800s, the population has declined drastically, and they are now classed as endangered. Several studies have shown that the introduction of the grey squirrel is the main factor in the red squirrel's decline, due to competition for food and shelter and the spread of the squirrelpox virus (which grey squirrels transmit to red squirrels).

F

However, again thanks in large part to the efforts of ordinary citizens, one area where the reds haven't disappeared is a small coastal town in the north-west of England called Formby, one of few red squirrel strongholds in England. Red squirrels can easily be spotted in gardens throughout the town, and the local residents are passionate about protecting them, with many volunteering with a local conservation group. This voluntary organisation manages the extensive woodland nearby, supplying additional food, and employing dedicated "squirrel officers" who help maintain "grey squirrel-free" habitats.

G

Elsewhere in the UK, most research and conservation is carried out in more rural areas. However, given the predicted future increases in urbanisation, managing urban sites like the one in Formby may be a better alternative, particularly as it makes the most of the benefits to animals of living alongside people, such as easy access to food and shelter. Of course, there are downsides too: road traffic poses an ever-present threat, as do pets. Even supplemental feeding can have unintended consequences, drawing animals from the safety of their nests and lairs and encouraging the spread of disease. Still, the benefits appear to outweigh the risks, and it is also worth noting that many native plant and bird species continue to exist in cities that were never designed with biodiversity protection in mind.

H

Humans rely on biological diversity, either directly for food, or indirectly, through nutrient cycling and pollination. As these community-based conservation management programmes show, with cameras offering fascinating insights into the secret lives of mammals, and local volunteers safeguarding endangered species, there are many courses of action we can take to help to counteract the damage brought by urbanisation and ensure that animals not only survive, but thrive in our towns and cities.

Questions 1–7

The reading passage has 8 paragraphs, **A–H**.

Which paragraph contains the following information?

Write the correct letter, **A–H**, next to questions 1–7.

NB You may use any letter more than once.

1 the pros and cons for animals living in cities ....

2 an example illustrating the benefit to research of working with non-scientists ....

3 an explanation for the drop in numbers of one type of animal ....

4 the likely proportion of local wildlife remaining once a location has been urbanised ....

5 the activities of a programme designed to help a particular at-risk species ....

6 the consequences of having too little information about wildlife numbers ....

7 an argument for more conservation programmes in cities rather than country areas ....

Questions 8–12

Complete the notes below.

Choose no more than ONE WORD AND/OR A NUMBER from the passage for each answer.

The Mammalweb Database

- It is a UK wildlife programme aiming to measure **(8)** ....

- Members of the public can apply to be something called a **(9)** ....

Findings:

- A total of **(10)** .... different types of animal have been recorded

- The most common animal recorded is a type of **(11)** ....

- One unusual report was of a **(12)** .... (it was later taken to a wildlife park)

Question 13

Choose the correct letter, **A**, **B**, **C** or **D**.

Which of the following is the most suitable title for this reading passage?

A   The hidden world of garden animals

B   It's time to limit urban development

C   How local residents aid conservation

D   Why the future looks bad for urban wildlife

10 Reaching for the skies

Space, the planets

Space

1.1 Answer these questions.

1 Would you like to travel into space? (Why? / Why not?)

2 What do you imagine it would be like?

3 What problems do you think you would experience in space?

1.2 Complete the text below with suitable words from the box.

astronauts   atmosphere   commercial   explorers
launch   outer   simulator   weightlessness

If you have ever dreamed of travelling in space then our (1).. space travel programme will make that dream a reality. Of course, passengers will need to prepare for this experience. However, unlike the months of training that (2).. undergo, our passengers will be ready for (3).. within two days. To prepare for a truly out-of-this-world experience, passengers will spend two days in our special training facility. There the passengers will be able to experience zero gravity in a special (4)..; this will allow the passengers to acclimatise. During the flight itself a rocket will propel the spacecraft into suborbital space in excess of 100,000 m above the Earth's (5).. . This will allow the passengers to experience (6).. . Our space (7).. will be able to float around the cabin and view the Earth and (8).. space for approximately ten minutes prior to re-entry and landing.

1.3 Read the text again and find words that match these definitions.

1 an actual event ....

2 go through an experience ....

3 the force or pull from the Earth ....

4 get used to a change in conditions ....

5 drive something forwards ....

6 more than ....

7 stay up in the air or in water ....

8 entering the Earth's atmosphere again

....

1.4 Complete the sentences with words from the text. You will need to change the form of the words.

1 Some people believe that space e.. is a waste of money.

2 Climbing extremely high mountains is made all the more difficult because of the drop in a.. pressure.

3 Spacecrafts need to reach extremely high speeds in order to escape the g.. pull of the Earth.

4 Last year the astronauts u.. a series of mental and physical tests in order to qualify for the mission.

5 This computer program s.. extremes of weather so that pilots can experience difficult flying conditions.

The planets

2.1 🎧 **10a** Listen to someone talking about the problems of forming colonies on other planets. Complete the table with NO MORE THAN TWO WORDS from the talk.

Planet	Physical features	Disadvantages
Venus	• same size as 1...............	• has no 2............... • covered in 3............... • constant 4...............
Mercury	• smaller than all other planets except 5...............	• has greatest range of temperatures of any planet in the 6...............
Saturn	• has many 7............... and 8...............	• much too hot

2.2 🎧 **10a** Listen again and complete the sentences below.

1 Venus is unusual because it .... in the opposite direction to other planets.

2 The .... of Venus has many craters caused by asteroids.

3 Mercury has no substantial ....

4 Mercury does not have any water so cannot .... life.

5 The Voyager space .... has provided us with pictures of Saturn's moons.

6 The .... of Saturn is mainly gas.

2.3 WORD BUILDING Complete the table.

Noun	Adjective
atmosphere	
	cosmic
	galactic
	gravitational
horizon	
	lunar
	meteoric
sun	
	stellar
	terrestrial
universe	

Vocabulary note

The suffix *-ic* tells us that a word is an adjective. How many adjectives in 2.3 end in *-ic*? Other common examples are: *economic, scenic, tragic*.

2.4 Complete the sentences with suitable words from the table in 2.3.

1 The moon appears much bigger when it is close to the ....

2 The Dog Star is the brightest star in our ....

3 Many scientists believe that dinosaurs became extinct when a .... hit the Earth.

4 A .... eclipse occurs when the moon is hidden by the sun.

5 Many people wonder if there is intelligent life elsewhere in the ....

6 The teacher told us to draw a .... line across the page.

7 The most successful products in the world are those that have a .... appeal.

8 .... energy is becoming more common nowadays.

3 Read this news report and decide whether the following statements are true or false. Give a reason for each answer using one of the underlined words in the text. Then check the meaning of any of the underlined words you don't know and write them in your notebook.

In May 1973, the USA launched its first <u>manned</u> space station. The station, called Skylab, managed to carry three different crews of astronauts over a nine-month period, in spite of the fact that it lost a meteor shield on launch. In February 1974, the final crew returned to Earth and, for the next five and a half years, the Skylab continued to orbit the Earth, <u>unmanned</u> and unused. Its low <u>orbit</u> gradually pulled the 77-tonne Skylab down towards the Earth, making a crash landing <u>inevitable</u> and causing a great deal of concern around the world. On 11 July 1979 the Skylab eventually crashed into the southern ocean off Esperance, Australia. Fortunately the <u>debris</u> fell in mostly <u>uninhabited</u> areas and locals scrambled to collect a souvenir. A 17 year-old from Esperance flew to America to claim a $10,000 reward for being the first to deliver a piece of the station to a newspaper. The local council of Esperance issued the USA with a $400 fine for littering. It has never been paid. There are currently approximately 8,000 pieces of <u>space junk</u> floating above our heads thanks to the satellites, space shuttles and space stations out there. One example is a screwdriver lost during a space shuttle mission in 1985, which has never been recovered.

Statements	True/False	Reason
1 In late 1974 there were people on board the space station.	....	It was ....
2 The Skylab may have floated in space for ever.	....	A crash was ....
3 Very few people lived in the area where it landed.	....	The area was ....

4 Complete the essay using suitable words from this unit and add a suitable conclusion.

'Space belongs to whoever gets there first.' Do you agree or disagree with this view?

Most of (1) p.................. Earth has already been mapped, so it is not surprising that explorers should turn their attention to other parts of the (2) u.................. The planets in our (3) s.................. s.................. have become the next frontier to be conquered, but who governs the vast area of space above us?

Some people believe that arriving first is key. In the 1960s, the US and USSR spent large sums of money in their attempts to be the first to (4) l.................. on the moon leading to a so-called (5) s.................. race. However, none of us think that the moon 'belongs' to the US simply because they planted a flag there. Furthermore, there are now thousands of (6) s.................. monitoring activities here on Earth, many of which are owned by big corporations, but this does not mean that they own the atmosphere above us. Therefore, arriving first is surely nothing more than a sign of wealth and technology.

There are other clear signs that no one 'owns' space. In the relatively short time that man has been travelling there, we have already left sufficient (7) d.................. behind to show that we are as careless in (8) o.................. space as we are on Earth. Broken equipment and shuttle parts have simply been left to (9) f.................. in the atmosphere and pose a very real threat if they collide with our planet. Clearly, some form of control is needed. Although there is an international (10) s.................. s.................., its activities are limited to research. Perhaps we need go further and establish some extraterrestrial laws.

5 PRONUNCIATION 🎧 10b Each of the following words has a weak sound (ə) or *schwa*, e.g. *about*. <u>Underline</u> the schwa in each word, then listen and check your answers. Practise saying the words. There may be more than one schwa in each word or phrase.

astr<u>o</u>naut   atmosphere   commercial   explorer   exploration   galaxy
horizon   horizontal   outer   satellite   solar system   sustain   universal

Test practice

Listening Part 3

 10c

Questions 1–4

Choose the correct letter, **A**, **B** or **C**.

Space exploration

1   John believes the main benefit of space exploration is
   A finding resources for use on Earth.
   B locating an alternative home for humans.
   C discovering more about the origins of Earth.

2   What problem do John and Susan identify with sending robots into space?
   A Their power supply is limited.
   B They are too reliant on humans.
   C Suitable robots would be too expensive.

3   What point does Susan make about space technology used in the 2000s?
   A It was out dated.
   B It was unreliable.
   C It was inexpensive.

4   What do John and Susan say is the biggest problem for missions to deep space?
   A the distance
   B the lack of fuel
   C the extreme temperatures

Questions 5–10

Choose TWO letters, **A–E**.

Questions 5 and 6

What **TWO THINGS** does John say about a mission to Mars?
A We should start preparing for it now.
B The ship could be ready sooner than expected.
C We already have the technology.
D It may take many years before it becomes a reality.
E It is unlikely to be approved in the next 10 years.

Questions 7 and 8

What **TWO POINTS** do John and Susan raise about living conditions on Mars?
A The soil may be toxic.
B Building would be impossible.
C Materials would need to be taken there.
D New types of metal may be discovered.
E It could be rich in resources.

Questions 9 and 10

What **TWO THINGS** do John and Susan say they would struggle with if they were going to Mars?
A the lack of water
B feelings of boredom
C the lack of routine
D the lack of greenery
E dealing with rubbish

Test Two (Units 6–10)

Choose the correct letter A, B, C or D.

1 People who are colour blind often can't .... between red and green.
    A see   **B** differ   **C** tell   **D** distinguish

2 Our car broke down twice on the way to the wedding. .... to say, we arrived two hours late.
    A Needless   **B** Pointless   **C** Regardless   **D** Worthless

3 I hope the lecturer wasn't referring .... my assignment when he made that remark.
    A in   **B** for   **C** to   **D** of

4 Languages .... over time so dictionaries need to be regularly updated.
    A eliminate   **B** evolve   **C** establish   **D** elicit

5 My teacher said my essay was .... She said she couldn't follow my argument.
    A incompetent   **B** inaccurate   **C** incoherent   **D** incisive

6 It's important to teach children not to .... lies.
    A say   **B** speak   **C** talk   **D** tell

7 These figures .... a peak in 1982 when over 2 million new machines were sold.
    A got   **B** increased   **C** rose   **D** reached

8 Air .... is cheaper than other forms of long-distance transport in my country.
    A trip   **B** journey   **C** travel   **D** travelling

9 A large number of houses were .... by the storm.
    A affected   **B** effected   **C** influenced   **D** involved

10 Many people believe that violent computer games can have a harmful .... on children.
    A affect   **B** effect   **C** damage   **D** involvement

11 The price of fresh fruit and vegetables .... considerably throughout the whole year.
    A rises   **B** peaks   **C** fluctuates   **D** decreases

12 The population of wild birds peaked .... approximately 400,000 before falling rapidly.
    A at   **B** for   **C** in   **D** of

13 My first job was to arrange the files into .... order from the oldest to the most recent.
    A alphabetical   **B** chronological   **C** numerical   **D** historical

14 The train whistle warned us of its .... departure.
    A previous   **B** imminent   **C** subsequent   **D** former

15 The majority of cave art was created in prehistoric ....

    A time   **B** stage   **C** era   **D** times

16 Computer viruses are a modern-........................... problem.

    A day   **B** era   **C** times   **D** time

17 I much prefer life in the twenty-first .... to that of the Middle Ages.

    A age   **B** era   **C** years   **D** century

18 It can take .... time for people to get used to a new system.

    A long   **B** a long   **C** so long   **D** too long

19 Many people are fascinated by the native .... of Australia, especially koalas and kangaroos.

    A fauna   **B** flora   **C** agriculture   **D** vegetation

20 The mother bird carries food back to the nest in its ....

    A feather   **B** wing   **C** beak   **D** paw

21 We must try to protect .... animals, otherwise when a species disappears the whole ecosystem is affected.

    A ecological   **B** endangered   **C** extinct   **D** exotic

22 I believe that farmers should be banned from using .... near waterways.

    A crops   **B** contamination   **C** pollution   **D** pesticides

23 Zoos should try to re-create the animals' .... habitat rather than keeping them in cages.

    A nature   **B** native   **C** natural   **D** naturalist

24 A plant is only as healthy as the .... it grows in.

    A habitat   **B** water   **C** soil   **D** vegetation

25 It must have been amazing to be the first astronauts .... space.

    A in   **B** of   **C** up   **D** to

26 I think we should spend more money taking care of our own ....

    A Earth   **B** atmosphere   **C** planet   **D** stars

27 I think we should spend more on space ....

    A explore   **B** explorer   **C** expansion   **D** exploration

28 Navigation around the globe is a lot simpler thanks to the information we receive from ....

    A satellites   **B** stations   **C** systems   **D** shuttles

29 I don't think we will ever find another planet that can .... life.

    A suspend   **B** survive   **C** supply   **D** sustain

30 I imagine astronauts spend a lot of time thinking about life .... Earth.

    A in   **B** of   **C** down   **D** on

11 Design and innovation

Building, engineering

Building

1.1 Which adjectives best describe your home?

A   old traditional modern

B   concrete brick steel timber

C   single-storey two-storey multi-storey / high rise

1.2 Complete the sentences using the words in brackets in the correct order.

1   It's a .... house. (brick, traditional)

2   I live in a .... apartment. (high-rise, lovely)

3   I'd rather live in a .... cottage. (small, country)

1.3 Now make a similar sentence about your own home.

I live in .... but I'd rather live
in ....

Vocabulary note

If we use more than one adjective they are normally in the following order: opinion, size, age, shape, colour, origin, material, type: An **ugly, old, brown, plastic shopping** bag. However, more than four adjectives together can sound awkward. NOT
~~An ugly, big, old, rectangular, brown, Italian, plastic bag~~.

2.1 🎧 11a   Listen to three people describing their homes and complete the table below.

	Type of building	Material(s) used	Favourite feature	Adjectives used to describe it
A				
B				
C				

2.2 🎧 11a   Listen again and answer the questions. Include the words from the recording that give you your answers.

Speaker A

1   Where did the stone come from?
....

2   What makes the ceilings ornate?
....

3   Is the house large or small?
....

Speaker B

1   Is the computer system new or old?
....

2   What makes the apartment functional?
....

3   Are the bedrooms large or small?
....

4   Are the buildings around it tall?
....

Speaker C

1   Is this house different from those around it?
....

2   Which room does the speaker say is bright?
....

3   What shape is the bottom of the staircase?
....

Error warning!

We say that you *build a house / a hospital* etc, NOT ~~build a building~~. *Build up* is not used to talk about construction. It refers to increasing or developing something: *He went to the gym to **build up** his muscles. We are trying to **build up** a relationship with a company in Japan. I had to **build up** the confidence to apply for the manager's job.* NOT ~~We need to build up a hospital.~~

Engineering

3.1 **Scan the article and underline these words.**

abandoned   collapsing   connecting   digging   emerging   expanding   flooding
impassable   ingenious   operation   prosperous   pump   tripled   scheme   struggled

Between 1760 and 1840, the Industrial Revolution brought about a major shift in Britain's population. People moved in their thousands from the farms of the countryside to the city-based factories, and the population of the nation's capital tripled in size. By 1825, London was the world's largest and most prosperous city, but its congested roads, which were in poor condition, were almost impassable, and the railways emerging in the north of the country had yet to reach the rapidly expanding capital. In addition, the river Thames, which had helped London become one of the most successful ports in the world, created problems with access: connecting two ports on opposite sides of a river is tricky, especially if they are not located close to bridges. Clearly, a land-based link was needed.

An attempt to build a tunnel beneath the river had already been made in 1798 by civil engineer Ralph Dodd, but the work was abandoned due to flooding, which became a constant problem, even when a steam-driven pump was employed. In 1805, a group of miners tried again, this time digging at a point further upriver. Once more work was halted due to the difficult conditions. The miners were used to dealing with hard rock rather than the soft clay beneath the river, which they struggled with daily. The tunnel walls were unstable, constantly crumbling and collapsing, and the miners were forced to give up. The failure of these projects led engineers to conclude that an underground passageway below the Thames was simply not feasible.

Nevertheless, Isambard Brunel, one of the most ingenious figures in engineering history, refused to accept defeat. Brunel had already drawn up plans for a tunnel under the River Neva in Russia, but this scheme never came about. Still, he believed he could solve the earlier issues using his new invention: a tunnelling shield. Brunel's innovative device protected the workers, allowing them to move through the tunnel while digging out the earth. Other men would then follow behind laying bricks to create the supporting walls and roof. The work was slow but effective, taking more than 18 years to complete. Finally, in 1843, the world's first underwater tunnel was completed, eventually becoming part of the London underground rail system, and is still in operation today.

3.2 **Decide if the following statements are True, False, or Not Given. Write the words you have underlined that helped you find the answers.**

1   By 1840, there were three times the number of people living in London than before the Industrial Revolution.
   ....*True (tripled = three times the number)*............

2   It was difficult to travel through the city of London in the early 1800s. ....

3   The first trains appeared in London in 1825. ....

4   There was a bridge joining London's two ports. ....

5   Ralph Dodd stopped his tunnel project due to problems with water. ....

6   The pump used by Dodd's team often broke down. ....

7   The miners were able to tunnel more easily than the previous workers. ....

8   The walls built by the miners were strong. ....

9   Brunel's approach had already been used in another project. ....

10   Brunel's tunnel has been in use since 1843. ....

3.3   Match the verbs (1–8) in column A with the definitions (A–H) in column B.

A   B

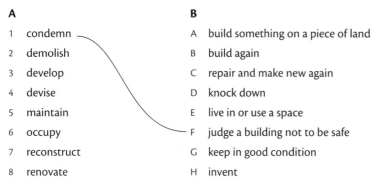

A		B	
1	condemn	A	build something on a piece of land
2	demolish	B	build again
3	develop	C	repair and make new again
4	devise	D	knock down
5	maintain	E	live in or use a space
6	occupy	F	judge a building not to be safe
7	reconstruct	G	keep in good condition
8	renovate	H	invent

3.4   Choose the correct words.

1   We can't move into the house until they have *developed / renovated* it.

2   No one has been allowed to occupy the building since it was *condemned / reconstructed*.

3   The architect *devised / demolished* a clever way of keeping the house cool in summer.

4   The tenants were offered a reduced rent if they agreed to *maintain / occupy* the property.

3.5   WORD BUILDING
          Complete the table.

Noun/person	Verb	Adjective or past participle
builder / building	build	
		constructed
	design	
engineer		
innovation		
	invent	
	occupy	
structure		

3.6   Complete the text with words from 3.5.

A group of (1) i................... architecture students has won this year's Timber Bridge Competition. The students' (2) d................... beat 17 others. The team used an (3) i................... approach to their bridge, which was (4) b................... entirely out of timber. They used traditional (5) c................... methods to avoid using nails or screws. The students demonstrated a good knowledge of fundamental (6) e................... principles. They (7) c................... a working model of the bridge, which (8) o................... an entire car park. This allowed them to test the bridge and ensure that the (9) s................... was sound.

4   PRONUNCIATION 🎧 11b Tick the correct sound for each of the letters underlined. Listen and check your answers, then practise saying the words correctly.

1	design	s	z	6	housing	s	z
2	please	s	z	7	fasten	s	z
3	device	s	z	8	destruction	s	z
4	devise	s	z	9	use (n)	s	z
5	residence	s	z	10	use (v)	s	z

Test practice

Academic Reading

Questions 1–5

The reading passage has five sections, **A–E**.
Choose the correct heading for each section from the list of headings below.
Write the correct number, **i–viii**, next to questions 1–5.

> **List of headings**
>
> | | |
> |---|---|
> | i | Outdoor spaces in the house of tomorrow |
> | ii | The house of the future helps in the battle of the sexes |
> | iii | The compact home of tomorrow |
> | iv | The multipurpose home of tomorrow |
> | v | Housework declines in the house of the future |
> | vi | Mixed success for visions of the future |
> | vii | The future lies in the past |
> | viii | A change of structure in the home of tomorrow |

1 Section A ....

2 Section B ....

3 Section C ....

4 Section D ....

5 Section E ....

The house of the future, then and now

A
The term 'home of tomorrow' first came into usage in the 1920s to describe the 'ideal house for future living' (Corn and Horrigan, 1984). In the 1930s and 1940s, advertisers picked up the concept, and a number of full-scale homes of tomorrow traveled through fairs and department stores. It was in this same era that American consumer culture was consolidated. In the 1920s, there were three competing conceptions of the home of the future. The first depicted the home of tomorrow as a futuristic architectural structure. The second conception was that of the mass-produced, prefabricated house, a dwelling potentially available to every North American. These first two failed to capture the imagination and the dollars of industrialists or of the public, but the third image did. From World War II until the present, the evolving story of the home of the future is a story of 'the house as a wonderland of gadgets' (Horrigan, 1986, p. 154).

B
In the 1950s, the home of the future was represented in and by one room: the kitchen. Appliance manufacturers, advertisers and women's magazines teamed up to surround women with images of the technology of tomorrow that would 'automate' their lives, and automation became a synonym for reduced domestic labor. In 1958, one author predicted 'Combustion freezers and electric ovens may someday reduce the job of preparing meals to a push-button operation' (Ross, 1958, pp. 197–8). 'Before long there will also be self-propelled carpet and floor sweepers, automatic ironers, and many additional push-button marvels.' (Ross, 1958, p. 200)

The postwar faith in and fascination with science is very apparent in future predictions made in the 1950s. The magazine *Popular Mechanics* did a special feature in February 1950, predicting that 'Housewives in 50 years may wash dirty dishes – right down the drain! Cheap plastic would melt in hot water.' It went on to claim that she would clean her house by simply turning the hose on everything, because furnishings, rugs, and draperies would all be made of synthetic fabric or waterproof plastic. The overriding message of the 1950s vision of the house of the future is that one can access the wonders of the future through the purchase of domestic technology today. 'Put them in your home – suddenly you're living in the future.' As Corn and Horrigan (1984) noted, 'by focusing on improving technology ... the future becomes strictly a matter of things, their invention, improvement, and acquisition'.

C

What is most striking in the 1960s home of the future is the recognition and incorporation of social and political turmoil into the representation of domestic technology. Technology moves out of the kitchen and spreads to the living room, bedroom and bathroom. While the home of the future was still a wonderland of gadgets, who was using the gadgets and why was finally being opened up to possible alternatives. Whirlpool dishwashers ran an advertisement explaining, 'How Whirlpool made my husband a man again'. Readers learned of the crisis of masculinity that can take place if a man helps with the housework. We learn that Barry is a great son, father and husband. He believed that the scrubbing of pots and pans was man's work and so he helped out at home. However, at work the men used to laugh behind his back because his hands were rough and red. The Whirlpool two-speed dishwasher stopped all that. Thus, a household appliance can preserve a man's masculinity by ensuring that he does not have to do 'women's work' in the home.

D

The broader social context continued to be reflected in the 1970s home of the future, but now the trend was to look backwards for the future, back to a proud pioneer heritage. In stark contrast to the 1950s, 'old-fashioned' is no longer used in a pejorative way; it is seen as a cherished value. Over the 1970s, North America experienced a certain erosion of trust in science and technology and there was less Utopian speculation about the technologically produced future. The previous unproblematic link between technology, the future and progress was being questioned (Corn, 1986).

From the space-age metals of the 1960s where every object had an electrical cord, we find a return to the traditional. The modernist or ultra-modernist designs of a few years earlier were all but gone. We also see the influence of the Green movement, and the energy crisis was making itself felt, reflecting fears about a future not quite as rosy as that predicted by *Popular Mechanics* in 1950.

E

In 1978, *House Beautiful* magazine, predicting what the homes of the 1980s would be like, suggested that self-indulgence was the wave of the future. 'Our senses are awakened, and a new technology is waiting to aid us in giving them a free rein. Bathroom spas and gyms, computerized kitchens, wide screen entertainment, even home discotheques are all on the way.' By the 1980s, the environmental and social movements of the 1970s were starting to ebb, significantly more women were working outside of the home, and computer technology was becoming more of a reality in the household. All these trends opened the door for a renewed love of technology.

The line between work and leisure became blurred in the 1980s. Forget about not being able to fit exercise into a hectic workday; in 1982, you can work and work out simultaneously. The Walking Desk, a computer workstation for the office at home, has a treadmill, stationary bike and stair climber installed underneath. The desk will also come with a compact-disc player and color monitor for viewing nature scenes on a computer break. Thus, in addition to turning exercise into work, we see that nature is being brought into the home – one never has to leave.

Questions 6–13

Look at the following list of statements (questions 6–13).
Match each statement or prediction with the correct time period, **A–F**.
Write the correct letter, **A–F**, next to questions 6–13.
NB You may use any letter more than once.

6   There was a loss of faith in automation. ....

7   Advertisers believed that houses would be made in a factory. ....

8   There were fewer housewives. ....

9   One writer envisaged furniture being made from fully washable materials. ....

10   People felt less optimistic about the future. ....

11   There was a link between our interest in the future and increased consumerism. ....

12   One magazine predicted that disposable plates would be used. ....

13   A new expression for 'the perfect home' was introduced. ....

List of time periods
A   1920s
B   1930s and 1940s
C   1950s
D   1960s
E   1970s
F   1980s

12 Information technology

Telecommunications, computers and technology

Telecommunications

1.1 Before you listen, answer these questions.

1 If you need to contact someone, do you prefer to
A send an email   B send a text message
C make a phone call?

2 How do you stay in touch with
A your friends   B work colleagues
C an elderly relative?

3 How would you describe your mobile phone?
A basic   B adequate   C state-of-the-art

4 What do you generally use your mobile phone for?

5 Do you prefer digital or printed books? What about newspapers and magazines?

1.2 🎧 12a Listen to a lady choosing a new mobile phone and match the comments below to

A the Nixon 10

B the Optima

C the LTC

Comments

1 it is very <u>small</u> ....

2 it can <u>follow and record</u> your exercise programme ....

3 has a better <u>display</u> for watching videos etc ....

4 on older phones, <u>moving the text up and down</u> was a problem ....

5 the <u>sound</u> quality is good ....

6 it can <u>hold</u> a lot of data ....

7 its <u>power supply</u> can be a problem ....

1.3 Complete the crossword with words from the recording.

Across

1 I've just bought a new phone so now I need to .... my favourite apps

6 moving text and images up and down on a screen

7 (see 9 down)

8 a portable energy source

10 easy to use

13 (see 11 down)

14 My phone is running really slow, I need to .... the software

15 I've got to delete some photos because I'm running out of ....

Down

2 app is short for ....

3 information stored electronically

4 My phone died because I didn't have my .... with me.

5 working well (a machine)

9 (and 7 across) an app that records your health and exercise progress

11 (and 13 across) Facebook, Twitter etc are types of ....

12 My phone switches on as soon as you touch the ....

1.4 **🔘 12b** Listen to six people speaking. Complete the sentences below with the technology or appliance they are talking about. Listen out for the verbs they use to help you.

1 She uses her .... every day.
2 The boy needs a ....
3 She would like to buy a ....
4 He appreciates having a ....
5 She'd like to get her mother a ....
6 A computer is more than a typewriter, it is a ....

Which two words needed the suffix 'or'?

Computers and technology

2.1 Read the article then look at the statements below. Write Yes if the statement agrees with the claims in the article, and No if it contradicts them. Underline the part of the text that gave you your answer and correct any incorrect statements.

From toasters to air conditioners, consumer goods often now have a chip inserted into them to collect and communicate data, allowing a 'dumb' device to become a 'smart' one that we can easily operate from anywhere. The idea of different devices being connected via the internet in some way is not new. It was first discussed in the 1970s and was given its current name, the 'Internet of Things,' in the 1990s. However, the concept didn't really take off until 2010, when the Smart phone put computers into our pockets, and the broadband and wireless networks that had emerged in the early 2000s became the norm in many households. The idea is now so widely accepted that it's often referred to just by its initials, *IoT*.

In the home, IoT aims to make our lives easier – on our way home from work, we can get our smart phone to tell our smart heating system to switch on, ready for my arrival. It's not just a case of being able to switch our appliances on and off remotely, of course. The chips also track and monitor usage on a much wider scale, which means that, across entire cities, devices can share data to help make public transport systems more efficient or even detect flooding, creating 'smart cities'.

Nevertheless, while the potential benefits of IoT are considerable, there are genuine concerns about its use. The reality is that everything with an internet connection can be hacked, and there are several examples of just how insecure smart devices can be. In 2015, a London hacker obtained the Wi-Fi passwords of various homes through their smart kettles, and in 2016 in Finland, the heating thermostat in two apartment buildings was hacked, leaving the residents in freezing cold for nearly a week. In the same year, the worst ever cyberattack was carried out, disabling online platforms in Europe and the US by hacking into digital cameras and video recorders. Security flaws like these are not the only issue. Even more concerning is the question of privacy and the possible use of tracking devices to carry out surveillance without our knowledge. Perhaps one day we will decide that disadvantages like these far outweigh the convenience of being able to switch the kettle on from your bed.

1 Everyday kitchen appliances can now store information. ...Yes...
2 The *Internet of Things* helped to make the Smart phone a reality. ....
3 In the early 2000s, most homes had broadband and wifi. ....
4 There are problems when IoT is used to control bus or train systems. ....
5 IoT may allow someone outside your house to obtain secret information. ....
6 People are most worried about IoT being used to shut down the internet. ....

2.2 Now match the words in bold in the text with these definitions.

1 an attempt to take over a computer through the internet
....

2 a person who accesses a computer without permission
....

3 to cause a machine or device to work ....

4 a system that allowed a lot of information to be communicated very quickly ....

5 an adjective used to show a machine can connect to the internet ....

6 protection, being safe ....

7 a tool or small machine invented for a specific purpose
....

8 to watch and check something ....

9 to discover something using special equipment ....

10 from a distance ....

2.3 COMPOUND WORDS Match a word from box A with a word from box B and use the compound words to complete the sentences below.

A	artificial	digital	internet	online
	remote	virtual		

B	age	control	connection	intelligence
	platform	reality		

1 Some people enjoy escaping to remote places where there is no ....

2 Many of the claims made about .... suggest that computers can think for themselves.

3 At home, I often lose the .... and have to turn on the TV manually.

4 Many people now do their shopping through an .... instead of going to physical shops.

5 The images in .... games can appear so real that it can be frightening.

6 We live in a ...., and so we expect all business to be done quickly and efficiently.

2.4 Correct the mistakes in the text. Use ONE WORD only. Hyphenated words (e.g. *state-of-the-art*) count as one word.

Today's [1]*advance* technology has brought many benefits. For example, nowadays we have many [2]*small tools* that can save time in the home and, if you have access [3]*with* a computer and a telephone [4]*connect* then you can work almost anywhere you choose. What is more, modern software [5]*programmes* are so user-friendly that you don't even need a great deal of computer knowledge to be able to [6]*play* them.

However, there are some disadvantages to the [7]*technology* era. For example, people today want to have the very [8]*last* technology but, as new technology dates very quickly, an increasing amount of computer hardware is being dumped. This adds to our already serious pollution problems. Furthermore, [9]*computerise* has led to fewer jobs and less human contact as many everyday transactions are now done [10]*with* computer rather than manually.

1 .....advanced.....   6 ....
2 ....   7 ....
3 ....   8 ....
4 ....   9 ....
5 ....   10 ....

Error warning!

Note the following spellings of the word *program*: computer **program** (UK and US spelling), television **programme** (UK spelling only). Note the different forms of *computer*: *computerise* (verb); *computerisation* (noun); *computerised* (adj): *We use a computerised system.* NOT *a computerise system.* *Automated* can be used in a similar way, but includes machines as well as computers: *Our processing system is fully automated.* We talk about *the computer era, the digital era* or *the technological era.* NOT *the technology era.*

Test practice

Speaking

Part 1 (4–5 minutes)

1   Can you tell me about your hometown?

2   Do you work or study?

3   What do you enjoy about your work (or study)?

4   What form of transport do you usually use?

5   When you are not working, what kind of things do you normally do?

6   What kind of things do you enjoy doing with your friends?

7   What did you do last weekend?

8   What are your plans for after this test?

Test tip

Ask a friend to help you practise. Stick to the time limit and record your interview. Give as much information as you can for each answer.

Part 2 (3–4 minutes)

In this part of the test you are going to talk about a topic for about 2 minutes. Here is a card with some questions on it. You have about 1 minute to prepare and you can make notes if you wish.

Describe a piece of technology you use often
You should say
- what the piece of technology is
- what it looks like
- what you use it for
and say whether you enjoy using it or not.

Part 3 (4–5 minutes)

We've been talking about technology, and I'd like to discuss with you one or two more general questions related to this. Let's consider, first of all, people's attitude to technology.

1   Some people always want to have the latest technology; why do you think that is?

2   Do you think people today use technology too often, for example, to find information? (Why is this a problem?)

3   Why do you think older people struggle so much with new technology?

4   Are there any ways we could help older people to adapt?

5   What changes in technology would you like to see in the future?

6   Do you think we should always try to improve on existing technology, or are some things better as they are? (Why?)

13 The modern world
Globalisation, changing attitudes and trends

Globalisation

1.1 **Answer these questions.**

1   How many of the following brand names do you know?
    Nike   Sony   Coca-Cola   Levi's   Versace   Gucci   Adidas

2   Can you name the countries these companies are from?

3   Can you name a product or brand from your country that is well known in other countries?

1.2 🎧 **13a** **Listen to two people, Amy and Bill, discussing globalisation. Who expresses the following opinions? Write A for Amy and B for Bill.**

1   Globalisation could harm the regional **way of life**. ....

2   Globalisation can help people who live **within a small area**. ....

3   **Worldwide**, more people eat traditional food than fast food. ....

4   People can enjoy products **from many different cultures** today. ....

5   **Large overseas companies have control over** the non-alcoholic drink market. ....

6   If not for globalisation, companies from different countries would not **join together** to do business. ....

7   People who travel prefer to see **unusual and exciting** things instead of **symbols** used by big companies. ....

8   Experiencing something from another country does not take away your **feeling of belonging to your country**. ....

9   **A range of different cultures** can be reflected in food bought overseas. ....

10 No single company **has complete control over** the fashion industry. ....

1.3 🎧 **13a** **Now listen again and write the words or phrases from the conversation that mean the same as the words in bold in 1.2.**

way of life = culture; ....

....

1.4 **WORD BUILDING**
Complete the table.

Noun	Adjective
culture	
	ethnic
globalisation	
	modern
	multicultural
nation	
	urban

Changing attitudes and trends

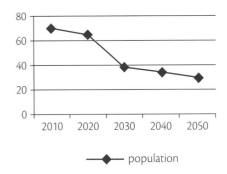

2.1 **Read the article and then look at the statements below. Write *Yes* if the statement agrees with the opinions in the text and *No* if it contradicts them. Underline the part of the text that gave you your answer.**

The past 50 years have seen astounding developments, including globalisation and the internet, and the next 50 years may bring even more profound changes. In order to predict the future we must first examine the past. Historians see history as being driven by a combination of cumulative long-term trends and short to mid-term <u>cycles, each of which contains the seeds of a subsequent but familiar situation.</u> There have been many projections about the future which, with the benefit of hindsight, seem rather ridiculous. Who can forget the predictions about the Y2K bug, when commentators believed that societies would collapse and satellites would fall from the sky? Unfortunately, as a result, many people today are more sceptical about current predictions concerning global warming.

One of the few areas in which long-term trends can be clearly seen is demographic statistics. These indicate that the population of the world will increase to about 8.5 billion by 2030 and continue to rise to 9.7 billion by 2050, after which growth will slow, then flatten out. Some societies have birth rates that are already locking their populations into absolute decline. Not only will the populations of each of these societies dwindle, but an increasing proportion will be moving into old age, when they are less productive and use more health resources. However, the weakness of all such predictions is that humans meddle with their own history. Predictions about the future affect how humans act or plan today and ultimately how events unfold. The challenge is to pick the trends that are likely to be prolonged, but to also factor in human influence.

1   A cycle is usually repeated at some time **in the future**. Yes

2   We can **look back and understand** past predictions. ....

3   Past predictions have caused people to **firmly believe in** current predictions. ....

4   **Population figures** can be predicted quite accurately. ....

5   Some **countries** are predicted to experience a **total** decline in population. ....

6   The **percentage** of elderly people will **dwindle** in some countries. ....

7   Elderly people **work less**. ....

8   To make accurate predictions we need to **take into account** the **effect** people have on their environment. ....

2.2 **Look at the words in bold in the eight statements and find the words or phrases in the text that are similar in meaning, or the opposite. The first one has been done for you.**

1   in the future – subsequent

2   ....

3   ....

4   ....

5   (×2)....................... ....

6   (×2) ....

7   ....

8   (×2) ....

Error warning!

Percent or *Per cent* is the word form of the symbol %. We can write *20%* or *20 per cent*. *Percentage* is the noun form: *The **percentage** of women in Parliament increased in 2001.* NOT ~~*The percent of women* ...~~

2.3 Correct the six mistakes in the text. Use the information in unit 23 to help you.

The graph displays the actual population of Australia in 2002 and the projected figures of 2101. The per cent of people aged 15–24 is predicted to fall significantly during this period, while there will be an increase of the percentage of people aged 55–64. In 2002, just under 15 percentage of the population was aged between 15 and 24, while in 2101 this is predicted to drop in approximately 10 per cent.

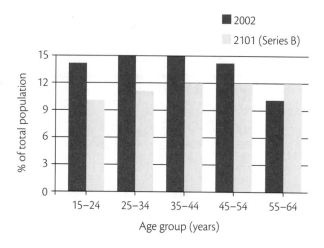

1 .....shows.....   4 ....

2 ....   5 ....

3 ....   6 ....

2.4 Complete the first half of this essay with suitable words from the box, then complete the essay.

ageing   challenges   compounded   declining   elderly   factors   implications   migrating
population   present   rates   trends

Statistics show that in several countries the population will decline in the next 50 years and the population of these countries will also age rapidly.
What problems might this cause? What can best be done to deal with these problems?

IIf current (1) .... continue, then in some countries the (2) .... is expected to dwindle within the next 50 years. This problem is (3) .... by the fact that not only is the number of inhabitants diminishing, but they are also growing older. This (4) .... population will bring several (5) ....

The first of these is economic. At (6) .... there are sufficient younger people to earn money and pay taxes to support the (7) .... However, within 50 years this will not be the case. The ageing and (8) .... population will therefore have important (9) .... for the economy of the country. In addition, there will be fewer young people to staff care homes and look after the older generation. As a result, their quality of life is also likely to suffer.

To find a solution, we need to first understand the causes, and there may be several possible contributing (10) .... here. Firstly, birth (11) .... in these countries are clearly falling. This may be due to economic issues, or to the fact that young people are (12) .... away from the area for work. If this is the case, then…

3.1 PRONUNCIATION Which of the patterns (A–F) matches the number of syllables and the stress pattern of the words below? (For example, pattern A matches the word *global* because it has two syllables with a stress on the first syllable.)

A	B	C	D	E	F
• —	• — —	— — • — —	— • —	— — — • —	— • —

global ....A....
globalisation ....
implication ....
isolation ....

culture ....
domestic ....
international ....
local ....

sceptical ....
modernisation ....
national ....
multicultural ....

projection ....
icon ....
multinational ....
population ....

3.2 🎧 13b Now listen and check your answers, then practise saying the words.

Test practice

Academic Writing Task 1

You should spend about 20 minutes on this task.

The chart below gives information about people of different ages and their reasons for walking less.

Summarise the information by selecting and reporting the main features, and make comparisons where relevant.

Write at least 150 words.

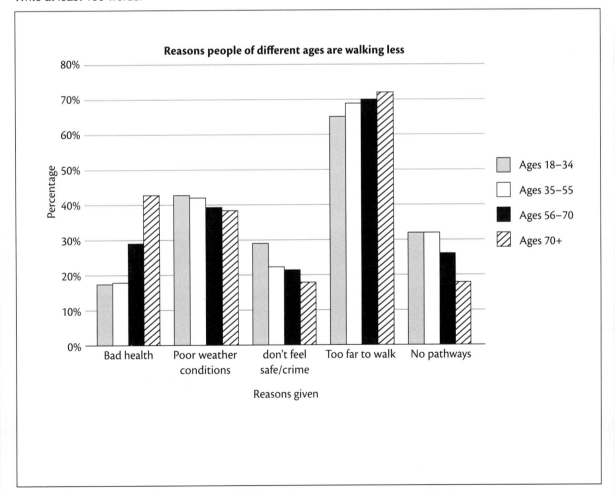

14 Urbanisation
Problems and solutions, big city life

Problems and solutions

1.1 Consider whether you can ever have *too much*, *too many*, *too little* or *too few* of the following.

time   traffic   people   money   space   work   rubbish

1.2 🎧 **14a** Listen to a conversation between two women and decide which two topics they talk about.

1.3 🎧 **14a** Listen again and write down all the verbs that are used with the words *problem* and *issue*.

....

....

....

....

1.4 Complete the sentences using the verbs you wrote in 1.3. There may be more than one possible answer, so try to use a different verb for each sentence.

1   One of the biggest problems .... the world today is poverty.

2   Your problems won't go away if you ignore them; you need to .... them.

3   The problem was .... by a blocked pipe, which eventually burst.

4   Here is a list of the issues that will be .... during the meeting.

5   Unfortunately we were unable to .... the issue, even after two days of talks.

6   The main speaker did not arrive, which .... an awkward problem for the organisers of the conference.

1.5 Match the nouns in column B with the correct verbs in column A. Which two verbs can be used with the words *problem* and *compromise*?

A	B
find	a compromise
overcome	an issue
solve	a situation
remedy	a difficulty
resolve	a solution
reach	a problem

1.6 Correct the mistakes in these sentences.

1   I am not sure we will ever solve the issue of unemployment.

2   We need to resolve a solution to this situation as soon as possible.

3   What can we do to solve this difficulty?

4   At last scientists have solution the problems associated with solar-powered cars.

5   Finally, the members of the city council were able to solve a compromise and the building work was allowed to start.

1   *solve the problem / resolve the issue*

2   4   ....

3   5   ....

1.7 Cross out the one word in each list that is NOT a synonym for the word in capitals.

1 PROBLEM   difficulty, dilemma, ~~benefit~~, challenge, obstacle

2 SOLUTION   answer, key, remedy, resolution, setback

3 WORSEN   compound, deteriorate, enhance, exacerbate

4 IMPROVE   advance, aggravate, flourish, progress, reform

5 CHANGE   acclimatise, adapt, adjust, amend, linger, modify, transform

> **Vocabulary note**
>
> We usually use a hyphen between two words if they are joined together to form an adjective: *user-friendly*. We don't use a hyphen if the first word ends in *-ly*: *environmentally friendly*.

1.8 Use a hyphen to combine one of the words in box A with one of the words in box B. Then complete the sentences.

A   double   long   short   one   *B*   edged   sighted   sided   term

1 We need a .... plan for our transport systems that will take into account future growth.

2 A warning sign was put at the site of the accident as a .... measure until a new wall was built.

3 This argument appears to be a little .... I'd like to hear the other side as well.

4 The management agreed to employ five more members of staff, which in hindsight was a very .... decision because within a few weeks we were again understaffed.

5 Globalisation is a .... sword. It promotes multiculturalism while it erodes the local culture.

Big city life

2.1 Complete the text with suitable adjectives from the box. More than one adjective may be possible.

adequate   basic   booming   catastrophic   decent
enormous   pressing   staggering

Megacities

The world's population is [1]..........................., nowhere more so than in its cities. Today, there are 33 megacities, each containing more than 10 million inhabitants, three-quarters of them in developing nations. By 2030, there are expected to be at least 27 megacities. Such a [2]........................... rate of urbanisation brings its own problems, especially in developing nations, where the majority of the megacities will be found.

Employment and educational opportunities are the main attraction of urban centres. But hopes for a better life are often dashed as overpopulation puts an [3]........................... strain on the infrastructure of the cities and their ability to provide [4]........................... necessities such as clean water and a place to live.

Many rural migrants fail to find [5]........................... work, and therefore cannot afford [6]........................... housing. In some megacities up to 50 per cent of the residents live in slums. This problem is [7]..........................., with the United Nations predicting that two thirds of the world's population will be living in cities by 2050. If the infrastructure within those cities does not grow at the same rate the result will be [8]........................... .

2.2 Find words in the text on page 73 that match these definitions.

1   People that live in a particular place. ....

2   Areas of the world that are poorer and have less advanced industries. ....

3   The process by which more people leave the countryside to live in the city. ....

4   The problem of having too many people. ....

5   The basic systems and services of a city. ....

6   Very poor and crowded areas of a city. ....

2.3 WORD BUILDING Complete the table.

Noun	Verb	Adjective
competition		
		excluded
	include	
	isolate	
		poor
responsibility	.... responsibility	
		tolerant

3.1 Answer these questions. Write one or two sentences.

1   What are the main problems associated with living in a big city?

2   Can anything be done to solve those problems?

3   Whose responsibility is it to solve these problems?

> **Ⓥ** *Vocabulary note*
>
> To refer to a group of people we can use *the* + adjective: *the elderly, the poor, the young*. E.g. *We should look after **the elderly***.

3.2 Now complete these answers to the questions with suitable words from 2.3.

1   Big cities can be overcrowded, so there are a lot of people c........................... for each job and for accommodation. The lack of jobs usually means that there is a lot of p........................... in big cities. And although there are a lot of people around them, many people feel very i........................... in big cities and it's particularly difficult for the elderly.

2   I think we need to be more t........................... of each other. I think it helps if we try to create small communities within the bigger city so we should try to i........................... people rather than e........................... them.

3   Well, we all have to t........................... r........................... for these problems and we can all do something to help. But the government is also r........................... to a certain extent as well. They need to make sure that the p........................... are looked after and that they have access to the facilities they need.

4 PRONUNCIATION Ⓞ 14b If we have *-ed* at the end of a word, it can be pronounced with a *t* or *d* sound. Look at the following words and write *t* or *d* depending on their sound. Now listen and check your answers, then practise saying the words.

> accepted   crowded   developed   excluded   included   isolated
> overpriced   overworked   resolved   stressed   solved

Test practice

Academic Reading

Rags, bones and recycling bins

Tim Cooper investigates the history of waste recovery.

Test tip

This reading text is also good practice for General Training Section 3.

As concern mounts that the consumer society may be ecologically unsustainable, historians have begun to interest themselves in past efforts to achieve efficient use of scarce resources. Far from being a recent innovation, recycling and reuse of household cast-offs have a long history. In early modern Britain, one of the most characteristic forms of recycling has been the trade in second-hand clothing, which has survived to the present day in the shape of the ubiquitous charity shop. The cost of buying new ensured that many among the lower orders of eighteenth-century English society relied on second-hand apparel. The rag fairs of the rapidly growing cities and a network of tradesmen and pawnbrokers supplied this trade. Some historians have argued that the second-hand trade played an important role in the nascent development of mass consumerism and fashion; in fact, demand was so high clothes were often a target for thieves.

Recycling was not restricted to the clothing trade. A much wider culture of reuse existed. This included, for example, the recycling of building materials from demolished buildings, the repair or reuse of most metal goods, and the use of old rags in the paper industry, which was almost wholly reliant upon recycling for its raw materials. Recycling was thus an important component of the pre-industrial economy, enabling it to cope with shortages of raw materials and aiding the poor. Pre-industrial recycling was largely a response to chronically low levels of production. After 1800, industrialisation, urbanisation and population growth saw the emergence of a new problem – waste – and gave a new significance to recycling. Of course, the generation of urban waste was not new in itself, but the scale of waste production after 1800 certainly was. The treatment and disposal of domestic waste became a problem of the first order. From the 1850s the problem of human waste disposal was being addressed by the construction of sewerage systems; the domestic refuse problem, however, remained relatively neglected until 1875.

To fully appreciate the complexities of this issue, some further context is needed. Nineteenth century Britain was very much dependent on coal, which was used domestically, for cooking and warmth, and in manufacturing. In the 1850s, the average amount of coal burned by each household in London alone was estimated at 11 tons per year. The coal ash produced by the fires was very much in demand for brick making, badly needed to house the rapidly expanding population. However, the ash was also in demand from the food and agricultural industry in the South East region of the country, where it was used to fertilise crops, again much needed by the growing urban population. Thus, the collection of domestic waste in all its forms created a flourishing trade.

Up until 1900 most urban areas relied on private contractors for waste disposal, who operated only with the minimum of environmental regulation. This was the context in which the Victorian dust-yards, immortalised in Charles Dickens' novel Our Mutual Friend, emerged.

These yards sprang up either in or around many major cities in the nineteenth century, but were particularly characteristic of London. The dust-yards made their money by employing men, women and children to sift and sort through the filth in search of items of value, such as rags and metals. These were then sold to contract merchants. A large proportion of the material that remained after sorting was dust and cinders; where possible these were sold as a fertiliser or fuel source, but where no market existed they were dumped either on land or at sea.

The dust-yards were the most notorious of the nineteenth-century waste trades. In *Dangerous Trade* (1902), industrial health expert Thomas Oliver stated that 'under all circumstances dust-sorting is dirty and disagreeable work'. The uniquely unpleasant conditions of the yards meant that dust-women formed 'a class by themselves, and so the work becomes more or less hereditary'. The workers also received marginal reward for their efforts. By 1900 the average wages of women in contractors' yards in London were only between seven and eight shillings per week. As a result the dust-yards were increasingly controversial by the end of the nineteenth century. At the same time, the waste continued to grow. The 1875 Public Health Act had given local authorities a legal responsibility to remove and dispose of domestic waste. However, the last years of the century saw a solution to the apparently insoluble problem of what to do with the refuse of Britain's cities. A means, in the eyes of experts, to achieve the perfect removal of waste without resort to either the dust-yard or the tip: the incinerator.

Test tip

For notes completion, and flowchart completion items, make sure that you stick to the word limit. Do not write extra unnecessary words. Check you have copied the words correctly from the text.

Questions 1–8

Complete the notes below. Choose **NO MORE THAN TWO WORDS** from the passage for each answer.

The history of recycling in the UK

Eighteenth-century Britain

- People recycled products such as
  - **(1)** .... (sometimes these had been stolen)
  - scrap from knocked down buildings
  - almost anything made from **(2)** ....
  - old cloth or rags.
- The making of **(3)** .... relied heavily on recycled materials.

- Recycling had two main advantages:
  - it provided necessary **(4)** .... (needed due to low levels of production)
  - it gave economic support to **(5)** ....

Nineteenth-century Britain

- The remains of fires were used to help grow **(6)** .... and to make **(7)** ....

  More refuse was created because

  i) there were more people & more big cities

  ii) increasing **(8)** ....

Questions 9–14

Complete the flowchart below using **NO MORE THAN TWO WORDS** from the text.

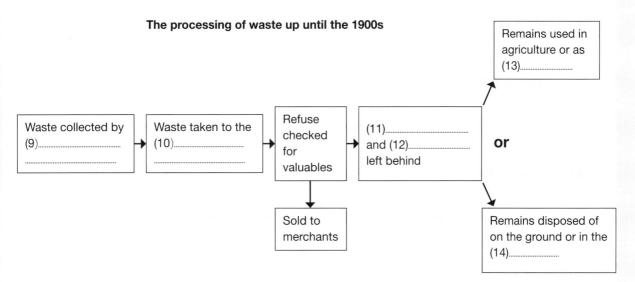

The processing of waste up until the 1900s

Remains used in agriculture or as (13)...........................

Waste collected by (9)........................... .... → Waste taken to the (10)........................... .... → Refuse checked for valuables → (11)........................... and (12)........................... left behind **or**

Sold to merchants

Remains disposed of on the ground or in the (14)...........................

Question 15

Choose the correct answer **A**, **B**, **C** or **D**.

In the final paragraph, what are we told about waste disposal at the end of the nineteenth century?
A It was a respected business.
B The work was relatively well-paid.
C Authorities decided to burn the waste.
D Disposal of waste had not yet been regulated.

15 The green revolution
The environment, climate change and pollution

The environment

1.1 Choose the words that reflect your opinion of these three statements from the first column of the table below. Write the words you chose in the *My opinion* column.

1 We should educate the public about our environment by handing out leaflets.

2 Within a few years we will have solved all of our pollution problems.

3 Within the next ten years the only chemicals we use will be environmentally friendly ones.

	My opinion	Speaker A	Speaker B
Statement 1 – useful / useless?			
Statement 2 – possible / impossible?			
Statement 3 – likely / unlikely?			

1.2 🎧 15a Now listen to two people (speakers A and B) giving their opinions about the same ideas and choose the words that reflect their opinions. Write them in the appropriate columns of the table.

1.3 Listen again or look at the recording script at the back of the book and write the adjectives the speakers used to express their opinions. Put the adjectives into the correct column according to their meaning.

useful	useless	possible	impossible	likely	unlikely
beneficial	....	....	....	....	....
....	....	....	....	....	....
....	....	....	....	....	....
....	....	....	....	....	....

> ### Ⓥ Vocabulary note
> The prefix *re-* often tells us that something is being done again: *reuse, revegetate.*
> The prefix *de-* often tells us that something is being removed: *decaffeinated, deforestation.*

Climate change and pollution

2.1 Complete the text with words from the box.

acid   biodiversity   contaminated   deforestation   ecosystems   emissions
environmental   erosion   exhaust   drought   fertilisers   greenhouse   waste

The advances made by humans have made us the dominant species on our planet. However, several eminent scientists are concerned that we have become too successful, that our way of life is putting an **unprecedented** strain on the Earth's (1)............................ and threatening our future as a species. We are confronting (2)............................ problems that are more **taxing** than ever before, some of them seemingly **insoluble**. Many of the Earth's crises are **chronic** and **inexorably** linked. Pollution is an obvious example of this, affecting our air, water and soil.

The air is polluted by (3)............................. produced by cars and industry. Through (4)............................. rain and (5)............................. gases these same (6)............................. fumes can have a **devastating** impact on our climate. Climate change is arguably the greatest environmental challenge facing our planet with increased storms, floods, (7)............................. and species losses predicted. This will **inevitably** have a negative impact on (8)............................. and thus our ecosystem.

The soil is (9)............................. by factories and power stations, which can leave heavy metals in the soil. Other human activities such as the overdevelopment of land and the clearing of trees also take their toll on the quality of our soil; (10)............................. has been shown to cause soil (11)............................. . Certain farming practices can also pollute the land though the use of chemical pesticides and (12)............................. . This contamination in turn affects our rivers and waterways and damages life there. The chemicals enter our food chain, moving from fish to mammals to us. Our crops are also grown on land that is far from **pristine**. Affected species include the polar bear, so not even the Arctic is **immune**.

Reducing (13)............................. and clearing up pollution costs money. Yet it is our quest for wealth that generates so much of the refuse. There is an urgent need to find a way of life that is less damaging to the Earth. This is not easy, but it is **vital**, because pollution is **pervasive** and often life-threatening.

2.2 Match the words in bold with these synonyms.

1 unspoiled ...*pristine*...
2 crucial ....
3 unparalleled ....
4 extremely harmful ....
5 insurmountable ....

6 unaffected ....
7 omnipresent ....
8 unavoidably (×2) ....
9 persistent ....
10 challenging ....

3 Consider how you would answer these questions.

1 What do you think is the greatest environmental threat we face today?
2 What can the government do to help protect the environment?
3 What can we as individuals do?

4.1 Use a dictionary to check the different forms of the words in the box as well as the prepositions used with them. Then complete the answers to the questions in 3 using the correct form of the word in brackets. You will need to add prepositions to the words that are underlined.

contaminate	danger	dispose	erode	pollute	recycle	risk	sustain	threat

1 I think our environment is ¹ ...*under threat from*... (*threat*) many different things. We have allowed too much ² .... (*pollute*) to enter our ecosystem and we are ³ .... (*danger*) poisoning ourselves as a result. I think soil ⁴ .... (*erode*) and water ⁵ .... (*contaminate*) are two of the most urgent problems that we need to deal with.

2 Clearly our current lifestyle is not ⁶ .... (*sustain*). The government should educate people about these problems and encourage us to change our habits. They need to show everyone that we are putting the very future of our planet ⁷ .... (*risk*).

3 We can make sure we don't throw ⁸ .... (*recycle*) items into our normal waste ⁹ .... (*dispose*) bins. We can also help protect our planet by not using phosphate-based detergents; this will help to keep ¹⁰ .... (*pollute*) out of our food chain.

4.2 Complete the sentences using the negative form of the words in brackets.

1 It is <u>unrealistic</u> (*realistic*) to expect everyone to change their buying habits overnight.

2 When it comes to protecting the environment, cost should be
.... (*relevant*).

3 It is .... (*reasonable*) for rich countries to expect developing countries to reduce carbon emissions immediately.

4 People who dump chemical waste into our waterways are very .... (*responsible*).

5 The oil spill has caused .... (*repairable*) damage to several marine species.

6 Scientists believe that the damage to this area is .... (*reversible*).

7 These species are ....(*replaceable*). Once they are lost our ecosystem will be changed.

8 It is a mistake to think that increased consumerism and environmental damage are .... (*related*).

> **Vocabulary note**
>
> The prefix *ir-* is often used with adjectives beginning with *r* to form the opposite or to mean lacking something: *reversible*, **ir**reversible, *regular*, **ir**regular. Some words beginning with *r* form their opposite with *un-*: *realistic*, *unrealistic*.

4.3 Spend 2 minutes speaking about the topic below. When you have finished, complete the writing task. For both tasks, try to use as many of the new words you have learned in this unit as you can.

Describe something that you often do to help the environment.

You should say
- **what you do**
- **why you think this helps the environment**
- **what other things you would like to do to help**

and say how you feel about helping the environment.

Your city council has asked for suggestions of ways that locals can help the environment.
Write a letter to the council. In your letter
- *suggest a way that locals and the council can help the environment*
- *explain why you think this would help the environment*
- *say why you think it is important to help the environment*
Write at least 150 words
Begin you letter as follows:
Dear Sir or Madam,

---

5 PRONUNCIATION 🎧 15b Some words have a different stress pattern and therefore a different pronunciation, depending on their meaning or part of speech. Circle the correct stress pattern for the words in *italics* in these sentences. Listen to the recording to check your answers and then practise saying the sentences.

1 I *refuse* to go. (r**e**fuse / ref**u**se)

2 Disposing of *refuse* is a growing problem. (r**e**fuse / ref**u**se)

3 There is a *conflict* here. (c**o**nflict / confl**i**ct)

4 The two reports *conflict* with each other. (c**o**nflict / confl**i**ct)

5 We all need to be *present* at the meeting. (pr**e**sent / pres**e**nt)

6 This issue *presents* an enormous problem. (pr**e**sents / pres**e**nts)

7 We are making a lot of *progress*. (pr**o**gress / progr**e**ss)

8 We need to *progress* at a faster rate. (pr**o**gress / progr**e**ss)

9 There has been an *increase* in carbon emissions. (**in**crease / incr**ea**se)

10 Temperatures are expected to *increase*. (**in**crease / incr**ea**se)

Test practice

Academic Writing Task 1

Test tip

Make sure that you include all of the stages in the process. You should follow a logical sequence and do not miss any stages out. Do not copy words directly from the question paper; instead try to change them. For example, you could use the verb *collect* instead of the noun *collection*. Study the information in unit 23 before you begin.

You should spend about 20 minutes on this task.

The diagram below shows the process for recycling of aluminium cans.

Summarise the information by selecting and reporting the main features, and make comparisons where relevant.

Write at least 150 words.

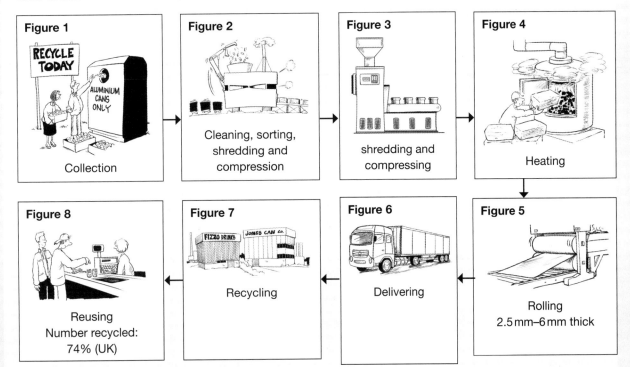

Figure 1

Collection

Figure 2

Cleaning, sorting, shredding and compression

Figure 3

shredding and compressing

Figure 4

Heating

Figure 5

Rolling
2.5 mm–6 mm thick

Figure 6

Delivering

Figure 7

Recycling

Figure 8

Reusing
Number recycled:
74% (UK)

Test Three (Units 11–15)

Choose the correct letter A, B, C or D.

1   The tallest building where I live has 75 ....
   A stores   **B** storages   **C** stories   **D** storeys

2   It is a very .... house – you can't really tell it apart from all the others in the street.
   A ornate   **B** innovative   **C** traditional   **D** state-of-the-art

3   I wish someone would invent a .... for opening milk cartons – my family always makes a mess of it!
   A devise   **B** device   **C** trigger   **D** pulley

4   Although it is an old house, it has been very well ....
   A maintained   **B** condemned   **C** occupied   **D** demolished

5   The latest .... for consumers is a system that allows shoppers to check out their groceries for themselves without having to wait in long queues.
   A innovate   **B** inventor   **C** innovator   **D** innovation

6   The developers .... a school on the new housing estate.
   A build   **B** building   **C** built   **D** built up

7   This machine performs the same .... as a washing machine but on a much larger scale.
   A function   **B** frame   **C** feature   **D** form

8   The Internet allows us to .... enormous amounts of information without leaving the house.
   A access   **B** accept   **C** scroll   **D** supply

9   My new fridge has a little screen on the outside that .... the internal and external temperature.
   A devises   **B** designs   **C** displays   **D** discovers

10 The whole system has been .... so we can no longer ask anyone for help.
   A automatic   **B** automated   **C** computerise   **D** digital

11 I found a very useful article .... the Internet.
   A by   **B** in   **C** for   **D** on

12 Our new house was designed .... computer.
   A by   **B** in   **C** on   **D** with

13 Many big cities today are ...., with inhabitants from all over the world.
   A culture   **B** cultural   **C** multiculture   **D** multicultural

14 International prices can also have an impact on the .... market.
   A domestic   **B** global   **C** urban   **D** worldwide

15   The graph shows the figures .... 2003 and 2005.
    A of   **B** to   **C** for   **D** about

16   The chart shows the .... of visitors and their country of origin.
    A per cent   **B** percentage   **C** %   **D** total

17   I think we all need to do more to help ....
    A old   **B** old person   **C** elderly   **D** the elderly

18   Our .... population will cause many problems in the future.
    A age   **B** ageing   **C** elderly   **D** old

19   We really need to find a way to .... this issue.
    A solve   **B** overcome   **C** prevent   **D** resolve

20   The bad weather and a lack of food simply .... our problems.
    A compounded   **B** enhanced   **C** salvaged   **D** transformed

21   Given the rapid growth of our population, there is a .... need to improve our infrastructure.
    A huge   **B** catastrophic   **C** pressing   **D** booming

22   If people were more .... of each other then there would be less fighting.
    A excluding   **B** exclusive   **C** tolerate   **D** tolerant

23   We all need to .... responsibility for improving our local community.
    A have   **B** make   **C** take   **D** give

24   After a few hours of discussion we finally reached a ....
    A compromise   **B** promise   **C** situation   **D** debate

25   Some scientists believe that we are in danger .... running out of oil within ten years.
    A from   **B** for   **C** of   **D** to

26   Many jobs are at .... if the current financial climate continues.
    A danger   **B** risk   **C** dangerous   **D** threat

27   Cleaning detergent is a common household .... that can be found in our waterways.
    A pollution   **B** pollutant   **C** polluter   **D** polluted

28   It is difficult to quantify the .... that household waste has on the environment.
    A affect   **B** effort   **C** impact   **D** implication

29   Every household should be more careful in the way that they .... of waste.
    A dispose   **B** disposal   **C** eliminate   **D** throw

30   The government have .... to fine anyone who pollutes the river.
    A endangered   **B** risked   **C** prevented   **D** threatened

16 The energy crisis
Natural resources, alternative fuels

Natural resources

1.1 **Answer the questions in this quiz.**

1   You decide to fly to an island 5,000 miles away for a holiday.
    How many trees would you need to plant to offset or make up
    for the CO_2 emissions produced by the flight?
    A   0.2   B   20   C   2

2   Which is the most environmentally friendly way to clean
    your clothes?
    A   Hand-wash the clothes in hot water.
    B   Take them to the dry cleaners.
    C   Machine-wash the clothes in cold water.

3   You are tidying up your house in the evening, going back and forth between the bedroom, kitchen and living room,
    spending five to ten minutes in each room as you sort out the clutter. What is the best way to make sure your lights aren't
    needlessly wasting energy?
    A   Keep the lights on as you go from room to room until the job is done.
    B   Turn the lights off every time you leave a room and then on again when you return.

4   You decide to cook a baked potato for lunch. Which is the most energy-efficient way of cooking the potato?
    A   Put it in an electric oven to cook slowly for an hour.
    B   Quickly zap it in the microwave.

5   You want to really make a significant contribution to the reduction of CO_2 emissions. Which of these would be of the most
    benefit over the course of a year?
    A   Taking the train instead of driving a car.
    B   Hanging your washing out to dry rather than using the tumble dryer.
    C   Working from home one day a week.

1.2   **16** **Listen to the answers to find out how environmentally aware you are.**

1.3   **Complete the text with one word in each gap. Then look at the recording script at the back of the book to check**
         your answers.

If we want to (1)................... energy then we need to change the way we behave. We need to buy appliances that are more
energy (2)................... and limit the amount of time we use them. To reduce the (3)................... the greenhouse gases have on our
(4)................... we should plant more trees. Trees can (5)................... carbon dioxide and so they help to (6)................... the fumes
produced by our cars. Turning off lights even for a few minutes can (7)................... the negative effects of turning them on
again later.

2.1 Read the text and then answer the questions below.

The future of energy

CO_2 plays a critical role in maintaining the balance in the Earth's atmosphere and the air that we breathe. It is also a waste product of the fossil fuels that almost every person on the planet uses for transport and other energy requirements. Because we create CO_2 every time we drive a car, cook a meal or turn on a light, and because the gas lasts around a century in the atmosphere, the proportion of CO_2 in the atmosphere is rapidly increasing.

The best evidence indicates that we need to reduce carbon dioxide emissions by up to 70 per cent by 2050. If you own a four-wheel-drive car and replace it with a hybrid car – a car that is powered by a combination of electricity and petrol – or a smaller standard-fuel car, you can achieve a reduction of that magnitude in a day rather than half a century. Unfortunately, our past history of change is considerably slower than this. Samuel Bowser first invented the petrol pump in 1885 but it wasn't until 1988 that all new cars manufactured in the UK were required to use unleaded petrol only.

Not only do fossil fuels pose an environmental hazard but there is also a pressing need to find an alternative energy source that is renewable. Opinions as to how much oil remains vary considerably. Some say that the Earth has produced only 18 per cent of its potential yield of oil; others say supplies may run out by 2051, with gas following 10 years later. To counter this, many countries are investing heavily in alternative energy sources such as solar energy or wind power, which uses large turbines to capture the energy of the wind.

1   How do you write CO_2 in full? ....

2   What do we call fuels such as coal, gas and oil?
....

3   What are two names for the substance that comes out of the exhaust of a car? ....

4   What do we call fuels that can be produced at any time?
....

5   Name two types of alternative energy.
....

6   What is a turbine most similar to?
A   a large engine   B   a windmill   C   a car

Alternative fuels

2.2 Complete the text with words from the box.

| alternative | converting | eco-friendly | emit | engine | fuel | fumes | greenhouse gases | plant | solar |

Fueling our cars

Our love of the fuel-burning car with its poisonous exhaust (1) .... has had a devastating effect both on our environment and on oil supplies. It is unlikely we will abandon our cars in large enough numbers to resolve this problem, so there is a pressing need to find an (2) .... fuel. Many car companies are exploring (3) .... energy sources, which have a surprisingly long history. In 1899, electric cars were very popular in the US, and in 1901, Ferdinand Porsche designed the first hybrid car. Both are now making a comeback and are likely to become much more commonplace in the future. Hydrogen vehicles can be traced back even further, to 1807. These use (4) .... panels to extract hydrogen from water are also likely to be readily available in the near future. As they (5) .... only water vapour, they do not contribute to (6) .... While countries such as Germany and Japan already have ambitious hydrogen plans, critics say that building a network of fuelling stations and (7) .... existing petrol stations to hydrogen will prove too costly and will limit this vehicle's potential.

Others believe that biofuels are the future. These fuels are based on (8) .... oils and so can be grown. The concept of using vegetable oil as a (9) .... dates back to 1895 when Dr Rudolf Diesel developed the first diesel (10) .... to run on vegetable oil. He demonstrated his engine at the World Exhibition in Paris in 1900 and described an experiment using peanut oil as fuel in his engine. In 1912, Diesel said, 'The use of vegetable oils for engine fuels may seem insignificant today. But such oils may become in the course of time as important as petroleum and the coal tar products of the present time.'

Error warning!

Gas is the American word for *petrol*. *Smoke* is produced when something burns. *Fumes* are the gases produced by chemicals such as petrol: *Older cars generate a great deal of* **fumes**. NOT *a great deal of gas* / *a great deal of smoke*

2.3 **Decide whether these sentences are true or false. Underline the parts of the text that gave you your answer.**

1 Cars that run on electricity and petrol first appeared in 1901. ....*True*........

2 Water is produced from the exhausts of hydrogen cars. ....

3 It will be relatively inexpensive to change current petrol stations for hydrogen cars. ....

4 Biofuels are non-renewable. ....

5 In 1912 vegetable oil was seen as an important fuel source. ....

2.4 **Which is the odd one out? Try to explain why.**

1 curb / limit / ~~promote~~ / restrict ....*The other words mean 'to reduce'.*....

2 electricity / nuclear energy / solar energy / wind power ....

3 economical / effective / efficient / emission ....

4 carbon / fuel / gas / petrol ....

5 emit / discharge / release / retain ....

6 renewable / disposable / rechargeable ....

7 diminish / dwindle / deplete / drastic ....

8 consume / extend / exhaust / expend ....

9 conserve / preserve / reserve / save ....

2.5 **Answer these questions using as many new words and phrases from this unit as you can. If possible, record yourself and then listen to your answers.**

1 Do you think that you waste too much energy in the home? (Why / Why not?)

2 What can the government do to encourage people to save energy in the home?

3 Why do you think some people prefer to drive a car instead of using public transport?

4 Do you feel optimistic about the future in terms of energy? (Why / Why not?)

5 What changes to transport do you think will happen in the next 20 years?

Test tip

In the speaking test you will be assessed on your 'lexical resource' – in other words, whether you can use a wide range of vocabulary accurately. Think about your answers to these questions. Did you have to hesitate to search for words? Which words did you manage to use? Which words do you still need to practise?

Test practice

Academic Reading

In 2011, the US Environmental Protection Agency honoured famous country and western singer Willie Nelson for his efforts to promote the use of biodiesel through his own 'BioWillie' brand, a vegetable oil-based fuel which was then being distributed at filling stations nationally. However, by 2014, the venture had failed. Clearly, many hurdles stand in the way of making such biofuels commercially viable with traditional sources. Indeed, it remains very difficult to forecast whether powering our vehicles with crop derivatives will ever be a truly economical proposition. Nevertheless, it is not too early to ponder what impact the widespread adoption of biofuels would have on our environment.

In 2006, Michael S. Briggs, a biodiesel advocate at the University of New Hampshire, estimated that the United States would need about 140 billion gallons of biodiesel each year to replace all the petroleum-based transportation fuels currently being used. Although one could make a similar appraisal for the amount of sugar-derived ethanol needed to meet our needs, it is unlikely that drivers would ever want to fill up their tanks entirely with ethanol, which contains only two-thirds of the energy of gasoline, whereas biodiesel is only 2 per cent less fuel-efficient than petroleum-based diesel. Hence a switch to biofuels would demand no new technology and would not significantly reduce the driving range of a car or truck.

The main source of biodiesel is plant oil derived from crops such as rapeseed. An acre of rapeseed could provide about 100 gallons of biodiesel per year. To fuel America in this way would thus require 1.4 billion acres of rapeseed fields. This number is a sizeable fraction of the total US land area (2.4 billion acres) and considerably more than the 400 million acres currently under cultivation. Consequently, the burden on freshwater supplies and the general disruption that would accompany such a switch in fuel sources would be immense.

Such calculations are sobering. They suggest that weaning ourselves off petroleum fuels and growing rapeseed instead would be an environmental catastrophe. Are more productive oil crops the answer? Oil palms currently top the list because they can provide enough oil to produce about 500 gallons of biodiesel per acre per year, which reduces the land requirement fivefold. Yet its cultivation demands a tropical climate, and its large-scale production, which currently comes from such countries as Malaysia and Indonesia, is a significant factor in the ongoing destruction of what rainforest remains there. Conservationists have been warning that palm oil production poses a dire threat to the dwindling population of orang-utans, for example, which exist only in the wild in Borneo and Sumatra. So here again, the prospect of dedicating sufficient land to growing feedstock for the world's transportation needs promises to be an environmental nightmare.

There is, however, a 'crop' that is widely recognised as having the potential to meet the demands of a biodiesel-based transportation fleet without devastating the natural landscape: algae. Algae is a single-celled plant, some varieties of which can contain 50 per cent or more oil. They also grow much more rapidly than ordinary plants and can double in quantity within several hours.

The US Department of Energy funded considerable research on biofuel production using algae after the oil problems of the 1970s, an effort known as the Aquatic Species Program. Although this programme was terminated in the 1990s, a lot of experience was gained through research and various demonstration projects. The results suggested that algae can be grown in sufficient density to produce several thousand gallons of biodiesel per acre per year – a full order of magnitude better than can be expected using palm oil and two orders of magnitude better than soybeans.

It is not surprising then that many scientists and entrepreneurs are once again looking hard at the prospects for using algae to produce transportation fuels and sizeable amounts of money are being invested in various schemes for doing so. David Bayless, a professor of mechanical engineering at Ohio University, has been working with scientists to engineer a device that can grow cyanobacteria (blue-green algae). It uses carbon dioxide from the gases emitted from power-plant chimneys and sunlight that is distributed to the growing surfaces through optical fibres. Bayless uses an enclosed bioreactor and claims to be able to produce as much as 60 grams of biomass per square metre of growing surface per day.

Another recent effort is being carried out in San Diego by KentSeaTech Corporation. This company gained experience growing algae as a part of its aquaculture operations so was quick to respond when the California state government started looking for ways to treat the huge quantities of nutrient-laden water which runs off from adjacent farm lands. 'It's no real difficult feat to turn nutrients into algae,' says director of research Jon Van Olst, 'but how do you get it out of the water?' This is what Van Olst and his co-workers have been trying to achieve.

The people working on these ventures are clearly eager to make growing algae a commercial success. Yet it is not hard to find experts who view such prospects as dim indeed. John Benemann, a private consultant in California, has decades of experience in this area. He is particularly sceptical about attempts to make algae production more economical by using enclosed bioreactors rather than open ponds. He points out that Japan spent hundreds of millions of dollars on such research, which never went anywhere. Even Van Olst has serious reservations. 'It may work,' he says, 'but it is going to take a while and a lot of research before we get anywhere.'

Questions 1–5

Classify the following characteristics as belonging to
- **A** biodiesel
- **B** ethanol
- **C** ordinary diesel

Write the correct answers **A–C** next to questions 1–5.

1 Produced by a popular American entertainer. ....

2 This fuel gives only slightly more power than its renewable equivalent. ....

3 Provides two-thirds of the power of standard petrol. ....

4 Your car's performance will be almost unchanged if you change to this fuel. ....

5 Production can have a negative impact on water resources. ....

Questions 6–12

Do the following statements agree with the claims of the writer in the reading passage?

Next to questions 6–12 write

Yes	if the statement agrees with the claims of the writer
No	if the statement contradicts the claims of the writer
Not given	if it is impossible to say what the writer thinks about this

6   2% of Americans already use biodiesel. ....

7   At present in America, 400 million acres of land are used for agriculture. ....

8   The use of palm oil as a fuel source will require more land than using rapeseed oil. ....

9   Growing biodiesel crops has had a positive effect on local wildlife in some areas. ....

10 One advantage of algae is the speed with which it grows. ....

11 David Bayless believes that algae can produce more energy than solar power. ....

12 It is easy to grow algae using agricultural waste water. ....

Question 13

Choose the correct answer, **A**, **B**, **C** or **D**.

13 What is the main purpose of this article?
   A   To prove that biofuels could totally replace petrol in America.
   B   To examine the environmental impact of standard fuel sources.
   C   To assess the advantages and disadvantages of different types of fuel.
   D   To show that an international effort is required to solve the fuel crisis.

17 Talking business

Employment, management and marketing

Employment

1.1 Answer these questions.

Have you ever worked in any of these places? If not, would you like to?

A   a shop   B   a restaurant   C   a hotel   D   an office

1.2 🎧 17a Listen and match the speakers to the correct industry. Write your answers in the second column. In the third column, write the adjectives the speakers use to describe their job.

advertising
building
hospitality
retail

Speaker	Type of industry	Adjectives used to describe work
1		
2		
3		
4		

1.3 🎧 17a Complete the sentences with words from the recording. If necessary, listen to the speakers again.

1   I'm employed on a casual basis, so my .... are paid at the end of each week.

2   Over 100 members of staff were made .... when the new machines were installed in the factory.

3   It is important to have experience in the .... as well as academic qualifications.

4   I do .... so I often have to sleep during the day.

5   The owners had a meeting with all of the .... to discuss the takeover.

6   The government may decide to raise the age at which people .... from work from 65 to 70.

7   My boss has asked me to work .... tomorrow, so I won't be home until late.

8   Our junior staff .... $12 per hour.

9   If they don't increase my .... this year then I'm going to look for another job.

10 Many young people today value .... over a big salary.

1.4 Complete the sentences using the correct form of the word *employ*.

1   The .... find it difficult to get an interview if they have not had a job for a long time.

2   All .... must apply in writing if they wish to request a holiday.

3   .... rose by 5 per cent due to the closure of two large factories in the area.

4   I was only .... as a cleaner, but the family expected me to look after their children as well.

5   I couldn't work when my daughter was sick. Fortunately, my .... is very understanding.

Ⓥ *Vocabulary note*

A *job* = the particular thing you do to earn money: *I'm hoping to get **a job** during the holidays.*
Occupation = a formal word for *job*.
Profession = a type of job that requires specialist knowledge: *He works in the medical **profession**.*
Work = something you do to earn money. It is a verb as well as an uncountable noun: *I'm hoping to find **work** during the holidays.* NOT ~~find a work~~.
Workforce = all the people working in a company/industry/country: *A company is only as good as its **workforce**.*
Workplace = the building or room where people work: *You really need experience in the **workplace** to get a good job.*

Management and marketing

2.1 **Think of a word or phrase that matches the definitions below.**

1   The business or trade in a particular product. m.............................

2   People who buy goods. c.............................

3   The materials in which objects are wrapped before being sold.
    p.............................

4   A new fashion or pattern of behaviour. t.............................

5   The fact that someone can be believed or trusted. c.............................

6   Make someone do something by giving them a good reason to do it.
    p.............................

7   A means of identifying a particular company. b.............................

8   The things a company makes to sell. p.............................

2.2 **Now read the following text and check your answers to 2.1.**

Luxury brands dominate both the cosmetic and skincare market. But consumers are looking for more than just beauty in sophisticated packaging. Companies offering products with healthy ingredients have set the trend in recent years. When consumers go shopping for cosmetics, they want to know the products they are buying won't harm their skin. To gain credibility, many cosmetic companies have persuaded dermatologists and pharmacists to endorse their brands. In the past, the target customers of most skincare and cosmetic brands were women between the ages of 20 and 50. Nowadays, however, men are also increasingly looking for products to give their skin a healthy look. Once seen as a niche market, this is a segment that is only expected to grow in the coming years. Besides men, teenagers are also trying to enhance the health and beauty of their appearance. With such a broad client base, it is not surprising that the industry shows no sign of slowing down.

Error warning!

Products is used to refer to things that are produced to be sold – the focus is on the company producing them. *Goods* is used to refer to things that are sold – the focus is on the buying or selling of these. *Goods* cannot be used in the singular. *We have tested each **product**.* NOT ~~We have tested each goods/good.~~

3.1 Use a dictionary to check the meaning of the words in the box. Then choose the correct words in the sentences.

income   salary   wages   earnings

1   Buying larger containers of food is a more *economic / economical* way of shopping.

2   I would like to increase my *income / money* so I'm going to invest in some shares.

3   I need to earn more *money / income* so that I can buy that new computer.

4   Nowadays people worry a great deal about *earnings / money*.

5   My *earnings / money* increased by 10 per cent last year.

> **Error warning!**
>
> *Economical* = something that does not use a lot of fuel or money: *My new car is really economical to use.* *Economic* = the money of a country: *A strong government needs good **economic** policies.* NOT ~~economical policies~~

> **Vocabulary note**
>
> *Advertisement* or *advert* = a picture or short film used to persuade people to buy a product or apply for a job: *Did you see the **advertisement** in the paper?* *Advertising* = the business of trying to persuade people to buy things.

3.2 Correct the mistakes in the text, then write your own answer to this question.

> ***There is very little that parents and teachers can do to help young adults to prepare themselves for the workforce. Do you agree or disagree?***

The number of ¹*unemployment* seems to increase each year and the competition for each ²*work* is also increasing. Consequently, young adults need to do as much as they can to prepare to enter the ³*working place*. There are several things that parents and teachers can do at school and at home to help them.

Firstly, once they reach 15 or 16 years of age, children should be encouraged to plan their ⁴*profession*. No matter what ⁵*work* they choose, choosing early will help them to make sure they learn the appropriate ⁶*knowledge* during their studies. For example, if they would like ⁷*working* in the ⁸*advertisement* industry, it can help if they study the arts. Teachers can also help by showing children the best way to respond to an ⁹*advertising* for a job.

At home, parents can teach children how to stick to a budget. If a country experiences an ¹⁰*economical* crisis, these skills are invaluable. They can begin by making children ¹¹*gain* their pocket money by doing ¹²*job* in the home. They could even be paid more or less ¹³*earnings* based on the quality of their ¹⁴*job*. If children develop a strong work ethic from an early age then this should ensure that they have enough money when they reach ¹⁵*retire* age. In conclusion, although some people may feel there is not a lot that adults can do to help children succeed in their work life, I believe that there are several key ways that both teachers and parents can prepare them for this stage. Therefore, I completely disagree with this statement.

1   *unemployed* ....
2   ....
3   ....
4   ....
5   ....

6   ....
7   ....
8   ....
9   ....
10 ....

11 ....
12 ....
13 ....
14 ....
15 ....

4.1 PRONUNCIATION 🔊 17b Which words are pronounced in a similar way? Put the words in the box into the correct column according to their sound. Then listen and check. Practise saying the words.

clerk   earn   first   floor   force   law
market   nurse   perk   poor   purse
target   walk   work

ɜː	ɑː	ɔː
bird	park	ball

Test practice

General Training Writing Task 1

You should spend about 20 minutes on this task.

You work in a busy but poorly organised office and you are keen to be promoted. Your employer needs to find a new supervisor for your department.

Write a letter to your employer. In the letter
- **ask to be considered for this job**
- **explain why you would be a suitable candidate**
- **outline the current problems and the changes you would like to make.**

You should write at least 150 words.
You do **NOT** need to write any addresses.
Begin your letter as follows:

Dear .....

Academic Writing Task 2

You should spend about 40 minutes on this task.

In today's job market, qualifications do not matter. It is far more important to have good practical skills than a good theoretical knowledge of your field.

To what extent do you agree or disagree with this opinion?

Give reasons for your answer and include any relevant examples from your own knowledge or experience.

Write at least 250 words.

18 The law
Crime, punishment

Crime

1.1 Put the following into order from least to most serious in your opinion. Which do you think are considered to be crimes?

arson   burglary   fraud   vandalism   kidnapping   murder   pickpocketing
smuggling   swearing   dumping toxic waste

1.2 Now read the text and decide whether statements 1–7 are true or false. Write the words from the text which mean the same as or the opposite of the words in *italics*.

Crime

Crime is defined by society and relative to the society defining it. Traditionally, crime is considered an offence, a violation of public rules or laws. Crime is defined within each society by specific criminal laws on a national, state and local level. Actions that are offensive to an individual or group of people but do not violate laws are not crimes. Punishment or other sanctions result from the violation of these laws, and the social system for monitoring and enforcing public rules or laws is put into action. The social system generally consists of an administrative authority that formally deals with crime and a force of representative officers to enforce the laws and act on behalf of society. Being guilty of a criminal act usually involves some form of conscious evil intent or recklessness. In unintentional cases, such as crimes committed by children or the insane, the criminal is not usually punished in the same manner as is intentional crime.

Theories of crime and criminal activity are numerous and varied, but the reasons behind crime remain elusive. Theories suggest many possible causes. One theory suggests that property crime depends on criminal motive and opportunities to perpetrate crime. It also contends that crime is influenced by the degree to which others guard over neighbourhoods and other people. This particular theory relates an increase in crime rate to an increase in crime opportunity and a decrease in protection. Research also shows that income inequality correlates to property crime.

1   Offence is another word for crime. _True – crime is considered an offence_

2   The word offensive is related to crime. ....

3   It is the duty of the police to *violate* the law. ....

4   Generally, people who are guilty of a crime are *aware* of what they are doing.
....

5   The explanations for crime are *difficult to find*. ....

6   Crime can increase if people *protect* their property less. ....

7   Crime on property *is linked* to the different amounts of money people earn.
....

1.3 WORD BUILDING Complete the table.

Noun	Verb	Adjective
crime	c.................... a crime	
	deter	
	enforce	
	offend	
prevention		
prison		
punishment		

Error warning!

A *convict* is a person who is in prison. To *convict* someone is to find them guilty in a court of law. You *commit a crime* or *convict a criminal*, not ~~convict a crime~~. We talk about *criminal acts*, NOT ~~criminal actions~~.

1.4 Complete the sentences with a suitable word from the table in 1.3.

1 All .... acts should be punished.

2 Every society needs a strong system of law ....

3 People who .... crimes are often victims themselves.

4 I think dumping toxic waste should be made a .... offence. There is little to .... people from doing this at the moment.

5 I think we could have .... this crime by fitting an extra lock on the door.

Punishment

2.1 Match the verbs in column A with the nouns in column B.

A	B
accept	a crime
commit	a law
convict	a fine
impose	the consequences
pass	a criminal

2.2 Match the people with the things they do.

List of people

1 The accused = .C.

2 The judge ....

3 The jury ....

4 The prosecutor ....

5 The lawyer ....

6 The victim ....

List of things they do

A ... tries to prove the accused is guilty.

B ... gives evidence against the accused.

C ... is the person who is on trial.

D ... decides whether the accused is innocent or guilty.

E ... tries to prove the accused is innocent.

F ... decides how a criminal should be punished.

2.3 COLLOCATION What words can you use with *crime* and *law*? Write in the boxes below.

	Crime	Law
Adjectives	serious	
Verbs		

2.4 🎧 18 Now listen and fill in any blanks you have in the table.

2.5 🎧 18 Complete the sentences with suitable words from the recording. You may need to change the grammatical form of the word. Listen and check your answers.

1 I consider myself to be a law-a.............. citizen. I've never broken the law in my life.

2 The laws in this country are rather s.............. – even chewing gum is banned.

3 Arson is a crime a.............. property, but sometimes people can get hurt as well.

4 I was given a parking f.............. again yesterday. It's costing me a fortune.

5 It is the responsibility of the police and the government to c.............. crime.

6 More money should be spent on crime p.............. than on building prisons.

7 Sometimes the police feel that they are a.............. the law and should not be punished for traffic offences.

8 It used to be against the law to go fishing on Sundays, but thankfully that law was a.............. years ago.

> **Vocabulary note**
>
> *Prevent* = to stop something from happening or someone from doing something: *I stayed away from the bully to **prevent** any trouble. This will **prevent** crimes from happening.* NOT *This will avoid crimes.*
> *Avoid* = to stay away from someone or something: *You should try to **avoid** dangerous situations.*

3.1 Improve the speaking test answers by replacing the underlined words. Then answer the questions yourself.

1 **Do you think we should punish people who commit crimes?**
'Yes. I think that, if people [1]*do* a crime, then they should be punished and made to accept the consequences of their [2]*acts*. If they don't receive a [3]*punish* then they're likely do the same thing again.'

2 **Should all types of crime receive the same punishment?**
'No, in my opinion, for [4]*small* crimes it's best to just [5]*find* people. But, for more serious [6]*offends*, then we need to [7]*prison* them'.

3 **What do you think we can we do to stop people committing crimes?**
'Well, sometimes a crime is [8]*happened* through need, for example, if someone is poor and hungry. So, first, we need to take care of everyone in society and not just worry about protecting our [9]*stuff*. But we can also [10]*past* new laws, and educate people about them, so that they act as a [11]*block*. That way, [12]*people* who do crimes will think twice before they act.'

1	commit	4	....	7	....	10	....
2	....	5	....	8	....	11	....
3	....	6	....	9	....	12	....

Test practice

General Training Writing Task 2

You should spend about 40 minutes on this task.

Write about the following topic.

Crime is increasing and the prisons are overcrowded; the only way to fix these problems is to build more prisons.

Do you agree or disagree?

Give reasons for your answer and include any relevant examples from your own knowledge or experience.

You should write at least 250 words.

Use the following questions to help you think about this issue, then make notes to help you plan your answer.

1   Is it true that crime is increasing and prisons are overcrowded? Why do you think this is happening?

2   Would building more prisons fix these problems? (Can you explain why or why not?)

3   Is this the *only way* to fix these problems? (If not, can you suggest any other ways?)

4   Think about the statement in the question, do you agree with it or not?

Use this space to plan your ideas:

Building more prisons to reduce crime and make prisons less crowded	Other ways to reduce crime and overcrowded prisons
This would / might help to:	Some other ways to solve these problems are:
It wouldn't/might not help with:	Reasons this could / might work:

19 The media

The news, fame

The news

1.1 **Answer these questions.**

1 Are you
   A   well-informed about current affairs?
   B   not interested in current affairs?

2 Do you consider newspapers to be
   A   biased   B   entertaining   C   informative?

3 Do you prefer to get the news from
   A   newspapers   B   the internet   C   the radio   D   the television?

1.2   🔊 **19a** **Listen and say whether the following statements are true or false according to the speaker. Correct the statements that are false.**

1 The speaker believes the general public is well-informed. _False – they are ill-informed._

2 The Manly University project focused on stories about famous people.

....

3 Dan Taylor believes that the main aim of today's mass media is to inform people.

....

4 The study revealed that newspapers avoid reporting on the gap between the rich and the poor.

....

5 Important news stories appear in the back pages because this highlights their importance.

....

1.3   🔊 **19a** **Listen again and find words or phrases that match these definitions.**

1 a situation in which newspapers, radio and television are allowed to express opinions openly

2 to send out a programme on television or radio

3 written about or spoken of in the news

4 large systems consisting of many similar parts, all of which are centrally controlled

5 newspapers, radio and television when seen as a group

6 the deliberate removal of sections of a text or film considered to be unsuitable

7 a popular newspaper with lots of pictures and short articles

8 words in large print at the start of a news story or the main stories in the news

1.4 Read the following information about the same story and complete the text with words from the box.

biased   controversial   exposés   front page   publications   press   safeguards   sources

In response to the study, Martin Dexter from the Associated Press said: 'This study seems to be rather a harsh attack on the ¹............................. and I can't agree with its conclusions. You need to remember that we have a broad range of media sources available to us nowadays. There is an enormous amount of alternative news sources that provide a healthy balance to the mainstream media. If people want to be informed, they are unlikely to turn to tabloid newspapers to do so. Instead, they can access a wide range of journals, magazines and smaller ²............................. . They can also search online for the most up-to-date information from any part of the world. On the negative side, there is a problem with editor verification with some stories reported on the internet because ³............................. can be unreliable. The ⁴............................. in place for traditional media just don't exist there at the moment.'

'I'll admit that stories about ⁵............................. issues are less likely to be seen by the tabloids as ⁶............................. news. But I would be more concerned about content which is politically ⁷............................. or motivated. I believe there are many publishers and broadcasters that do still have a strong tradition of ⁸............................. and investigative journalism. If there is an emphasis on entertainment rather than more serious issues, then this is being driven by consumer demand. Perhaps ultimately we only get the media we deserve.'

1.5 Now answer these questions.

1 What do we call newspapers when seen as a group?

2 What phrase is used to refer to traditional news sources (i.e. newspapers, TV and radio)?

3 What two problems with new media does Martin Dexter mention?

4 What do we call the type of journalism that tries to discover the truth behind issues that are of public interest?

5 What reason does Martin Dexter give for newspapers not focusing on serious issues?

Fame

2.1 Use a dictionary to check the meaning of these verbs. Find out the noun and adjective forms and write them in your notebook.

bias   exploit   expose   inform   intrude   invade   investigate   publish   publicise
sensationalise   verify   speculate

2.2 Use a suitable form of the words in 2.1 to replace the words in bold.

1 There has been a lot of **gossip** .....*speculation*..... in the media about the identity of the victim.

2 Not surprisingly, the reporter was unable to **prove the truth behind** .... the claims.

3 The government has agreed to launch an official **inquiry** .... into the matter.

4 There has been a great deal of **media hype** .... about the new James Bond movie.

5 I'm not sure celebrities are being **used** ....; they often seem to court fame.

6 Most people believe that this newspaper favours the government too much to provide an **impartial** .... coverage of the election.

Vocabulary note

We say something/someone **has a / is a** good/bad/positive or negative **influence on** someone/something: John's new friends **are a** really bad **influence on** him. Influence can be a verb or a noun: The media **influences** the way many people think. The media **has a** major **influence on** the way many people think.

Remember that effect is a noun and affect is a verb. These can be used in a similar way to influence: The media **affects** the way many people think. The media **has a** major **effect on** the way many people think.

Error warning!

We say **on** the radio, **on** television, **on** screen, **on** the computer, **on** the Internet. We use **in** with printed media: We learn all about celebrities **in** magazines or **on** television. NOT ~~in magazines or television~~. These materials are freely available **on** the Internet. NOT ~~in the Internet~~.

3.1 These adjectives can be used to talk about the media or people in the media. Decide whether they are used in a negative or a positive way and put them in the correct box.

artificial   biased   distorted   factual
informative   invasive   intrusive
pervasive   realistic   sensationalist
superficial   unbiased   attention-grabbing

Positive	Negative

3.2 Think about your answers to these questions. Try to use as many of the adjectives from 3.1 as you can.

1   Would you like to be famous? (Why? / Why not?)

2   Do you think famous people have a positive or a negative influence on young people?

3   Nowadays we have access to the news 24 hours a day. What effect does this have?

3.3   🎧 19b Complete these answers to the questions in 3.2 with a suitable word or phrase. Then listen and check your answers.

1   I think a lot of people want to be famous nowadays and that's why reality TV is so popular. But I wouldn't like to be famous at all. Being famous nowadays simply means that you're in the ¹t............................ a lot and you're followed by the ²p............................ everywhere you go. I'd find that very ³i............................ . Famous people have no ⁴p............................ at all in any part of their life. Their life also seems to be very ⁵s............................ because they spend all of their time going to parties and trying to look glamorous. It all seems very ⁶a............................ to me – they just don't seem to be part of the real world at all.

2   I think they should have a positive ⁷i............................ on young people, but many of them don't. Some personalities are good role models and use their ⁸c............................ status to encourage people to think about important issues, but we often see photos of famous people behaving badly.

3   I think it can ⁹a............................ us in both positive and negative ways. On the one hand, it's very convenient to be able to catch up with what's happening in the world at any time of the day or night, no matter where you are. But on the other hand, this kind of news can give you a ¹⁰d............................ view of what's happening, because even minor news ¹¹s............................ are given more importance than they perhaps should have.

4.1   PRONUNCIATION Which of the following sounds do these words have: s (**stop**), z (**zoo**), ʒ (A**s**ia) or ʃ (**sh**op)?

artificial ....ʃ....   censor ....   intrusive ....   invasive ....
attention ....   exposed ....   intrusion ....   publication ....
biased ....   exposure ....   invasion ....   superficial ....

4.2   🎧 19c Now listen and practise saying the words.

Test practice

General Training writing Task 1

You should spend about 20 minutes on this task.

You have seen an interesting article in a magazine. You have a very good friend who you think will be interested in this topic.

Write a letter to your friend. In your letter
- **explain what the article is about**
- **say why you think your friend would be interested in this article**
- **tell your friend where they can find this article.**

Write at least 150 words.
You do **NOT** need to write any addresses.
Begin your letter as follows:

Dear .....,

Test tip

In General Training writing task 1, remember to think about the tone of the language you use. If you are asked to write a letter to a family member or a friend, your tone should be less formal than when writing a business letter.

Academic Writing Task 2

You should spend about 40 minutes on this task.

Write about the following topic:

It is now very easy to get all the news we need online, so there is no longer any need to pay for newspapers or expensive magazines.

Do you think this is a positive or a negative development?

Give reasons for your answer and include any relevant examples from your own knowledge or experience.
Write at least 250 words.

Test tip

General Training candidates can also practise with this task 2 question. When thinking about the positives or negatives of a development, think about any advantages or disadvantages this change has brought.

20 The arts
Art appreciation, the performing arts

Art appreciation

1.1 Which art forms are shown in these pictures? What do we call the people who do these things?

1.2 Which of these art forms do you enjoy the most/least? Why? What type of art/music do you prefer? Why?

1.3 Read the text, making sure you understand the meaning of the words in bold. Use a dictionary if necessary.

The brain of the beholder

The cave figures of Lascaux, Leonardo da Vinci's *Mona Lisa*, a Cubist painting by Pablo Picasso and the African **artefact** that **inspired** Picasso's work. These works of art are separated by great gulfs in time, different social and political systems, and language divides. Yet despite these variations, there is art in each place and era. That there is a seemingly **universal impulse** to express oneself this way suggests that human beings are neurologically hardwired for art.

Imagine yourself in the Louvre in Paris, pushing through the throngs to behold the Mona Lisa's enigmatic smile. Or recall the first time you ever saw the Sydney Opera House. Most likely your skin tingled, you felt a thrill and you paused for a moment of **reflection**. Even glimpses of **mundane** objects such as the latest curvaceous kettle can inspire something similar. Art and design critics will describe how formal qualities like proportion are **choreographed** to produce the viewer's **rush**. But the fact that **aesthetic** experience can inspire such a biological response suggests that it's a stimulus neuroscientists could analyse just as **deftly**.

And that's exactly what they are doing. In laboratories and galleries around the world, researchers are showing how the organisation of the brain relates to the **conception** and experience of art. This is the **burgeoning** field of neuroaesthetics, in which scientists are discovering that – rather than **transcending** the ordinary – art and aesthetics are part of everyday experience. They're also finding that, in some **fundamental** ways, art really is an expression of human nature.

1.4 Write *Yes* if these statements agree with the information in the text or *No* if the statements contradict the information. Write the words in bold that helped you with your answer.

1 Pablo Picasso got the idea for one of his paintings from an ancient work of art from Africa.
   Yes – artefact, inspired

2 The desire to create art is limited to certain parts of the world. ....

3 When people look at works of art it provokes serious and careful thought. ....

4 Ordinary objects can be aesthetically pleasing. ....

5 Art critics believe that artistic elements are arranged and combined together in order to create a feeling of excitement. ....

6 Researchers are analysing how the brain creates the idea of art. ....

7 Neuroaesthetics is failing to catch on in the world of science. ....

8 Scientists have discovered that art is a way of rising above everyday life. ....

▉ The performing arts

2.1 🔊 20a You will hear a radio broadcast about three different arts festivals on Bethania island. Listen and complete column A below. Write NO MORE THAN ONE WORD for each answer.

A	B
Living (1) .... **Week**	1 *the study of art in relation to its beauty =* ....
• Talks	
• (2) .... lunches	2 *organised sets of special events =* ....
• Book (3)	
• (4) .... for children	
• This year's (5) .... is Island Life	
The (6) .... **Arts**	3 *skilled =* ....
• A painting (7)	4 *creations =* ....
• Discussion of the (8) .... process	5 *represent or show something in a picture or story* = ...
• Workshops at local (9)	
• Display of local (10)	6 *make shapes in wood or stone with a knife* = ...
• (11) .... **of Voices**	7 *describes a show that involves the audience* = ...
• Several performances will be (12)	8 *the people gathered to listen to a performance* = ...
• (13) .... theatre	9 *take part =* ....
• Free (14)	10 *musical performances =* ....

2.2 🔊 20a Now listen again and find words or phrases to match the definitions in column B.

2.3 WORD BUILDING Complete the table.

Noun	Verb	Adjective
		creative
culture		
	influence	
	inspire	
imagination		
	participate	
		rich

3.1 Try to talk for two minutes about the following topic. Use words from the table in 2.3 if you can.

> Describe the type of music that you like.
> You should say
> - what type of music you prefer to listen to
> - when and how you like to listen to this type of music
> - why you enjoy listening to this type of music
> and say how listening to this music makes you feel.

3.2 🔊 20b You will hear somebody answering the question in 3.1. Listen and complete the text with no more than two words from the text. You may need to listen twice.

My taste in music is quite [1] .... and there isn't really one [2] .... of music that I like. I listen to everything from [3] .... music to [4] .... Music [5] .... a very important [6] .... in my life, and I listen to it almost constantly. I find that it helps to [7] .... or to change a [8] .... So I tend to choose my music according to who I'm with or what I'm doing. For example, if I'm driving long distances in my car I prefer to play something [9] .... to help keep me awake, but if I'm having a dinner party with friends then I play something more [10] .... I think that music helps to [11] .... me when I'm working, although my colleagues find it [12] .... so I tend to listen with [13] .... on. In that way I can [14] .... into my own little world. When I was younger I would definitely have said that I preferred live music. The [15] .... in a live [16] .... can be [17] .... Nowadays, though, a lot of popular groups only perform at very large [18] .... in front of [19] .... of 20,000 or more and I don't really like that. I prefer the [20] .... of listening to recorded music, and the sound quality is better as well. Music really [21] .... our lives – it can turn a boring, monotonous period of time into a [22] .... So I think it's essential to have music and, in fact, all of [23] .... in your life.

4 PRONUNCIATION 🔊 20c Each of the following words has a weak sound or *schwa* (ə), e.g. *about*. Underline the weak sounds in each word then listen and check your answers. Practise saying the words. There may be more than one schwa in each word.

atmosphere   classical   edition   festival   fundamental   imagination
literary   monotonous   musical   performance   popular   visual

Test practice

Academic Reading

You should spend about 20 minutes on questions 1–12, which are based on the reading passage.

Storytelling

Dr Tom Sjöblom, University of Helsinki, explores the link between narratives and memories.

Storytelling seems to be a fundamental feature of human existence. In a recent article, Paul Hernadi points out that storytelling and narratives are such widespread phenomena that they could justifiably be included in the list of human universals (Hernadi, 2001). But our craving for narratives, or stories, goes deeper than this. It is embedded in our mental images of whatever happens around us (Boyer, 2001). In other words, creating narratives is our way of connecting and interacting with our environment (Mink, 1978).

As a species, we humans appear to have a much more active attitude towards our environment than any other species. Our bodies and minds not only adapt to the surrounding world, but we actively shape and construct our environment to better suit our needs (Plotkin, 1993). From this perspective, culture is nothing more than an environment that we create ourselves. Culture is not something in opposition to nature. Instead it is a part of it; it is – in a way – nature modified to better suit the requirements of the human life form. Thus, culture and all aspects of it are basically products of natural selection and, more specifically, the evolution of the human mind (Boyer, 2001).

Between 60,000 and 20,000 years ago the first signs of art and religion appeared and humans started to build houses and invent more sophisticated tools and weapons, such as bows and arrows. This period has been called the 'big bang' of human culture. There is still much controversy over how to explain this period of innovation, but a growing consensus connects the greater cultural energy and innovation of the period to the emergence of individuals as creative beings (Mellars, 1994).

The archaeologist Steven Mithen has suggested that this creativity can be explained by the emergence of a 'cognitively fluid' mentality – in other words, an ability to link together information from different areas of our life. Cognitive fluidity makes it possible for human beings to emerge from the concrete situational present and to adopt a more general and abstract approach (Mithen, 1996). As Gerald Edelman puts it: 'With that ability come the abilities to model the world, to make explicit comparisons and to weigh outcomes; through such comparisons comes the possibility of reorganizing plans.' (Edelman, 1992)

Edelman goes further than this and argues that it is the flexibility of our memory system which is the key for understanding how cognitive fluidity affects our ability to learn new things in general (Edelman, 1992). The basic idea here is that our memory does not really represent the past as it happened. In most of the cases it does not even represent it as it is stored and coded into our brains. Instead, our memory prefers creating the past from the perspective of how relevant it is to our present situation. Striving for this kind of coherence, our mind combines stored representations and blends information stored in them (Holyoak & Thagard, 1995). Thus, all things being equal, we do not remember the past, we create it.

The medieval art of memory, known as *memoria*, has interested historians for a long time, but seldom from a psychological or cognitive perspective. Recently, this has been changed through the work of Mary Carruthers. According to Carruthers, *memoria* was the reason why literature, in a fundamental sense, existed in medieval Europe. It was the process by which a work of literature became both institutionalised by the group and learned by its individual members (Carruthers, 1990).

For those medieval experts who were educated in the art of memory there were two principal strategies for achieving their goal. The first and older of these strategies, attributed to Aristotle, relied on the concept of 'mental images'. Supporters of this strategy argued that remembering was to see mental pictures, which are firmly imprinted upon the memory. Thus, the best way to memorise narratives is to stimulate the act of memorising by using visual aids such as emotion-provoking representations, or so-called 'word pictures'. Descriptive language can also be used to create a kind of mental painting, although no actual pictures are present (Carruthers, 1990). As Albertus Magnus (1193–1280) puts it: 'something is not secure enough by hearing, but it is made firm by seeing' (Albertus I.1. II. 6–7).

The second, and more popular, strategy for memorising narratives was by rote learning. This was achieved by the frequent repetition of a text until it was accurately memorised. In this case, the process of memorising was aided by the use of rhythmic and/or formulaic expressions, and by breaking longer texts into numbered segments and then memorising them one by one (Carruthers, 1990).

The followers of this strategy criticised the use of visual imagery because of its inaccuracy. It was argued that the use of visual aids was marginally helpful at best, providing cues for recollection, but could not in itself guarantee the accuracy of the memorising process (Carruthers, 1990). The latter countered the criticism by arguing that, while in ordinary circumstances the accuracy of visual imagery could not be trusted, this problem would disappear if the visual imagery was strong enough to make a person emotionally engaged with the text. Indeed, they argued, it is the creation of strong emotional responses that makes the use of visual images such a powerful tool for memory creation (Carruthers, 1990).

Questions 1–8

Look at the following theories (questions 1–8) and the list of people below.
Match each person with the correct theory.
Write the correct letter (**A–H**) next to questions 1–8.

1   Early European storytelling came about because of a traditional form of memorising. ....

2   Cognitive fluidity allowed early humans to make and change arrangements. ....

3   Telling stories allows us to relate to our surroundings. ....

4   The brain changes our recollection of past events to match our current circumstances. ....

5   Telling stories is a trait which is common to all nations. ....

6   Early humans became more inventive when they were able to make a connection between different ideas. ....

7   Your memory of something will be improved if you visualise it rather than just listen to it. ....

8   Humans adjust to their surroundings as well as changing them. ....

List of people

A Hernadi   E Edelman
B Mink   F Holyoak & Thagard
C Plotkin   G Carruthers
D Mithen   H Albertus

Questions 9–13

Complete each sentence with the correct word, **A–H**, below.
Write the correct letter (**A–H**) next to questions 9–13.

Competing theories about memorising

In medieval times, the most commonly used memorising strategy involved (**9**) .... pieces of a text. People who used this strategy believed it was superior to Aristotle's method, which was based on (**10**) .... ideas. Rote learners claimed that results from using this older strategy were too (**11**) .... However, Aristotle's followers pointed out that only the use of (**12**) .... images would be problematic. Regardless of the strategy used, it has been claimed that the tradition of memorising advanced the art of (**13**) .... in medieval Europe.

A emotional
B mundane
C painting
D repeating
E unreliable
F visualising
G vivid
H writing

Test Four (Units 16–20)

Choose the correct letter A, B, C or D.

1   People would use a lot less power if they bought household goods that were energy ....
    A effective   **B** efficient   **C** economical   **D** ecological

2   The .... from car exhausts have a significant effect on global warming.
    A emissions   **B** smoke   **C** gases   **D** acid

3   Our greatest problem is that we are .... more and more fossil fuels each year and supplies are dwindling.
    A conserving   **B** consuming   **C** producing   **D** preserving

4   We need to persuade people to change their habits so that they .... more energy.
    A consume   **B** conserve   **C** produce   **D** use

5   In the future we will need to use .... energy sources such solar power.
    A recycled   **B** reinvented   **C** renewable   **D** reusable

6   If oil supplies run out in 2051 then we need to find .... energy sources soon.
    A alternate   **B** alternating   **C** alternative   **D** altering

7   I need to earn a lot more .... before I can afford to buy that car.
    A payment   **B** salary   **C** wages   **D** money

8   I am writing to complain about a recent problem I had with a member of your ....
    A company   **B** employees   **C** staff   **D** workplace

9   The company lost a great deal of money when one of their .... was found to be faulty.
    A goods   **B** products   **C** manufacture   **D** business

10   The government should do more to help the .... find a job.
    A employed   **B** employment   **C** unemployment   **D** unemployed

11   Taking a packed lunch to work can be a lot more .... than buying it every day.
    A economical   **B** economics   **C** expenditure   **D** expenses

12   I'd really like to find a .... during the summer holidays.
    A job   **B** work   **C** profession   **D** career

13   I think that people who .... serious crimes should be punished.
    A convict   **B** commit   **C** offend   **D** offence

14   I had to pay a .... for parking my car in a restricted area.
    A fine   **B** find   **C** fee   **D** form

15 Helping poor people to find a job may help to .... crime.
    A avoid   **B** deter   **C** impose   **D** prevent

16 I don't agree with .... very young or petty criminals.
    A committing   **B** enforcing   **C** imprisoning   **D** offending

17 In most countries, it is .... the law to steal other people's property.
    A against   **B** by   **C** for   **D** with

18 The government should .... a law to make computer hacking illegal.
    A abolish   **B** bring   **C** enter   **D** pass

19 I don't like this newspaper – the reports are really .... towards the government.
    A biased   **B** prejudiced   **C** reliable   **D** well-informed

20 Tabloid newspapers are a good example of .... media.
    A masses   **B** mass   **C** main   **D** multi

21 I think following celebrities on their holidays is an .... of privacy.
    A avoidance   **B** invasive   **C** intrusion   **D** invasion

22 The popular press often contains a lot more .... than hard facts.
    A speculation   **B** realism   **C** influence   **D** tolerance

23 When celebrities behave badly it can have a negative influence .... young people.
    A for   **B** in   **C** on   **D** to

24 I enjoy learning about celebrities in magazines and .... TV.
    A by   **B** from   **C** in   **D** on

25 I think successful writers and artists are very ....
    A imaginative   **B** imagination   **C** inspiration   **D** inspire

26 This artist helps to preserve our local .... by using traditional themes in his work.
    A culture   **B** creation   **C** events   **D** skills

27 I don't really appreciate classical music. I prefer the .... arts such as painting and sculpture.
    A festival   **B** literary   **C** performing   **D** visual

28 The .... enjoyed the performance so much that they gave a 10-minute standing ovation.
    A artists   **B** audience   **C** players   **D** participants

29 My friends and I have the same .... in music.
    A type   **B** topic   **C** theme   **D** taste

30 I was so embarrassed when my teacher made me .... my song in front of the whole school.
    A participate   **B** participant   **C** perform   **D** performance

21 Language building 1

Using a dictionary, word families

Using a dictionary

1.1 **Answer these questions about your dictionary.**

1 What type of dictionary do you have?
   A English → English   B English → your language   C Your language → English

2 When do you use it?
   A When reading.   B When writing.   C Whenever I am studying.

3 Which of the following is true for you?
   A I just look up words online or use a translation tool.
   B I stop and look up every word I don't know.
   C I only use a dictionary to check words after I have done an exercise.
   D I rarely use a dictionary.

Study Tip

Whether you look up words in an online dictionary, or a printed version, or just use an online translation tool, it is important to make sure you are using a reliable source of information. If possible, use a monolingual dictionary as this will help you to practise your English more. The best dictionaries not only contain the words you need to look up but they will also give you example sentences and information about words and how they are used. If you would like to buy a dictionary, exercises 1.3 and 1.4 might help you to assess the different dictionaries you find.

You cannot use a dictionary in the IELTS test so, when you are using this book, don't use your dictionary to look up every new word. Instead, use the context to work out the meaning of a word as you complete the exercises. Only use your dictionary when you have finished. When you are writing, use your dictionary to help with spellings as well as the correct usage of words and make a note of any words you repeatedly need to look up.

1.2 **The words in column A are all related to dictionaries. Match the words to the correct meaning in column B.**

A		B	
1	monolingual	A	a large amount of written material organised to show how language works
2	bilingual	B	written in only one language
3	corpus	C	a word that means the same
4	synonym	D	a dictionary containing synonyms and antonyms
5	antonym	E	the sound and pronunciation of words
6	thesaurus	F	written in two different languages for translation purposes
7	phonology	G	the origin of words
8	etymology	H	a word that means the opposite

1.3 **Do you know how your dictionary is organised?**

1 How can you tell whether the word is a noun/verb/adjective etc?

2 How does it tell you the pronunciation of the word?

3 Does it give you other words in the same family?

4 Does it give you example sentences?

5 Does it tell you whether a word is informal, slang or taboo?

6 Does it show differences between the US and UK version of the word?

7 Does it tell you which other words can / need to be used with this word?

8 A printed dictionary often has information at the beginning. Does your dictionary give:
   • information about measurements?
   • information about grammar?
   • hints on how to use the dictionary?
   • an explanation of the phonetic script used?
   • a list of abbreviations used?

> **Study Tip**
>
> If you look up a verb in your dictionary, you should see the following in brackets after it: *vt* or *vi* (sometimes simply *t* or *i*). This tells you whether the verb is *transitive* or *intransitive*. A transitive verb needs, or can have, an object, e.g. *put:* I **put** *the vase on the table. Put* is transitive because it must have an object (the vase). NOT ~~I put on the table~~.
> An *intransitive* verb does not need, or cannot have, an object, e.g. *rise: The sun* **rises** *every morning. Rise* is intransitive because it has no object. Not ~~I rise the table~~. Some verbs can be transitive or intransitive, e.g. *carry:* I **carried** *the table to another room.* (Transitive, the object = *the table.*) *His voice* **carried** *across the room.* (Intransitive, his voice didn't carry anything.)

1.4 **Look up the words *develop, exist, swerve* and *vanish* in your dictionary and then answer these questions.**

1 Which verb(s) are transitive and which are intransitive? ....

2 Which verb(s) can be either transitive or intransitive? ....

3 Which verb(s) can have an object and which verb(s) cannot have an object? ....

4 Which verb(s) has the following meaning?:
   A move uncontrollably .... B be ....
   C disappear? .... D change or grow

5 Which word does the verb *swerve* rhyme with   A curve   B halve   C mauve? ....

1.5 **Abbreviations are often used in a dictionary to give you information about words. What do the following abbreviations stand for? Choose a word from the box that you might find these abbreviations next to.**

		because of good well traffic differ
1	adj = ...*adjective: good*............................	
2	conj	
3	vi	
4	U	
5	adv	
6	prep	

1.6 Some words can have more than one meaning so don't assume the first reference you find is the meaning you are looking for. Match the words in column A to two possible meanings in column B. Use a dictionary to help you if necessary.

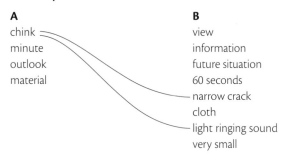

A
chink
minute
outlook
material

B
view
information
future situation
60 seconds
narrow crack
cloth
light ringing sound
very small

1.7 🎧 21 A dictionary can also help you to pronounce words correctly using phonetic symbols. Listen to the recording and then match the vowel sounds that are underlined with the correct phonetic symbol.

p<u>u</u>t   th<u>e</u>se   <u>i</u>n   s<u>o</u>me   b<u>a</u>ll   ch<u>oo</u>se   w<u>or</u>d   <u>a</u>bout   g<u>ue</u>st   wh<u>a</u>t   att<u>a</u>ck   h<u>ar</u>d

Phonetic symbols

iː these	uː	ɜː	ɑː	ɔː	e
ɒ	ʌ	æ	ə	ʊ	ɪ

Study Tip

A good dictionary will also tell you which other words can or need to be used with the word you are checking. This is called *collocation*. Collocation will help you to use new words accurately in a sentence. When you look up a new word in your dictionary, make a note of the words that collocate with it. The example sentences can help with this.

Study the following extract from the *Cambridge Advanced Learner's Dictionary*. You will see that the word *choice* can be used in several different ways and have a variety of collocations.

WORDS THAT GO WITH **choice** ACT

have a choice • make a choice • give/offer sb a choice • be **faced with** a choice • an **informed** choice • a choice **between** [two things or people] • a choice **of** sth • **by/ from** choice

choice ACT Ⓔ /tʃɔɪs/ *noun* [C or or S U] an act or the possibility of choosing: *If the product doesn't work, you are given the choice of a refund or a replacement.* ○ *It's a difficult choice to **make**.* ○ *It's your choice/The choice is yours* (= only you can decide). ○ *It was a choice **between** pain now or pain later, so I chose pain later.* ○ *Now you know all the facts, you can make an **informed** choice.* ○ *I'd prefer not to work but I don't **have much** choice* (= this is not possible). ○ *He **had no** choice **but to** accept* (= He had to accept). ○ *Is she single **by** choice?*

WORDS THAT GO WITH **choice** VARIETY

a bewildering/excellent/wide choice • offer a choice of sth • a choice of sth

choice VARIETY ❶ /tʃɔɪs/ *noun* [S or U] the range of different things from which you can choose: *There wasn't much choice on the menu.* ○ *The evening menu offers a **wide** choice of dishes.* ○ *The dress is available **in a choice of** colours.*

Word families

Vocabulary note

A prefix is a letter, or group of letters, that can be added to the beginning of a word to make a new word. Prefixes can help you to work out the meaning of unknown words. The prefix *re* means to do again, e.g. *use*, **re***use* = to use again. A suffix is a letter, or group of letters, that can be added to the end of a word to form a new word. The suffix *able* means it is possible to do something, e.g. *assess*, *assess***able** (= it is possible to assess). In your dictionary, a prefix will be shown with a hyphen after it (*re-*); a suffix will be shown with a hyphen in front of it (*-able*).

2.1 Use your dictionary to check other words that can be made from the same base word. Put the following words into the correct columns to make new words.

approach   assess   assume   create   define   distribute   establish   identify   interpret   represent   vary

-ment	-tion	-able	mis-	re-	un-

2.2 Consider one of the longest words in the English language: *antidisestablishmentarianism*. Base form = *establish* (+ *-ment*) = *establishment* (+ *dis-*) = *disestablishment* (+ *-arian*) = *disestablishmentarian* (+ *-ism*) = *disestablishmentarianism* (+ *anti-*) = *antidisestablishmentarianism*.

Which of the groups of letters in column A are prefixes and which are suffixes? Match them to the meanings in column B.

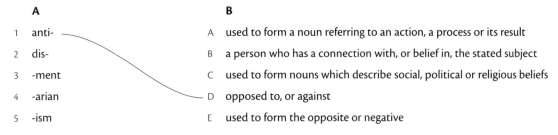

A
1 anti-
2 dis-
3 -ment
4 -arian
5 -ism

B
A used to form a noun referring to an action, a process or its result
B a person who has a connection with, or belief in, the stated subject
C used to form nouns which describe social, political or religious beliefs
D opposed to, or against
E used to form the opposite or negative

2.3 Think of an example word for each of the prefixes and suffixes in column A above.

22 Language building 2
Learning vocabulary, collocation

Learning vocabulary

1.1 Create a list.

Each week, try to build up a list of new words you have seen or read. These may be words you are familiar with but don't know well enough to use actively or accurately. Don't make the list too long – ten should be enough. Here are ten useful words for this week.

1 analysis   6 environment
2 benefit   7 occur
3 consistent   8 period
4 create   9 significant
5 define   10 theory

1.2 Check the meaning.

Make sure you understand the meaning of each of the words in **1.1**. Which of them is closest in meaning to each of the following?

A happen ....   F length of time ....
B make ....   G advantage ....
C reliable; unchanging ....   H opinion or explanation ....
D close examination ....   I explain the meaning or limits of something ....
E important ....   J surroundings ....

1.3 Find out the different forms of each word.

1 Look again at the words 1–10 in **1.1**. Write *N* next to the nouns, *V* next to the verbs and *A* next to the adjectives.

2 Which word can be a noun or a verb? ....

3 Which of the words can have the following prefixes: *in*, *re*?

1.4 WORD BUILDING Complete the table with the different forms of each of the words in 1.1.

	Noun	Verb	Adjective		Noun	Verb	Adjective
1				6			
2				7			
3				8			
4				9			
5				10			

1.5 Learn how to pronounce the words.

1 🎧 **22a** Listen and practise saying each word.

2 🎧 **22b** Now listen to ten sentences (a–j). Each contains a word from **1.1**, but in a different form. Write down each word and its form (noun, verb etc).

A environmentalist (noun) ....

B ....

C ....

D ....

E ....

F ....

G ....

H ....

I ....

J ....

3 🎧 **22b** Now listen to the sentences again and mark the stress on each of the words you have written. Practise saying the sentences.

1.6 Know how to spell the words.

Study the spellings of words 1–10 in **1.1**, then cover up the words. Now underline the correct spellings below.

1 analasis   <u>analysis</u>   analisis

2 beneficial   benefitial   benefisial

3 consistent   consistant   concistent

4 recretion   recreation   recration

5 defined   defind   defende

6 enviroment   environment   environement

7 occurred   ocurred   ocured

8 periodicaly   periodicly   periodically

9 sinificant   singificant   significant

10 theoretical   theretical   theorretical

> ### Study Tip
> When you are learning new words, look carefully to see if there are any spelling rules that can help you. Make a note of any double letters. It is sometimes easier to break the longer words up, e.g. *en-vi-ron-ment*.

1.7 Use the words.

Complete this text with the correct form of the words in 1.1.

Nowadays we hear the word 'sustainable' being used a great deal in academic journals and [1] <u>periodicals</u> . [2] .... in particular are very concerned that any development should be 'sustainable'. They argue that sustainable practices have great [3] .... for us and can have a [4] .... impact on the future of our planet.

However, the word 'sustainable' needs to be clearly [5] .... Sustainable development [6] .... in exploiting our natural resources without destroying them. We need to establish whether this can be put into practice or whether it is a mere [7] .... There needs to be a thorough [8] .... of any development plans before they are allowed to proceed, as once an area has been destroyed it is almost impossible to [9] .... it. We should do our best to ensure that there is no [10] .... of the logging and land clearing that destroyed so many forests at the start of the twentieth century.

> ### Study Tip
> Try to use new words as often as possible when speaking and writing. They should start to become part of your active vocabulary. Look back at new words as often as you can and test yourself on the meaning, pronunciation and spelling.

1.8 ⊕ 22b **Remember the context.**

Look at the following ideas or contexts, which were all used in the sentences in **1.4**. Which words from **1.4** do you associate them with? Listen again to check your answers.

1   very bad storms ....occurred....

2   global warming ....

3   the student council ....

4   growing plants ....

5   eating fish ....

6   studying chemistry ....

7   video games and violence ....

8   space exploration and Mars ....

9   a teacher commenting on an essay ....

10 young children and the impact of school ....

> **Study Tip**
>
> When you are trying to remember a word, it often helps to think about the context in which you last heard or read it. Think about where you were and what you were doing, or try to remember what the reading or listening text was about.

1.9   **Use spelling rules to help you edit your work.**

1   Change these words by adding the endings in brackets.

A   surprise ...surprising... (*ing*)

B   true .... (*ly*)

C   advance .... (*ment*)

D   happy .... (*est*)

E   worry .... (*ed*)

F   worry .... (*ing*)

G   unplug .... (*ed*)

H   stop .... (*ed*)

I   slope .... (*ed*)

J   change .... (*able*)

2   Add an appropriate prefix (*dis*, *im*, *in* or *un*) to these words.

A   suitable ...unsuitable...

B   appropriate ....

C   similar ....

D   noticed ....

E   interested ....

F   patient ....

G   ability ....

H   organised ....

I   polite ....

J   employment ....

Collocation

2.1   **Learn important collocations. Correct the collocation errors in these sentences.**

1   After a careful analysis from the situation we decided to cancel the trip.

....

2   Regular exercise can be to benefit for people with asthma.

....

3   These results are consistent to the ones we obtained last month.

....

4   We need to create for a new design.

....

5   I am looking up the definition from this word.

   ....

6   We should use products that are environmentally good.

   ....

2.2   **Complete the sentences with the correct prepositions from the box.**

1   The president refused to comment .... the problem.

2   I found out about the hotel .... the Internet.

about	for	in	on	to	with	of

3   I would like to apply .... the position of head chef.

4   The students were allowed .... participate .... the basketball tournament.

5   I was completely satisfied .... the service at your hotel.

6   My mother is concerned .... the amount .... money I spend each week.

7   The cost .... living has increased by 5 per cent this year.

8   There are several reasons .... this increase.

2.3   **Which word in each list cannot collocate with the word in bold?**

1   difficulty / ~~knowledge~~ / need / opportunity / problem   **arise**

2   draw / work / need / pay / receive / seek   **attention**

3   assess / cause / inflict / repair / take   **damage**

4   attract / develop / excite / feign / give / lose   **interest**

5   acquire / learn / speak / tell / use   **language**

6   control / an exam / a law / judgment / the time   **pass**

2.4   **Choose the correct adverb in each sentence.**

1   I was _completely_ / _utterly_ satisfied with my test result.

2   It is highly _likely_ / _possible_ that the president will resign today.

3   The machine was _slightly_ / _utterly_ useless.

4   I am _extremely_ / _totally_ concerned about your behaviour.

5   It was _bitterly_ / _completely_ cold in the winter.

6   I was _absolutely_ / _totally_ freezing by the time we arrived.

7   The oil spill had a _big_ / _heavy_ impact on the surrounding environment.

8   It is _absolutely_ / _very_ impossible to predict the future with any certainty.

> ### Vocabulary note
>
> When using an adverb with an adjective, note the following:
> _extremely_ = 'to a large degree' so it should not be used with adjectives that have an extreme meaning, e.g. _terrified_. You need to use a neutral adverb, e.g. _completely, really_: _completely terrified_. NOT ~~_extremely terrified_~~.
> _slightly_ = 'to a small degree', so cannot be used with extreme adjectives: _slightly scared_. NOT ~~_slightly terrified_~~.
> _significantly_ is often used with comparative adjectives: _significantly greater_. NOT ~~_significantly great_~~.
> Other collocations just have to be learned.

Study Tip

Once you have done all of these things, you should be able to say that you _know_ a word.

Academic Writing Task 1

Data, graphs and tables, diagrams and processes

Data, graphs and tables

Test tip

You will increase your writing task 1 score if you include an overview of the information and if you select only the most significant information (i.e. *the main features*) to include in your summary.

Error warning!

Make sure you spell these words correctly:
pie chart NOT *pie / pie chat*; *graph* NOT *graft*.

1.1 **Match the labels to the correct illustrations.**

1 pie chart 2 table 3 bar chart / bar graph 4 line graph 5 diagram 6 flowchart

A

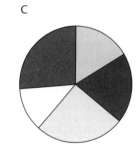

B

1. collect rubbish

2. sort

3. wash glass bottles

4. crush

C

D

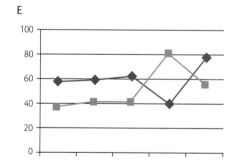

sugar cane crushing machine heater clarifier

filter evaporator vacuum pan centrifuge stored sugar

to refinery

E

F

Sydney	3.6
Melbourne	2.9
Brisbane	2.6
Canberra	1.8

1.2 Look at this writing task. Which data do you think is the most significant?

The graph below shows the amount of domestic waste collected and recycled in one country between 1960 and 2020.

Summarise the information by selecting and reporting the main features, and make comparisons where relevant.

Write at least 150 words.

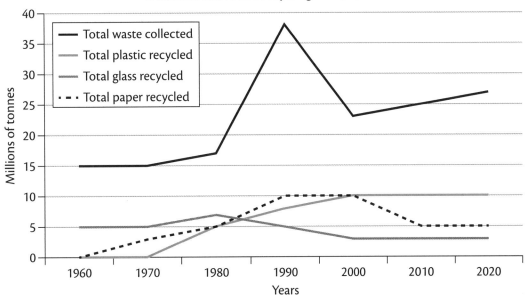

Domestic waste and recycling rates, 1960 to 2020

1.3 Look at the sentences and decide which sentence A) gives an overview of the information in the graph? B) does NOT belong in a Task 1 summary? C) has inaccurate information?

1   The total amount of waste collected rose from 15 million tonnes to approximately 17 million tonnes between 1970 and 1980.
2   The amount of paper being recycled reached a peak in 1990 then levelled out until 2010.
3   The amount of garbage being collected rose sharply between 1980 and 1990.
4   While the figures for all types of waste varied over this period, overall, far more waste was collected than recycled.
5   Unlike other forms of recycling, glass recycling has not fallen below 10 tonnes and, since 2010, more glass has been recycled than any other material.

1.4 Put these words and phrases into the correct column according to the trend they can be used to describe. Some of the words can be used to describe more than one pattern.

unchanged	fall	rise	drop	remain steady	reach a high
fluctuate	plunge	upward trend	downward trend	plateau	sharp
steep	unpredictable	static	significant	wildly	constant
reach a low	steadily	rapidly	fixed	peak	

↘	↗	→	↘ ↗ ↘ ↗
fall	rise	unchanged	fluctuate

1.5 **Correct the preposition mistakes in these sentences. You will need to refer to the writing task in 1.2.**

1 The amount of paper being recycled rose ~~by~~ 10 million tonnes between 1980 and 1990. ....*to*....

2 The amount of plastic being recycled rose consistently in 1970 and 2000. ....

3 The amount of paper being recycled rose from 5 million tonnes between 1980 and 1990. ....

4 The amount of glass being recycled fell by approximately 7 million tonnes to around 3 million tonnes per year between 1980 and 2000. ....

1.6 **Change the sentences below from *adjective + noun* to *verb + adverb*, or vice versa. Use your notebook.**

1 There was a significant increase in the number of birds in 1994.

2 The number of people attending fell considerably in 2002.

3 The percentage of female students rose dramatically in 1990.

4 There was a noticeable drop in temperatures between 1880 and 1885.

5 The figures changed constantly between 2001 and 2006.

6 There was a slight increase in temperatures in 1909.

Error warning!

When comparing statistics we usually say: ***Comparing*** *the figures for 1999 and 2000, we can see an increase of 20%.* NOT ~~Compared the figures for 1999.~~ We use ***compared to*** or ***compared with*** as follows: ***Compared to*** *the number of males, the number of females is relatively low.* NOT ~~Comparing with the number of males...~~ Or: *The number of males is quite large* ***compared to/with*** *the number of females.* NOT ~~comparing to the number of ...~~

Vocabulary note

Note the way we use prepositions with numbers and dates:

35%	10%
1995	1997

In *1997 the number fell* ***to*** *10%;* ***In*** *1997 the number fell* ***by*** *25%;* ***In*** *1997 the number fell* ***from*** *35%.* NOT ~~in 35%~~; *The number dropped* ***to*** *10%* ***between*** *1995 and 1997.* NOT ~~reduced to~~; ***By*** *1997 the number had fallen* ***to*** *10%.* See also units 7 and 13.

Vocabulary note

You can use a combination of verb + adverb, or adjective + noun, to avoid repeating the same phrases and to add extra meaning: *There was a* ***significant increase*** *in the numbers. The numbers* ***increased significantly***. Notice that you need a preposition when you use the noun form: *There was an* ***increase in*** *attendance; There was a* ***drop of*** *10%.* NOT ~~There was an increase attendance. There was a drop 10%.~~

1.7 **Complete this task 1 answer based on the graph in 1.2 with the correct word from the box. There are more words than you need, so you will not need to use them all.**

rate	from	doubled	in	dropped	until
consistently	by	overall	steady	peak	
trend	significantly	rose	plateaued	to	

The graph shows the amount of household garbage collected and recycled in one country between 1960 and 2020. While the figures for almost all types of waste varied over this period, [1]................, far more waste was collected than recycled. With total household waste, in the first 20-year-period the amount collected remained relatively [2]................ However, from 1980 to 2000, the figure [3]................ sharply and the amount collected had more than [4]................ in size by 1990, reaching a peak [5]................ approximately 37 million tonnes. It then fell [6]................ over the following decade, before rising again at a slower [7]................ between 2000 and 2020.

In terms of recycling, the largest amounts collected were in plastic and paper. These rose fairly [8]................ initially, and each has reached a [9]................ of 10 million tonnes. However, only plastic, which was not recycled [10]................ 1970, has maintained these numbers; recycled paper [11]................ between 2000 and 2010 and has remained at 5 million tonnes. In contrast, glass, the main recycled material up to 1980, experienced a downward [12]................ over the next twenty years and has [13]................ at around 3 million tonnes to be the lowest of all three recycled materials [14]................ 2020.

Describing a diagram or a process

2.1 Look at the following diagram and answer the questions.

1 At what stage is something added?

2 At what stage is something separated?

3 How many different stages are there altogether?

How chewing gum is made

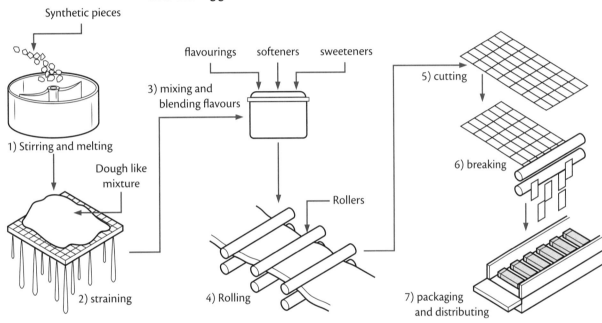

2.2 Write an introduction and overview sentence for the summary below. Use the answers to questions 1–3 in 2.1 to help. Then complete the summary with the correct form of the words in the box. You will need to use some of the words more than once.

add	container	first	finally
melt	ingredient	liquid	machine
mixture	next	pass	pieces(n)
place	shape(n)	then	travel

The diagram shows…

....

....

In the 1) .... stage of this process, (3) .... of synthetic material are put into a (4) .... and stirred and (5) .... until they form a single mass that resembles dough. This is (6) .... strained until all of the (7) .... has been eliminated. (8) ...., the solid gum is (9) .... into another (10) .... At this point, the desired flavourings, sweeteners and softeners are (11) .... This (12) .... is then blended until all of the (13) .... are mixed together. The gum then (14) .... to a different (15) ...., which uses rollers to flatten it out. (16) .... the thin sheets of gum are cut into rectangular (17) .... and broken up into individual (18) .... of chewing gum.(19) ...., the gum (20) .... along a conveyor belt, where it is enclosed in packaging ready to be distributed.

24 Academic Writing Task 2
Linking words, opinion words, register

Getting started

Test tip
Before you start writing, read the question very carefully and be sure to address all of the points raised. Use your introduction to rephrase the question. Don't repeat words and phrases from the question.

1.1 Look at this writing task 2 question and decide whether you agree or disagree with this opinion.

Students learn all they need to know about writing at primary school and there's no need for teachers to focus on writing after that.

To what extent do you agree or disagree?

1.2 Replace the underlined words in the introductory sentences below with the most suitable word or phrase from the box. There are more words than you need.

everything   this stage   that   young children   practising   they   kids   education

> Writing is an important skill and <u>students at primary school</u> spend a lot of time <u>focusing on</u> it. I completely disagree that <u>students</u> learn <u>all they need to know</u> about writing at <u>primary school</u>.

Linking words

2.1 These words and phrases can be used to link ideas together. Put the words and phrases into the correct column according to their function. Use your notebook.

similarly	that is	now
as a result	alternatively	in other words
indeed	and	consequently
nonetheless	while	to illustrate this
finally	whereas	firstly
however	in conclusion	therefore
although	but	because
secondly	because of	or
despite	not only … but … also…	also
in addition	furthermore	on the other hand
such as	to summarise	for example

Vocabulary note
Because is a conjuction and is used to give a reason: *The car crashed **because** the brakes didn't work. Because of* is a preposition and means *as a result of*: *The hospital closed **because of** a lack of funds.*

Sequencing ideas	Adding supporting ideas	Introducing a contrasting idea	Giving examples	Giving an alternative	Giving an explanation	Drawing a conclusion
firstly						

Test tip

Support your ideas with evidence and relevant examples.
Make sure that your ideas are well organised and easy to
follow by using the correct linking words.

2.2 Underline the correct linking words in the following
sentences.

Vocabulary note

The following linking words and phrases must be followed
by a noun and cannot be followed by a clause: *because of,
as a result of, in spite of, despite*: *I enjoyed my holiday **in spite
of** the bad weather.* NOT ~~in spite of the weather was bad.~~

1   It can be difficult to write an essay, *because / although* there
are several things you can do to make the job easier.

2   There are several things you can do to make writing easier.
For example / However, it can be helpful to make a rough
plan of your ideas.

3   It can be helpful to practise writing within the time limit. You can time yourself with a clock *and / or* a stopwatch.

4   You will not be allowed to use equipment *as a result / such as* a dictionary during the test.

5   I think I did well in the test, *although / in spite of* I did run out of time at the end.

6   I think that my vocabulary has improved *because / as a result of* reading this book.

2.3 Complete the paragraphs in this essay by inserting the correct linking words and phrases. There may be more than
one possible answer. You can use any word or phrase more than once.

in other words   therefore   however   firstly   as a result   furthermore
but also   thus   nevertheless   such as   as well as

Writing is an important skill and young children spend a lot of time practising it. (1) ...., I completely disagree
that they learn everything about writing at this stage.

Children learn a considerable amount about writing at primary school. (2) ...., they have to learn to hold a pen
correctly, (3) .... how to form individual letters neatly. Once they have mastered these basics, they are then faced
with the conventions of written language, (4) ...., the complex rules of spelling and grammar. (5) ...., as
children move through the school system, they have to learn to not only connect their ideas together (6) ....
to adapt the tone of their writing to different situations. (7) ...., by the age of ten or eleven, children are already
quite skilled writers.

(8) .... there is still a great deal to learn. In the higher levels of education, children must become independent
learners. (9) ...., they must learn to think for themselves and how to express their own ideas clearly, which is not
at all an easy task. If students do not have help from their teachers at this stage, they are likely to struggle and, (10) ....
..............., their school work may suffer. (11) ...., they may perform badly in exams. (12) ...., it seems clear
that older students also need the guidance of their teachers when it comes to writing.

Opinion words

 Vocabulary note

We often use adverbs to show our opinion of an idea.

3.1 Match the adverbs in column A with the correct meaning in column B.

A		B	
1	personally	A	it is easy to understand
2	unfortunately	B	it is easy to understand
3	clearly	C	it is well deserved
4	obviously	D	this is my own opinion
5	justifiably	E	I believe this is a sad thing
6	thankfully	F	I believe this is a good thing
7	fortunately	G	I believe this is a good thing

Error warning!

Be careful with punctuation. You must use a comma after the following words and phrases when they are used at the start of a sentence: *In addition, Also, For example, In conclusion, Finally, However, Furthermore, Lastly, In my opinion, Similarly, To summarise, Therefore, Unfortunately, To sum up,* e.g. *To sum up, in my opinion taking a gap year is a very good idea.* NOT ~~*To sum up in my opinion...*~~

3.2 Complete the sentences with adverbs from 3.1. Don't forget the necessary punctuation.

1 _Personally_, I think learning vocabulary is a good idea.

2 .... I remembered how to spell the word correctly on the day of the exam.

3 When I received my results I was .... proud.

4 .... my friend didn't study for the test so he didn't do very well.

5 .... if you work hard then you will improve.

Finishing off and register

Test tip

Use your conclusion to summarise your main points. When you have finished, carefully edit your work and check your spelling.

4.1 **It is easy to make careless spelling mistakes if you are writing quickly. Read the following paragraph and correct the spelling mistakes.**

Recnet resaerch at an Engilsh uinervtisy sugegsts taht it deosn't mttaer waht oredr the ltteers in a wrod are in; the olny impotarnt tihng is that the frist and lsat ltteers are in the rghit pclae. Eevn thuogh the mddile ltteers mghit be mxied up, people dno't hvae a prolbem raeding the wrods. Tihs is becuase we raed the wrod as a wohle rahter tahn eevry ltteer by iteslf.

> **Test tip**
>
> The IELTS test is a formal situation, so you should never use informal words, e.g. ~~kids, guys~~. You should also avoid using abbreviations: **number** NOT ~~no.~~ , **for example** NOT ~~e.g.~~ , **you** and **your** NOT ~~U/UR~~. Your dictionary should tell you if a word is *slang* = very informal, or *taboo* = this word will offend people.

4.2 **Correct the mistakes with register and spelling that have been underlined in the conclusion. Which words do you have to change because of register?**

> In conclusion, [1]through some [2]peple might think [3]kids learn everything they're ever [4]gonna need to know about [5]writting in primary school, in my view, there's still [6]lots of stuff for them to learn beyond this. [7]Personaly, I [8]belive that writing is such an important and complex skill [9]too master, that we are never [10]to old to need help.

1	though	7	
2		8	
3		9	
4		10	
5		11	
6		12	

25 General Training Writing
Vocabulary for Writing Tasks 1 and 2

Writing Task 1

1.1 Put the words into the correct column according to the type of letter they might be used in. Use your notebook.

apologise	applicant	appreciate	forgive
attend	be considered	excuse	invitation
confirm	dissatisfied	interview	would be
grateful	help	suggest	delighted
propose	sorry	ask	
unhappy	wonder	complain	

Acceptance	Application	Apology	Complaint	Enquiry	Recommendation	Thanks
would be delighted						

1.2 Use a word from the table in 1.1 to complete the sentences.

1 I am writing to ....*apologise*.... for my behaviour last night. It was inexcusable.

2 I would like to .... about the treatment I received at your hotel.

3 I hope that you will .... me for behaving in this way.

4 I am very .... for the amount of time you have given up to help me.

5 Unfortunately, I will not be able to .... the party.

6 I am writing to .... for your help in finding a place to live.

1.3 Underline the correct preposition in each sentence. Sometimes no preposition is necessary.

1 I am sorry *for* / *from* the damage that I caused.

2 The manager told *–* / *to* me that there were no rooms available.

3 I was unhappy *for* / *with* the way I was treated by your staff.

4 I would like to enquire *about* / *for* renting a car.

5 I would like to be considered *in* / *for* the position advertised.

6 I am available to attend *–* / *to* an interview at any time.

7 I would like to explain *–* / *of* what happened.

8 Would you be able to help *–* / *to* me?

9 Thank you *about* / *for* all of the help you have given me.

10 I am looking forward *for* / *to* seeing you soon.

Vocabulary note

Note that the phrasal verb *to look forward* is always followed by *to + ing*: *I am **looking forward to** catching up with you soon.* In formal letters we use the simple present tense rather than the present continuous: *I **look** forward to hearing from you in the near future.*

1.4 Match the words in column A with the words in column B to form some common phrases used at the end of letters.

A	B
Thank you	my CV
I would be	faithfully
I look	in advance
I have enclosed	sincerely
Best	regards
Kind	grateful if you could
Yours	wishes
Yours	forward to

> ## Vocabulary note
>
> Be careful with the spelling of the following words: *grateful, sincerely, faithfully*. Register is important when writing a letter. Make sure the language you use is not too informal if the letter is a very formal one, or too formal if the letter is to someone you know well.

1.5 What is the best way to begin and end a letter to these people?

1 a friend, or someone you know well and address by their first name

2 your employer

3 a person you have never met

4 a person you have met only briefly, but whose name you know

Writing Task 2

> ## Test tip
>
> Writing Task 2 is a discursive essay. You will be given a topic to write about. You should write a plan so that your ideas are organised logically and coherently. Try to use a wide variety of vocabulary and don't copy words from the question paper. Try not to repeat the same words or ideas. When you have finished, check your spelling and make sure you have written at least 250 words.

2.1 Look at this writing task 2 question and decide whether you agree or disagree with this opinion.

You should spend about 40 minutes on this task.

Students learn all they need to know about writing at primary school and there's no need for teachers to focus on writing after that.

Do you agree or disagree?

Give reasons for your answer and include any relevant examples.

Write at least 250 words.

2.2 Replace the underlined words in the introductory sentences below with the most suitable word or phrase from the box. There are more words than you need.

everything   this stage   that   young children   practising
they   kids   education

> Writing is an important skill and <u>students at primary school</u> spend a lot of time <u>focusing on</u> it. I completely disagree that <u>students</u> learn <u>all they need to know</u> about writing at <u>primary school</u>.

Linking words

3.1 These words and phrases can be used to link ideas together. Put the words and phrases into the correct column according to their function. Use your notebook.

similarly	in addition	but	first
as a result	such as	because of	therefore
nonetheless	that is	not only … but … also…	because
finally	alternatively	furthermore	or
however	and	to summarise	also
although	while	now	on the other hand
secondly	whereas	in other words	for example
despite	in conclusion	consequently	

Sequencing ideas	Adding supporting ideas	Introducing a contrasting idea	Giving examples	Giving an alternative	Giving an explanation	Drawing a conclusion
first						

3.2 Underline the correct linking word in the following sentences.

1 It can be difficult to write an essay, *because / although* there are several things you can do to make the job easier.

2 There are several things you can do to make writing easier. *For example / However*, it can be helpful to make a rough plan of your ideas.

3 It can be helpful to practise writing within the time limit. You can time yourself with a clock *and / or* a stopwatch.

4 You will not be allowed to use equipment *as a result / such as* a dictionary during the test.

5 I think I did well in the test, *although / in spite of* I did run out of time at the end.

6 I think that my vocabulary has improved *because / as a result of* reading this book.

> **Ⓥ Vocabulary note**
>
> The following linking words and phrases must be followed by a noun and not a clause: *because of, as a result of, in spite of, despite*: *I enjoyed my holiday in spite of the bad weather.* NOT *in spite of the weather was bad.*

3.3 Complete the paragraphs in this essay by inserting the correct linking words and phrases. There may be more than one possible answer.

in other words   therefore   however   firstly   as a result   furthermore
but also   thus   therefore   nevertheless   such as   as well as

Writing is an important skill and young children spend a lot of time practising it. (1) ...., I completely disagree that they learn everything about writing at this stage.

Children learn a considerable amount about writing at primary school. (2) ...., they have to learn to hold a pen correctly, (3) .... how to form individual letters neatly. Once they have mastered these basics, they are then faced with the conventions of written language,
(4)..................., the complex rules of spelling and grammar. (5) ...., as children move through the school system, they have learn to not only connect their ideas together (6) .... to adapt the tone of their writing to different situations.
(7) ...., by the age of ten or eleven, children are already quite skilled writers.

(8) .... there is still a great deal to learn. In the higher levels of education, children must become independent learners. (9) ...., they must learn to think for themselves and how to express their own ideas clearly, which is not at all an easy task. If students do not have help from their teachers at this stage, they are likely to struggle and, (10) ...., their school work may suffer. (11) ...., they may perform badly in exams. (12) ...., it seems clear that older students also need the guidance of their teachers when it comes to writing.

Opinion words

Vocabulary note

We often use adverbs to show our opinion of an idea.

4.1   Match the adverbs in column A with the correct meaning in column B.

A		B	
1	personally	A	it is easy to understand
2	unfortunately	B	it is easy to understand
3	clearly	C	it is well deserved
4	obviously	D	this is my own opinion
5	justifiably	E	I believe this is a sad thing
6	thankfully	F	I believe this is a good thing
7	fortunately	G	I believe this is a good thing

4.2   Complete the sentences with adverbs from 4.1.

1   <u>Personally</u>, I think learning vocabulary is a good idea.

2   ...., I remembered how to spell the word correctly on the day of the exam.

3   He worked very hard, so when he received his test results he was .... proud.

4   ...., my friend didn't study for the test so he didn't do very well.

5   ...., if you work hard then you will improve.

Finishing off and register

Test tip

In formal essay writing you must use the correct register. This means you should avoid using informal words e.g. ~~kids, guys~~. You should also avoid using abbreviations and write out the words in full: **number** NOT ~~no.~~, **for example** NOT ~~e.g.~~

5   Correct the mistakes with register and spelling that have been underlined in the conclusion. Which words do you have to change because of register?

In conclusion, [1]<u>through</u> some [2]<u>peple</u> might think [3]<u>kids</u> learn everything they're ever [4]<u>gonna</u> need to know about [5]<u>writting</u> in primary school, in my view, there's still [6]<u>lots of stuff</u> for them to learn beyond this. [7]<u>Personaly</u>, I [8]<u>belive</u> that writing is such an important and complex skill [9]<u>too</u> master, that we are never [10]<u>to</u> old to need help.

1	<u>though</u>	5	....	9	....
2	....	6	....	10	....
3	....	7	....	11	....
4	....	8	....	12	....

Test Five (Units 21–25)

Choose the correct letter A, B, C or D.

1 John .... on the table and called for everyone's attention.
    A held   **B** placed   **C** put   **D** stood

2 We have decided to .... a new industrial zone to encourage more businesses to move into the area.
    A evolve   **B** grow up   **C** develop   **D** exist

3 The word *put* rhymes with ....
    A suit   **B** cut   **C** foot   **D** blood

4 I never met our old school principal, but the new one seems very ....
    A approachment   **B** approachable   **C** misapproach   **D** unapproach

5 We don't encourage .... social behaviour such as vandalism.
    A anti-   **B** dis-   **C** pre-   **D** un-

6 The word *organise* is a .... of the word *arrange*.
    A antonym   **B** corpus   **C** collocation   **D** synonym

7 There are other books on this topic but Smith's is thought to be the .... work.
    A definite   **B** definition   **C** definitive   **D** define

8 .... many elderly people struggle to meet their everyday living expenses.
    A Now days   **B** Nowday   **C** Nowdays   **D** Nowadays

9 You need to choose a new assignment topic – this one is not .... to the one you chose last term.
    A dissimilar   **B** insimilar   **C** nonsimilar   **D** unsimilar

10 There are several reasons .... this change in decision.
    A by   **B** for   **C** of   **D** why

11 The lecturer .... our attention to a large screen at the back of the room.
    A drew   **B** pointed   **C** gave   **D** paid

12 This medicine should help, but if the problem .... come and see me again.
    A ocurs   **B** occurs   **C** recurs   **D** reccurs

13 It is .... likely that the government will back down and agree to the tax cuts.
    A completely   **B** fully   **C** highly   **D** totally

14 In 1990 the figures rose .... a previous high of 75% to a staggering 89%.
    A by   **B** from   **C** in   **D** with

15 The following year this figure .... noticeably from 72% to only 55%.

    A drop   **B** dropped   **C** dropping   **D** drops

16 There was a .... increase between 1989 and 2005.

    A significant   **B** significantly   **C** slightly   **D** steep

17 The bread .... baked in a hot oven and then put into bags ready for sale.

    A has   **B** is   **C** were   **D** can

18 We might be able to persuade more people to use the bus, but it is .... impossible to stop people from driving cars altogether.

    A absolutely   **B** highly   **C** very   **D** a little

19 There were losses in the car industry last year .... the tourism industry boomed.

    A in addition   **B** because   **C** similarly   **D** while

20 We made a significant profit last year .... the losses made by our international office.

    A although   **B** despite   **C** however   **D** as a result

21 I think school holidays are too long, ... I do think that children need more breaks than adults.

    A despite   **B** in spite of   **C** although   **D** furthermore

22 .... I believe that banning smokers from public places is a very good idea.

    A Clearly   **B** Fortunately   **C** Justifiably   **D** Personally

23 A .... study has shown that fewer children are taking up smoking.

    A recnet   **B** recent   **C** rescent   **D** resent

24 The female birds eat very little food .... the males.

    A comparing to   **B** compared to   **C** comparing with   **D** comparing

25 Generally speaking, ... have totally different interests from older people.

    A kids   **B** guys   **C** youth   **D** the young

26 I am writing to .... for the position of tour guide advertised in your newsletter.

    A application   **B** apply   **C** invitation   **D** invite

27 I would be .... if you could send me a brochure.

    A greatful   **B** gratefull   **C** grateful   **D** greatfull

28 I really must apologise .... the way that I behaved during my stay at the hotel.

    A by   **B** for   **C** of   **D** to

29 I .... like to accept your kind offer of a free meal in your restaurant.

    A could   **B** can   **C** will   **D** would

30 I am really looking forward .... you again soon.

    A to seeing   **B** to see   **C** seeing   **D** see

Answer key

Unit 1

1.2

Speaker	Topic (1–4)	Words that helped you	Person/People they would talk to
B	1	academically, struggling with an assignment	tutor
C	3	get a car	(big / older) brother
D	2	violin, piano, cello, popular bands, singers, classical music	grandad

1.3

2 A   3 D   4 B

1.4

1 in common
2 bond / connection (bond is usually used to describe a very close relationship between people)
3 have / establish / develop … with
4 break down
5 between
6 conflict

2.2

1 nurture   2 accommodating   3 sibling   4 relate
5 adolescence   6 rewarding   7 interaction

2.3

1 True (*Children who experience a rewarding friendship before the birth of a sibling are likely to have a better relationship with that brother or sister that endures throughout their childhood*)
2 False (*When early friendships are successful, young children get the chance to master sophisticated social and emotional skills, even more than they do with a parent.*)
3 False (*When parents relate to a child, they do a lot of the work, figuring out what the child needs and then accommodating those needs … However, this is not usually the case when two children are interacting.*)

4 True (*children who as preschoolers were able to coordinate play with a friend, manage conflicts, and keep an interaction positive in tone were most likely as teenagers to avoid the negative sibling interaction that can sometimes launch children on a path of anti-social behavior*)
5 True (*From birth, parents can nurture and help develop these social competencies (or skills) by making eye contact with their babies, offering toys and playing with them*)

2.4

1 family   2 adopt   3 relationship (*correlation* is also possible, but not *relation*)   4 relative
5 related   6 nurture   7 conflict   8 relation

3.1 and 3.2

immediate family, extended family, family gatherings, sibling rivalry, stable upbringing, active role, family resemblance, physical resemblance, striking resemblance*, maternal instinct
* does not appear in the recording

3.3

1 close-knit   2 ties   3 alike   4 temperament
5 stubborn   6 inherited

Test practice
Listening Part 1

1 Alex/Alexandra
2 3/three
3 8 November / November 8 / 8.11 / 11.8
4 5/five
5 108 Park Road
6 grandmother
7 sleeping / falling asleep
8 dress / get dressed
9 Monday (and) Tuesday
10 4:00 / 4pm / four o'clock

Unit 2

1.2

1 behaviour   2 gestures   3 Toddler   4 independent
5 climb   6 make-believe / imagination   7 outside world
8 immature   9 rapid   10 teeth / eyes   11 eyes / teeth
12 skills

1.3

1 acquired   2 imitating   3 unassisted / without support
4 spontaneously   5 mastered   6 stage, period

1.4

Verb	Noun	Adjective
develop	development	developed / developing / overdeveloped
grow	growth	fully-grown / overgrown
mature / reach maturity	maturity	mature

2.1

2 rate   3 peers   4 consequence   5 unparalleled
6 may / typically   7 abstract   8 concept

2.2

Childhood	Parenthood
crawling	nurturing
immature	overindulgent
irresponsible	overprotective
rebellious	patient
throw a tantrum	tolerant
unsteady	

2.3

1 period   2 growth   3 grew   4 gained   5 rate
6 significantly

3

2 D   3 G   4 F   5 C   6 B   7 H   8 A

4.2

reminisce, look back, remind, memory, memorise, forget, reminder

4.3

2 ~~reminders~~ memories   4 ~~memory~~ memorise
3 ~~remember~~ remind   5 ~~remind~~ remember

Test practice
General Training Writing Task 1
Model answer

Dear Sir or Madam

I recently spent 3 nights in your hotel. On my final day, I was told that my flight was leaving earlier than planned and so I had to pack my things very quickly. Because I was in such a hurry, I didn't have time to check that I had everything with me, and I have realised that I have forgotten to collect some papers from your business centre.

The document concerned is actually a very important contract that I had left with the staff in the business centre so that it could be photocopied. This is the original signed copy and I am going to need it within the next few days.

If possible, can you please scan a copy of the contract and attach it in an email to me? I will be able to get it printed off again at the business centre in my next hotel when I arrive. The contract is highly sensitive, so I would be grateful if you could then post the original to my office as soon as possible.

Thank you for your help in this matter.

Kind regards

Unit 3

1.2

1 variety   2 nutrients   3 servings   4 maintain
5 overweight   6 factors   7 overeating   8 ingredients

1.3

1 vital   2 dietitians   3 moderate   4 portions
5 skipping   6 curb   7 appetite   8 eliminate
9 allergy   10 trigger

2.1

1 muscle   2 fat   3 blood flow   4 carries blood
5 blocked   6 treatment   7 brain   8 cure
9 clear   10 risk

2.2

1 (any three) walking, jogging, running, swimming, cycling
2 B briskly   C gradually   D recommendation
   E pace   F overdoing   G recover   H alternate

3

Noun	Verb	Adjective
allergy		allergic
benefit	benefit	beneficial
harm	harm	harmful opp. = harmless
health		healthy opp. = unhealthy
infection	infect opp. = disinfect	infectious
nutrition	nourish	nutritious
obesity		obese
prevention	prevent	preventable
recommendation	recommend	recommended
variety	vary	various / varied

4.1

θ	ð
bath, birth, breath, death, growth, health, mouth (n), teeth	bathe, breathe, mouth (v), teethe, writhe

4.2

1 breath   2 teething; teeth   3 health   4 birth
5 writhing   6 breathe

5

2 variety of   3 vital   4 overweight   5 prevent
6 obesity   7 recommend   8 alternate

6 Model answer

1 I think in some ways we are less fit than 50 years ago because obesity was less of a problem then. But we're also healthier in that we are more aware of the risks of smoking. Although exercise has become more popular, fewer children participate in sports than 50 years ago because now they spend too much time playing computer games, which weren't around 50 years ago.

2 When I was young my mum cooked all of our meals and she would spend a lot of time in the kitchen. Now that I live by myself I find I'm too busy to cook or shop for food, so I tend to eat too much junk food.

3 I hope that they will stop making food with so many additives in and that fast food will become a lot healthier. I also think there will be more variety in fast food.

Test practice

General Training Reading Section 1

1 D (just be warned that it's not ideal for longer training sessions)

2 A (the highest setting doesn't require a lot of effort, so you'll need to use it longer to get a good workout if you are used to something more demanding.)

3 C (if you suffer from arthritis, you should probably avoid this one as the motion can put stress on the knees)

4 B (The *Rower 2000* works the back, arms, and legs simultaneously, offering as close to a complete workout as possible from a machine)

5 E (although it's quite a lot more expensive, it's best to opt for the motorized version)

6 C (beginners may struggle and find this stepper machine strenuous)

7 D (This model has a fairly hard seat, but if you prefer, there's a softer cushioned version you can buy separately)

8 B (Unless you're used to rowing, the motion can initially feel strange)

9 C (The best versions are equipped with handrails and wide pedals for your feet, but sadly this one doesn't and feels a little unstable and flimsy.)

10 False (A&E does this 'Less severe injuries can be treated in an Urgent Care Centre.')

11 Not given (There is no advice given about phoning ahead)

12 False (It is important to note that arriving by ambulance does not necessarily mean you'll be seen sooner than patients who take themselves to A&E)

13 True (you may be sent to an Urgent Care centre)

14 False (the hospital will do this: In all cases, the hospital will inform your doctor that you have been to A&E.)

Unit 4

1.2

1 realist   2 risk-taker   3 pessimist   4 optimist

1.3

Speaker 1	work hard for a living; achieve anything in your life; life has its ups and downs
Speaker 2	live life on the edge; feel alive; your quality of life
Speaker 3	have a negative attitude; life is full of disappointments
Speaker 4	have a positive outlook on life; live life to the full; lead a happy life

2
1 lifetime (one word)   2 living   3 life   4 life
5 living   6 lifelong (one word)   7 living   8 living

3.1
1 True (*Probably no one would consider <u>acting</u> to have the
same characteristics <u>as roller-skating</u> or playing baseball, but
men and women who act as a hobby report <u>feeling an intense</u>
<u>sense of belonging to a group, much the same way others do in</u>
<u>playing sports</u>*) strong = *intense*; feeling = *sense*
2 False (*And <u>activities providing the strongest sense of</u>
<u>competition are not sports</u>, but card, arcade and computer
games, he found.*) taking part in = *participating in*; desire to
win = *sense of competition*
3 True (*coin collecting … <u>fulfil their need for 'creativity'</u>*) satisfies
people's desire = *fulfil their need*; making things = *creativity*
4 False (*but nobody explains why skiing really appeals to people.*)
attracts = *appeals to*
5 True (*<u>Fishing</u>, generally considered more of an outdoor
recreational activity, for example, <u>is a form of self-expression</u>
like quilting or stamp collecting, because <u>it gives people the</u>
<u>opportunity to express some aspect of their personality</u>*) the
type of person you are = *personality*

3.2
1 personal fulfilment   2 insight   3 aspect   4 leisure
activity, hobby, recreational activity   5 daily routine

4.1
make a decision, make a change, make a choice, meet a need,
miss a chance, miss an opportunity, play a role, put pressure
(on), set a goal, take a chance, take an opportunity

4.2
Everyday life today is much more complicated than in the past.
Even in our leisure time we have to ~~take~~ **make** so many choices
about what to do or even what to watch on TV. We are often
spoilt for choice and this can leave us feeling confused and
dissatisfied. We all know that it is important to ~~get~~ **achieve** a
balance between work and play, but many of us do not succeed.
Instead, we ~~make~~ **put** extra pressure ~~for~~ **on** ourselves by trying
to be as successful in our work life as in our personal life.

Life in the past was much simpler as many people worked to
~~get~~ **meet** their basic needs. Today, for many of us, our job is not
just a way of making a ~~life~~ **living**. For many, work ~~is~~ **plays** an
important role in our everyday life and gives us a strong sense
of personal fulfilment. What is more, we have become much
more materialistic. Many people ~~get~~ **set** themselves goals such
as buying a new house or car and so we measure our success

by the material things we own. Desiring these luxuries is what
motivates us to work much harder than in the past, so in many
ways we ~~choice~~ **choose** this way of life.

We have worked hard to improve our standard of living, but
it may have come at a very high price. We need to ~~take~~ **make**
some changes in our priorities so that family occasions are as
important as business meetings. We should also ~~make~~ **take**
every possible opportunity to relax and enjoy our leisure time.
Once you have ~~given~~ **made** the decision to do this, you should
find that your quality of life also improves. My ultimate aim is to
have a happy family life. If I ~~get~~ **achieve** this goal then I know I
will not regret any chances I have ~~lost~~ **missed** to stay longer at
the office.

Test practice
Listening Part 2
1 C (*you're rushing to pull everything together for the new term
… those initial few days are actually <u>a great opportunity to</u>
<u>make lists and stock up on school supplies</u>*)
2 B (*<u>always book ahead</u> and get your tickets online*)
3 A (*They do usually only change <u>once a week</u>, so <u>it's best not</u>
<u>to go more often than that</u>*)
4 J (*pull out the kit … then <u>just leave them to it!</u> For me, that's
the real benefit*)
5 E (*the kids will even learn <u>a bit about chemical reactions</u>,
which is a nice added bonus*)
6 G (*you do need to <u>spend several hours hiding the clues and</u>
<u>making the treasure map</u>*)
7 I (*you do <u>need access to a digital camera</u>*)
8 A (*The only thing parents will need to think about is <u>cleaning</u>
<u>up afterwards</u>*)
9 C (*<u>I'd caution against getting the under-5s involved</u> as they're
likely to get hurt*)
10 H (*There is <u>some building involved</u>, so <u>if you're not handy</u>
<u>in that way yourself, you may need to find a friend or</u>
<u>relative who is</u>*)

Unit 5

1.2
1 overcome   2 study   3 concentrate / study
4 organise   5 taking / studying   6 learn   7 doing
8 revise   9 review   10 taught

1.3
1 studious   2 distractions   3 background noise
4 project, assignment   5 revise   6 curriculum
7 review   8 struggle

1.4

2 find out   3 know   4 learned   5 know   6 study
7 learn how   8 learn from

2.1

Other possible answers are in italics.

1   kindergarten / *nursery*
2   primary / *elementary*
3   junior
4   grade / year
5   senior
6   scholarship / *grant*
7   high / *secondary* (*high school* = US and Australia, *secondary school* = UK)
8   private / *public* (UK)
9   single-sex
10 mixed / coeducational

2.2

Subject	Person	Adjective
architecture	architect	architectural
archaeology	archaeologist	archaeological
biology	biologist	biological
economics	economist	economic (economical is related to saving money or fuel)
geology	geologist	geological
geography	geographer	geographical
journalism	journalist	journalistic
languages / linguistics	linguist	linguistic
law	lawyer	legal
mathematics / maths	mathematician	mathematical
science	scientist	scientific

2.3

2 architectural   3 linguist   4 economic   5 journalism
6 geography

3.1

1 topic   2 thesis   3 (current) literature   4 knowledge
5 relevant   6 limits / scope   7 controversies
8 financial resources   9 funding / a grant   10 tutor

3.2

dissertation = thesis, *easier* = more straightforward, *wide* = broad, *field of study* = area of specialisation / research area, *establish* = ascertain, *consider* = ask yourself, *think about* = take into account, *results* = findings

4

ass**i**gnment, consider**a**tion, c**o**ncentrate, c**o**ntroversy (UK) or contr**o**versy (US), cond**u**ct (v), distr**a**ction, dissert**a**tion, ec**o**nomist, educ**a**tional, **e**ducated, r**e**search (n), th**e**sis, th**e**ory, theor**e**tical

Test practice
General Training Reading Section 2

1 field (of study) (*A placement <u>can be unrelated to your field of study</u>*)
2 (individual) case manager (*<u>case manager, who will determine the minimum level of academic achievement</u> required*)
3 education authority (office) (*The <u>education authority</u> is responsible for the recruitment … <u>Applicants apply in person</u> to our office*)
4 post-secondary (*Our internship program is designed specifically for post-secondary students*)
5 six months (*… already graduated may … be considered <u>provided that they apply within six months</u>*)
6 academic institution / university (*<u>academic institution</u> … <u>will determine the duration of a work assignment</u>*)

Test One

(*Unit numbers in brackets show the unit where the vocabulary tested can be found.*)

1 B (Unit 1)	11 C (Unit 2)	21 C (Unit 4)
2 B (Unit 1)	12 A (Unit 2)	22 A (Unit 4)
3 D (Unit 1)	13 B (Unit 3)	23 C (Unit 4)
4 A (Unit 1)	14 A (Unit 3)	24 D (Unit 4)
5 B (Unit 1)	15 D (Unit 3)	25 B (Unit 5)
6 B (Unit 1)	16 B (Unit 3)	26 A (Unit 5)
7 A (Unit 2)	17 A (Unit 3)	27 D (Unit 5)
8 C (Unit 2)	18 B (Unit 3)	28 B (Unit 5)
9 D (Unit 2)	19 D (Unit 4)	29 D (Unit 5)
10 A (Unit 2)	20 B (Unit 4)	30 C (Unit 5)

Unit 6

1.2

A (at the beginning), F, G

1.3

1 translate   2 accuracy   3 language barrier
4 native speaker   5 fluency   6 function

2.1

1 You can say that again! (= I totally agree with you)
2 having said that (= despite this)
3 There is something to be said for (= It has some advantages)
4 to say the least (= it is in fact even more important than I have just said)
5 When all is said and done (= After everything else; remember this)
6 Needless to say (= This is to be totally expected)
7 That is to say (= In other words)
8 have a say (= be involved in making a decision)

2.2

1 ~~talks~~ shows / tells
2 ~~speaking~~ saying
3 ~~tell about~~ talk about / tell you about
4 ~~talk~~ speak
5 ~~said~~ spoken
6 ~~says~~ shows

2.3

1 recall (= *remember*)
2 express (= *say*)
3 stutter (= *speak with difficulty, pausing at the start of a word or repeating the beginning*)
4 conjecture (= *a guess not based on any proof*)
5 demonstrate (= *show how something works*)
6 state (= *say*)
7 gesture (= *using your hands to help you communicate an idea*)
8 contradict (= *state the opposite*)

3.2

2 False (*it was* spontaneous)
3 True (*it became more* sophisticated)
4 False (*they did not develop a way of* distinguishing *left from right*)
5 True (*must have some* inherent *tendency to link gestures to meaning*)

4.2

Other possible answers are in italics.

1 accuracy / *grammar*   6 explain
2 fluent   7 follow / *understand* / *comprehend*
3 speak / *talk*   8 first / *native*
4 native   9 pronunciation
5 speak   10 pronounce

Test practice

Academic Reading

1 C (*Pinpointing* the origin of language *might seem like idle speculation*)

2 D (*FOXP2 …* may be about 200,000 years old)

3 B (*How could our speechless* Homo sapiens *ancestors colonise the ancient world, spreading from Africa to Asia, and perhaps making a short sea-crossing to Indonesia, without language?*)

4 A (*Nevertheless,* the complexity of human expression may have started off as simple stages in animal 'thinking' or problem-solving *– for example, number processing (how many lions are we up against?)*)

5 A (*Apes are reliant on grooming to stick together, and* that basically constrains their social complexity to groups of 50.)

6 B (*Davidson and Noble, who reject Dunbar's gossip theory,* suggest that there was a significant increase in brain size from about 400,000 years ago)

7 D (*Giselle Bastion …* argues that gossip has acquired a bad name)

8 B (*William Noble and Iain Davidson … conclude that* language is a feature of anatomically modern humans, and an essential precursor *of the earliest symbolic pictures in rock art, ritual burial, major sea-crossings, structured shelters and hearths – all dating, they argue, to the last 100,000 years.*)

9 A (*Marc Hauser … In other words, we* can potentially track language by looking at the behaviour of other animals.)

10 C (*Dunbar notes that* just as grooming releases opiates that create a feeling of wellbeing in monkeys and apes, so do the smiles and laughter associated with human banter.)

11 B (*William Noble and Iain Davidson …* look for the origin of language in early symbolic behaviour *and the evolutionary selection in fine motor control. For example, throwing and making stone tools could have developed into simple gestures like pointing that eventually entailed a sense of self-awareness.* They argue that language *is a form of symbolic communication that* has its roots in behavioural *evolution.*)

12 E (*Dean Falk … suggests that before the first smattering of language there was* motherese, *that musical gurgling between a mother and her baby*)

13 C (*Robin Dunbar … believes they were probably talking about each other – in other words, gossiping.*)

14 C (*Dunbar argues that* gossip provides the social glue permitting humans to live in cohesive groups up to the size of about 150)

Unit 7

1.2

Speaker	Type of place	Words that helped you decide
1	rural	quaint, village, countryside, scenic, peaceful, fresh air, sleepy, local produce
2	coastal	beach, sand, water, crystal clear, sea, surf, water sports, snorkelling, scuba diving, deep-sea fishing
3	urban	skyscrapers, shopping malls, cosmopolitan, traffic jams, public transport, sports stadium, polluted
4	mountainous	above sea level, overlook, valley, picturesque, crisp air, steep, breathtaking

1.3

A 3   B 4   C 1   D 2

1.4

1 trends   2 of, of   3 peaked   4 travelling, reached
5 low   6 lows / troughs   7 peaks, troughs   8 at

2.1

Thanks to modern transport people can now ~~journey~~ **travel** a lot more easily than in the past. However, modern-day ~~trip~~ **travel** also has its problems: airports can be very crowded and there are often long queues of people waiting to collect their ~~luggages~~ **luggage / suitcases**. One way to make this job easier is to tie a colourful ribbon around each of your ~~luggage~~ **suitcases / pieces of luggage** so they are easier to spot on the conveyor belt. If you are going away on a short ~~journey~~ **trip** of only a few days then you may be able to limit yourself to hand luggage and save even more time. For longer ~~travels~~, **journeys / trips**, make sure you take plenty of snacks and drinks, especially if you are ~~trip~~ **travelling** with small children.

2.2

1 itinerary   2 in advance   3 access   4 peak
5 essential   6 identification   7 fluctuate
8 destination

2.3

1 transport   2 remote   3 effect   4 tourists   5 affects
6 tourism   7 trend   8 eco-tourism

Model answer

People often want to take a break from their ordinary life and explore faraway places. So many people want to do this that crowds flock to popular tourist destinations. This has advantages and disadvantages for the people who live there.

Tourism certainly has its disadvantages for local people in pristine parts of the world. Firstly, the arrival of large groups of tourists can mean the end of peace and quiet. As the beaches and different forms of transport all become overcrowded, local inhabitants may feel that they can no longer enjoy their own area. Furthermore, the development of hotels and holiday apartments may make the area too expensive for locals, who must surely resent the impact all of this has on the surrounding environment. Therefore, it is not surprising that some do not welcome these visitors.

Nevertheless, tourism also has several positive effects. Firstly, there is a clear boost to the local economy. In remote regions, young people are often forced to leave to find work, so the tourism industry provides much-needed employment opportunities and can help struggling communities to thrive. In addition, although tourism has been shown to negatively affect the environment, the growing trend of ecotourism may help to reverse this. Furthermore, the invasion of tourists is relatively short-lived, and is mainly limited to the peak tourist season; the rest of the year locals can relax and enjoy their beautiful surroundings. Thus, the benefits of tourism do appear to mitigate any problems it brings.

In conclusion, in my view, although large numbers of tourists can cause problems when they visit popular tourist destinations, the economic advantages more than make up for these. If it is managed well, tourism can help such areas far more than it hinders them.

3

ɜː (as in bird)	ʊə (as in pure)	ʌ (as in cup)
journey journal	tourism tourist	country double enough rough trouble southern
aʊ (as in cow)	**ɒ (as in not)**	**ɔː (as in ball)**
boundary doubt drought south	cough trough	bought course nought

Test practice
General Training Reading Section 1
1 E (*There are beautiful <u>beaches, coastal</u> villages, unspoilt <u>coves and bays</u>, clear turquoise <u>waters</u>, breathtaking scenery, <u>mountains</u>*)
2 D (*whale watching*)
3 C (*We can provide top-quality chalets, hotels or apartments*)
4 A (*Our holidays are ideal for young people <u>travelling by themselves</u>*)
5 C (*<u>skiing and snowboarding</u> are just some of the many activities on offer*)
6 E (*There is plenty to see and do and <u>families are particularly well-catered for.</u>*)
7 A (*<u>budget</u> accommodation, we're sure you will not find better value elsewhere*)
8 B (*our five-star hotel*)

Unit 8

1.2
1 C   2 B   3 A

1.3
1 lose (all) track of time
2 save time
3 spend time
4 time-consuming
5 took so long (not ~~so long time~~)
6 the right time … on time
7 in time
8 take my time

1.4
1 after   2 before   3 before   4 before
5 (one) after (another)   6 before   7 before
8 (very soon) after

2.1
1 8000 BC (see timeline)
2 radiocarbon dating (*Exact dates are not possible, since dates are inferred from minute changes in physical measurements, such as the radiocarbon dating method.*)
3 (in the) 1960s (*In the 1960s a car park was built over these.*)
4 hunter-gatherers (*the hunter-gatherers that erected the postholes*)
5 because it has eroded (*Many visitors to Stonehenge fail to notice the 'henge' since the ditch and bank have been greatly eroded over the passing millennia.*)

2.2
1 period   2 ancient   3 spanned   4 prehistoric
5 chronologically   6 phase   7 eroded   8 millennia
9 excavation   10 era   11 predate

2.3
1 chronological   2 the Middle Ages   3 ancient
4 era   5 age   6 consecutive

3.2
1 ~~nostalgia~~ nostalgic; ~~look backwards~~ look back;
2 ~~the modern time~~ the modern age / modern times; ~~history~~ historical
3 ~~stage~~ period; ~~go back in times~~ go back in time; ~~period~~ age

Test practice
Listening Part 4
1 drill
2 worms
3 olive oil
4 onions
5 ear
6 chewing (sticks / twigs)
7 (dental) specialists / specialism
8 (food) market
9 (fellow) sailors
10 sugar (acids)

Unit 9

1.1
Possible answers:
A elephant, giraffe, lion, hippopotamus, ostrich, rhinoceros
B carnation, daisy, lily, rose, tulip
C apple, banana, grape, grapefruit, mango, melon, orange, pear, pineapple
D emu, echidna, dingo, kangaroo, koala, platypus
E gum, maple, oak, pine, palm
F aubergine or eggplant, broccoli, courgette or zucchini, carrot, cauliflower, pea, pumpkin, potato

1.2

Animals	*Plants*
coat, claw, beak, fauna, fur, feathers, hide, horn, paw, predator, scales, trunk	*branch, flora, petal, root, thorn, twig, trunk, vegetation*

A *trunk* can be part of a tree or on an elephant. *Coat, feathers, fur, hide* and *scales* are all associated with the skin or covering of animals.

1.3

2 animal   3 human   4 nature   5 animal   6 natural
7 natural   8 human

1.4

1 semi-arid   2 vegetation   3 burrows/dens   4 den
5, 6, 7 insects/spiders/snails (in any order)   8 roots

2.1

2 soil (the others are verbs)
3 crop (the others are single plants)
4 chemical (the others mean without chemicals)
5 arid (the others are all wet climates)
6 tropical (the others are all dry climates)
7 introduced (the others all refer to things that naturally belong to an area)

2.2

1 True (*pesticides* = chemicals to kill pests)
2 True (*paddocks* = fields)
3 True (*eradicated* = killed off)
4 False (*native* is the opposite of *introduced*)
5 False (*very successful* is the opposite of *catastrophic*)

2.3

1 vulnerable   2 repercussions   3 become resistant
4 endangered   5 extinct   6 genetically modified
7 disastrous   8 ecological balance

2.4

Noun	Adjective	Adverb	Verb
agriculture	agricultural	agriculturally	
ecology	ecological	ecologically	
evolution	evolutionary		evolve
extinction	extinct		become extinct
nature	natural	naturally	
genetics / genes	genetic	genetically	

3

1 crops   2 genetically modified   3 eradicate
4 agriculture   5 insects   6 pesticides   7 soil
8 vegetation   9 habitat   10 become resistant to
11 ecological balance   12 endangered

4

adapt   agriculture   catastrophe   chemical
climate   disastrous   endangered   genetically
human   natural   vulnerable

Test practice
Academic Reading

1 G (*the benefits of living alongside people, such as providing food and shelter. Of course, there are downsides too …*)
2 C (*Using the general public in this way means they are able to have far more cameras out in the field than any single researcher could manage*)
3 E (*due to competition for food and shelter and the spread of the squirrelpox virus (which grey squirrels transmit to red squirrels)*)
4 A (*researchers estimated that cities accommodate only 8% of the bird species and 25% of the plants that would have lived in those areas prior to urban development*)
5 F (*This voluntary organisation manages the extensive woodland nearby, supplying additional food, and employing dedicated "squirrel officers" who help maintain "grey squirrel-free" habitats*)
6 B (*When data is limited, it is difficult to understand the bigger picture: we can't know if populations are becoming more or less abundant and why; or whether conservation is needed*)
7 G (*However, managing urban sites like the one in Formby may be a better alternative, particularly as it makes the most of the benefits of living alongside people*)
8 biodiversity (*are helping to assess* biodiversity)
9 spotter (*Anyone with access to a camera can register to take part and become a 'spotter'*)
10 34 (*recorded* 34 *species*)
11 squirrel (*the American grey squirrel – is the most frequent sighting*)
12 raccoon (*Another remarkable discovery was a North American* raccoon *… transfer it to a wildlife park*)
13 C (*The main idea throughout this passage is how ordinary people can help with animal conservation.*)

Unit 10

1.2

1 commercial   2 astronauts   3 launch   4 simulator
5 atmosphere   6 weightlessness   7 explorers   8 outer

1.3

1 a reality   2 undergo   3 gravity   4 acclimatise
5 propel   6 in excess of   7 float   8 re-entry

1.4
1 exploration   2 atmospheric   3 gravitational
4 underwent   5 simulates

2.1
1 Earth   2 oceans   3 cloud   4 thunderstorms   5 smaller
6 solar system   7 rings / moons   8 moons / rings

2.2
1 rotates   2 surface   3 atmosphere   4 sustain
5 shuttle   6 composition

2.3

Noun	Adjective
atmosphere	atmospheric
cosmos	cosmic
galaxy	galactic
gravity	gravitational
horizon	horizontal
moon	lunar
meteor	meteoric
sun	solar
star	stellar
Earth	terrestrial
universe	universal

2.4
1 horizon   2 galaxy   3 meteor   4 lunar   5 universe
6 horizontal   7 universal   8 Solar

3
1 False (unmanned)
2 False (inevitable)
3 True (uninhabited)

4
1 planet   2 universe   3 solar system   4 land
5 space   6 satellites   7 debris   8 outer
9 float   10 space station

5
atmosphere   commercial   explorer   exploration
galaxy   horizon   horizontal   outer
satellite   solar system   sustain   universal

Test practice
Listening Part 3
1 C (*there are so many important things that space exploration can teach us, especially about the history of our own planet*)
2 B (*Robots can't just react to situations independently … they need to be told what to do*)
3 A (*they were still using a lot of technology from the 1960s and 1970s rather than anything state of the art*)
4 A (*The real concern is simply how far away the craft will be*)
5&6 A, D (in any order) (D: *It's never too soon to start*; A: *Sometimes you have to start a project even if you're not going to see it finished … even if there's no real progress for ten or more years*)
7&8 A, E (in any order) (A: *even the dirt on the ground could kill us.* True; E: *I suppose the ground would likely contain a lot of resources. Yes, a lot of building materials could be sourced there*)
9&10 B, D (in any order) (B: *For me, the worst would be trying to keep myself occupied. Yes, I mean we worry now about tedious long-haul flights, with Mars you're talking about years of watching the same movies on some little screen*; D: *I need nature and open spaces. I agree, that would have a big impact on me too*)

Test Two
(*Unit numbers in brackets show the unit where the vocabulary tested can be found.*)

1 D (Unit 6)	11 C (Unit 7)	21 B (Unit 9)
2 A (Unit 6)	12 A (Unit 7)	22 D (Unit 9)
3 C (Unit 6)	13 B (Unit 8)	23 C (Unit 9)
4 B (Unit 6)	14 B (Unit 8)	24 C (Unit 9)
5 C (Unit 6)	15 D (Unit 8)	25 A (Unit 10)
6 D (Unit 6)	16 A (Unit 8)	26 C (Unit 10)
7 D (Unit 7)	17 D (Unit 8)	27 D (Unit 10)
8 C (Unit 7)	18 B (Unit 8)	28 A (Unit 10)
9 A (Unit 7)	19 A (Unit 9)	29 D (Unit 10)
10 B (Unit 7)	20 C (Unit 9)	30 D (Unit 10)

Unit 11

1.2
1 traditional brick
2 lovely high-rise
3 small country

2.1

	Type of building	Material(s) used	Favourite feature	Adjectives used to describe it
A	(a) single-storey (cottage)	timber and stone	ceilings	traditional, ornate, cosy
B	(a) high-rise (flat)	glass, concrete and steel	balcony	ultra-modern, state-of-the art, functional, cramped
C	(a) two-storey (house)	brick	staircase	conventional, typical, spacious, light, airy

2.2
A
1 the local *quarry*
2 (they are decorated with) *pretty details*
3 small *(cosy)*
B
1 new *(state-of-the-art)*
2 it has a space *to suit every purpose*
3 small *(cramped)*
4 no (his building *towers over everything else*)
C
1 no, it is *conventional, typical*
2 the living room (it is *light and airy*)
3 *curved*

3.2
1 True (the population... <u>tripled</u> in size)
2 True (<u>congested roads</u>, which were <u>in poor condition</u>, were almost <u>impassable</u> = difficult to travel through)
3 False (<u>railways emerging</u> (= appearing) in the north <u>had yet to reach London</u>)
4 False (<u>connecting</u> (= joining) ports... is tricky... they were <u>not close to bridges</u>)
5 True (the work was <u>abandoned</u> (= stopped) due to <u>flooding</u> (= a problem with water))
6 Not Given (we know they used 'a steam-driven pump' but we do not know if it often broke down)
7 False (they <u>struggled</u> daily (this means they did not do it 'easily'))
8 False (the walls were unstable, constantly crumbling and <u>collapsing</u> (= falling down / not strong))
9 False (this <u>scheme</u> (= approach / plan) never came about)
10 True (it was completed in 1843 and is still <u>in operation</u> (= in use) today)

3.3
2 D 3 A 4 H 5 G 6 E 7 B 8 C

3.4
1 renovated 2 condemned 3 devised 4 maintain

3.5

Noun/person	Verb	Adjective or past participle
building / builder	build	built
construction / construction worker	construct	constructed
design / designer	design	designed
engineering / engineer	engineer	engineered
innovation / innovator	innovate	innovative
invention / inventor	invent	inventive
occupancy / occupant	occupy	occupied
structure	structure	structured

3.6
1 inventive
2 design
3 innovative
4 built
5 construction
6 engineering
7 constructed
8 occupied
9 structure

4
1 z 2 z 3 s 4 z 5 z 6 z 7 s 8 s
9 s 10 z

Test practice
Academic Reading
1 vi (This section talks about two previous ideas of the future house which were not popular as well as the idea that eventually became popular.)
2 v (This section refers to the fact that the kitchen was the centre of the 'home of tomorrow' and would be full of the *technology of tomorrow* that would 'automate' their lives, and automation became a synonym for reduced domestic labor.)
3 ii (This section refers to appliances that enable men to help with the housework.)

4 vii (*now the trend was to look backwards for the future, back to a proud pioneer heritage. In stark contrast to the 1950s, 'old-fashioned' is no longer used in a pejorative way; it is seen as a cherished value.*)

5 iv (*Bathroom spas and gyms, computerized kitchens, wide screen entertainment, even home discotheques are all on the way ... The line between work and leisure became blurred in the 1980s. Forget about not being able to fit exercise into a hectic workday; in 1982, you can work and work out simultaneously.*)

NB For questions 6–13, don't confuse the letters used in the box of options with the letters used for the different paragraphs in the text.

6 E (*Over the 1970s, North America experienced a certain erosion of trust in science and technology*)

7 A (*In the 1920s ... mass-produced, prefabricated house*)

8 F (*By the 1980s ... significantly more women were working outside of the home*)

9 C (*in the 1950s ... furnishings, rugs, and draperies would all be made of synthetic fabric or waterproof plastic*)

10 E (*Over the 1970s ... there was less Utopian speculation about the technologically produced future ... reflecting fears about a future not quite as rosy as that predicted by* Popular Mechanics *in 1950.*)

11 C (*The overriding message of the 1950s vision of the house of the future is that one can access the wonders of the future through the purchase of domestic technology today. ... by focusing on improving technology ... the future becomes strictly a matter of things, their invention, improvement, and acquisition*)

12 C (*Housewives in 50 years may wash dirty dishes – right down the drain! Cheap plastic would melt in hot water.*)

13 A (*The term 'home of tomorrow' first came into usage in the 1920s to describe the 'ideal house for future living'*)

Unit 12

1.2 and 1.3

1 A, compact
2 A, track; keep track of
3 B, screen
4 C, scrolling
5 B, audio
6 C, store
7 B, battery

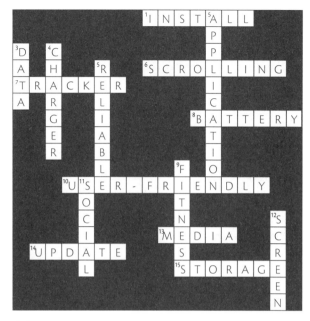

1.4

1 hairdryer   2 tin opener / can opener   3 blender
4 calculators   5 dishwasher   6 word processor
Processor and calculator end in *or*.

2.1

1 Yes

2 No (*The smart phone helped make the IoT a reality – the concept didn't really take off until 2010, when the Smart phone put computers into our pockets.*)

3 No (they *emerged in the early 2000s* and in 2010 they *became the norm in many* homes.)

4 No (it helps *make public transport systems more efficient*)

5 Yes (*a London hacker obtained the Wi-Fi passwords.*)

6 No (*more concerning are the issues of privacy* and ... *surveillance*)

2.2

1 cyberattack   2 hacker   3 operate   4 broadband
5 smart   6 security   7 device   8 monitor   9 detect
10 remotely

2.3

1 internet connection   2 artificial intelligence
3 remote control   4 online platform   5 virtual reality
6 digital age

2.4

1 advanced / high / modern / state-of-the-art / cutting-edge / leading-edge
2 gadgets / appliances / devices
3 to
4 connection
5 programs
6 use
7 technological / digital / computer
8 latest
9 computerisation
10 by

Unit 13

1.1

2
Nike = US   Sony = Japan   Coca-Cola = US   Levi's = US
Versace = Italy   Gucci = Italy   Adidas = UK

1.2

1 B (At this rate our culture will disappear altogether and we'll all end up eating the same bland food.)
2 A (a lot of people are worried about globalisation and the impact it could have on the local people. But actually I'm beginning to think it works the other way around.)
3 A (and globally, pizzas are actually more popular than burgers.)
4 A (globalisation could mean that we end up living a more interesting and multicultural life.)
5 B (the soft drinks market is totally dominated by just one or two big companies.)
6 A (Without globalisation, international companies just wouldn't merge like that.)
7 B (they want to see something exotic, not the same icons they see all around them at home!)
8 A (I doubt the local people feel they are losing their national identity just because a fast food outlet has opened up.)
9 A (And anyway, the nice thing about it is that in many places, these chains have to change the food they sell to suit the local culture. So there is a lot of give and take going on and you still get cultural diversity to some extent.)
10 B (I guess no one big multinational has a monopoly over the fashion market either, does it?)

1.3

2 local
3 globally
4 multicultural
5 multinationals, is dominated by
6 merge

7 exotic … icons
8 national identity
9 cultural diversity
10 has a monopoly over

1.4

Noun	Adjective
culture	cultural
ethnicity	ethnic
globalisation	global
modernisation	modern
multiculturalism	multicultural
nation	national
urbanisation	urban

2.1

2 Yes (There have been many projections about the future which, with the benefit of hindsight, seem rather ridiculous.)
3 No (… many people today are more sceptical about current predictions …)
4 Yes (One of the few areas in which long-term trends can be clearly seen is in demographic statistics.)
5 Yes (Some societies have birth rates that are already locking their populations into absolute decline.)
6 No (an increasing proportion will be moving into old age)
7 Yes (into old age, when they are less productive)
8 Yes (pick the trends that are likely to be prolonged, but to also factor in human influence.)

2.2

2 look back and understand = with the benefit of hindsight
3 firmly believe in (opp) are sceptical about
4 population = demographics; figures = statistics
5 countries = societies; total = absolute
6 percentage = proportion; dwindle (opp) increase
7 work less = are less productive
8 take into account = factor in; effect = influence

2.3

The graph ~~displays~~ shows the actual population of Australia in 2002 and the projected figures ~~of~~ for 2101. The ~~per cent~~ percentage of people aged 15–24 is predicted to fall significantly during this period, while there will be an increase ~~of~~ in the percentage of people aged 55–64. In 2002, just under 15 ~~percentage~~ % / per cent of the population was aged between 15 and 24, while in 2101 this is predicted to drop ~~in~~ to approximately 10 per cent.

2.4

1 trends   2 population   3 compounded   4 ageing
5 challenges   6 present   7 elderly   8 declining
9 implications   10 factors   11 rates   12 migrating

3.1

A = global, local, culture
B = national, sceptical
C = international, multicultural
D = domestic, projection
E = globalisation, modernisation
F = isolation, implication

Test practice
Academic Writing Task 1
Model answer

The chart shows 5 reasons given for walking less and what percentage of people of different ages give this reason. Overall, for all age groups, distance and bad weather are the most commonly cited issue, while the other problems vary by age group.

The youngest age groups, 18 to 34, and 35 to 55, are more likely to walk in spite of the distance than any other age group and least likely to have a health problem preventing them from walking. These age groups are, however, least likely to walk in bad weather, when there are insufficient pavements, and where they feel unsafe, though far more 18–34 year-olds give this as a reason.

Responses from people aged 56 to 70 differ mainly in terms of health, with more than double the percentage of people in this age group citing this as a reason compared with 18 to 34 year-olds. However, this group are far less concerned about pathways and crime.

Similarly, approximately 43% of the oldest group, aged 70 and over, stated that poor health prevented them from walking more, but they are the least worried about pavements and crime at 18%.

Unit 14

1.1

Too much / too little can be used with uncountable nouns: traffic, time, money, space, work, rubbish.
Too many / too few can be used with countable nouns: people.

1.2

They talk about work and traffic and to a limted extent, time.

1.3

face   deal with   cause   tackle   address   raise
resolve   present   identify

1.4

1 facing
2 address / resolve / deal with / tackle (*face up to* is also possible)
3 caused
4 raised / addressed / tackled
5 resolve
6 presented (*posed* is also possible)

1.5

find a solution, overcome a difficulty, solve or resolve a problem, remedy a situation, resolve an issue or problem, reach or find a compromise

1.6

2 ~~resolve~~ *find* a solution
3 ~~solve~~ *overcome* this difficulty
4 ~~solution~~ *solved / resolved / found a solution to* the problems
5 ~~solve~~ *reach / find* a compromise

1.7

1 benefit (= *advantage*)   2 setback (= *problem*)
3 enhance (= *improve*)   4 aggravate (= *make worse*)
5 linger (= *stay a long time*)

1.8

double-edged   long-sighted   long-term   short-sighted
short-term   one-sided
1 long-term   2 short-term   3 one-sided
4 short-sighted   5 double-edged

2.1

1 booming / enormous / staggering   2 staggering
3 enormous   4 basic   5 adequate / decent
6 decent / basic / adequate   7 pressing / enormous / catastrophic   8 catastrophic

2.2

1 inhabitants   2 developing nations   3 urbanisation
4 overpopulation   5 infrastructure   6 slums

2.3

Noun	Verb	Adjective
competition	compete	competitive
exclusion	exclude	excluded
inclusion	include	included
isolation	isolate	isolated
poverty		poor
responsibility	take/accept responsibility	responsible
tolerance	tolerate	tolerant

3.2

1 competing; poverty; isolated
2 tolerant; include; exclude
3 take responsibility; responsible; poor

4

d sound: accepted, crowded, excluded, included, isolated, resolved, solved
t sound: developed, overpriced, overworked, stressed

Test practice
Academic Reading

1 second-hand (used) clothes / clothing / apparel
2 metal
3 paper
4 raw materials
5 the poor
6 crops / food
7 (building) bricks
8 industrialisation
9 (private) contractors
10 dust-yard(s)
11 & 12 dust / cinders (in any order)
13 fuel
14 sea
15 C (A is wrong because we are told: '*under all circumstances dust-sorting is* <u>*dirty and disagreeable work*</u>'. B is wrong because we are told: *The workers also received* <u>*marginal reward*</u> *for their efforts*. D is wrong because we are told: *The 1875 Public Health Act had given local authorities a legal responsibility to remove and dispose of domestic waste.* C is correct because: *the last years of the century saw a solution to the apparently insoluble problem of what to do with the refuse of Britain's cities … : the incinerator.*)

Unit 15

1.2

Statement 1: Speaker A, useful   Speaker B, useless
Statement 2: Speaker A, impossible   Speaker B, possible
Statement 3: Speaker A, unlikely   Speaker B, likely

1.3

useful	useless	possible	impossible	likely	unlikely
beneficial	pointless	conceivable	unattainable	liable	improbable
worthwhile	futile	feasible	impracticable	probable	questionable
advantageous	fruitless	viable	unfeasible		doubtful
		achievable			

2.1

1 ecosystems   2 environmental   3 emissions   4 acid
5 greenhouse   6 exhaust   7 drought   8 biodiversity
9 contaminated   10 deforestation   11 erosion
12 fertilisers   13 waste

2.2

2 vital   3 unprecedented   4 devastating   5 insoluble
6 immune   7 pervasive   8 inexorably, inevitably
9 chronic   10 taxing

4.1

1 (being threatened by *also possible*)
2 pollution
3 in danger of
4 erosion
5 contamination
6 sustainable
7 at risk
8 recyclable
9 disposal
10 pollutants

4.2

2 irrelevant   3 unreasonable   4 irresponsible
5 irreparable   6 irreversible   7 irreplaceable
8 unrelated

4.3
Model answer

Dear Sir or Madam

I saw your notice asking for ideas about how to take care of the environment and would like to offer some suggestions. Firstly, one important way that everyone in the local area can help with is picking up litter along the river bank. In addition, if the council installs more rubbish bins at popular places along the river banks, this would also help enormously, and would encourage people not to litter in the first place.

These actions would help in two ways. Removing litter from the riverside areas will mean that less plastic and waste ends up in the river system. More importantly, it will also help local wildlife, who sometimes become caught in plastic containers when looking for food.

Taking care of our environment is a wonderful ideas because will benefit all of us in many ways, not only in making our town a better place to live but also in showing we care about our local wildlife.

Kind regards

5

2 r**e**fuse   3 c**o**nflict   4 confl**i**ct   5 pr**e**sent
6 pres**e**nts   7 pr**o**gress   8 progr**e**ss   9 **in**crease
10 incr**ea**se

Test practice
Academic Writing Task 1
Model answer

The diagram shows how aluminium cans are recycled. This is a process that involves both heavy machinery and the involvement of the general public.

The process begins when people take their used cans to a special collection centre once they have finished with them. The cans are collected from here and taken to a factory where they are first sorted and then cleaned. Next, the cans are shredded and crushed in a special machine until they form one solid block. The metal is then heated to a high enough temperature to allow the aluminium to melt. It is then rolled out flat to a thickness of between 2.5 mm and 6 mm. The aluminium sheets are now taken to a can-making factory to be made into new cans. From here, they are delivered to a soft drinks factory to be filled.

The new cans are now delivered to shops where they can now be once again sold to the public and reused. In the UK, 74 per cent of all aluminium cans that are sold are recycled.

[177 words]

Test Three

(Unit numbers in brackets show the unit where the vocabulary tested can be found.)

1 D (Unit 11)	11 D (Unit 12)	21 C (Unit 14)
2 C (Unit 11)	12 A (Unit 12)	22 D (Unit 14)
3 B (Unit 11)	13 D (Unit 13)	23 C (Unit 14)
4 A (Unit 11)	14 A (Unit 13)	24 A (Unit 14)
5 D (Unit 11)	15 C (Unit 13)	25 C (Unit 15)
6 C (Unit 11)	16 B (Unit 13)	26 B (Unit 15)
7 A (Unit 12)	17 D (Unit 13)	27 B (Unit 15)
8 A (Unit 12)	18 B (Unit 13)	28 C (Unit 15)
9 C (Unit 12)	19 D (Unit 14)	29 A (Unit 15)
10 B (Unit 12)	20 A (Unit 14)	30 D (Unit 15)

Unit 16

1.1

1 C   2 C   3 B   4 B   5 A

1.3

1 save (*conserve* is also possible)   2 efficient
3 effect (*impact* is also possible)   4 atmosphere /

environment   5 absorb   6 counter / offset
7 offset / counter

2.1

1 carbon dioxide   2 fossil fuels   3 exhaust fumes / emissions   4 renewable   5 solar power, wind power
6 B

2.2

1 fumes   2 alternative   3 eco-friendly / alternative
4 solar   5 emit   6 greenhouse gases   7 converting
  8 plant   9 fuel   10 engine

2.3

2 True (*These vehicles emit only water vapour*)
3 False (*critics say that … converting existing petrol stations to hydrogen will prove too costly*)
4 False (*These fuels are based on plant oils and so can be grown.*)
5 False (*Diesel said 'the use of vegetable oils for engine fuels may seem insignificant today'*)

2.4

2 electricity (the others are all alternative energy sources and are renewable)
3 emission (the others are all adjectives that describe reduced energy use)
4 carbon (the others are all different terms used for petrol)
5 retain (*retain* means *to keep* or *store*, the others all mean the opposite)
6 disposable (this means that you *throw it away*, the others can be made again)
7 drastic (this is an adjective meaning *severe*, the others are all verbs meaning *decrease*)
8 extend (this means to *cause something to last longer*, the others are mean to *use* or *use up*)
9 reserve (this means to *book a table or a seat*, or *to keep something for a particular time* but cannot be used with *energy*. The others all mean the same as *save* and can be used with the word *energy*)

Test practice
Academic Reading

1 A (*famous country and western singer Willie Nelson … the use of biodiesel through his own 'BioWillie' brand*)
2 C (*biodiesel is only 2 per cent less fuel-efficient than petroleum-based diesel*)
3 B (*ethanol, which contains only two-thirds of the energy of gasoline*)
4 A (*Hence a switch to biofuels would demand no new technology and would not significantly reduce the driving range of a car or truck.*)

5 A (*The main source of* <u>*biodiesel*</u> *is plant oil derived from crops such as rapeseed … Consequently, the burden on* <u>*freshwater supplies*</u> *… would be immense.*)

6 Not given (although we are told it is available, we are not given any information about how many Americans currently use it)

7 Yes (*considerably more than the* <u>*400 million acres currently under cultivation*</u>)

8 No (*Oil palms …* <u>*reduces the land requirement fivefold*</u>)

9 No (*Conservationists have been warning that palm oil production poses a dire threat to the dwindling population of orang-utans*)

10 Yes (*They also* <u>*grow much more rapidly*</u>)

11 Not given (we are told his programme uses sunlight (solar energy) but there is no comparison made)

12 Yes ('*It's no real difficult feat to turn nutrients into algae*')

13 C (A ✗ this is shown to be doubtful at present; B ✗ only alternative fuels are discussed; C ✓ the suitability of several different fuels is assessed; D ✗ although other countries are mentioned, there is no suggestion that they should work together)

Unit 17

1.2

Speaker	Industry	Adjectives
1	retail	unskilled, monotonous
2	hospitality	demanding, exhausting
3	building / construction	physical, manual
4	advertising	rewarding

1.3

1 wages   2 redundant   3 workplace   4 shift work
5 staff   6 retire   7 overtime   8 earn / are paid
9 salary   10 job satisfaction

1.4

1 unemployed   2 employees   3 Unemployment
4 employed   5 employer

2.1

1 market   2 consumers / customers   3 packaging
4 trend   5 credibility   6 persuade   7 brand
8 products

3.1

1 economical   2 income   3 money   4 money
5 earnings

3.2

2 job   3 workplace   4 career
5 profession / occupation   6 skills   7 to work
8 advertising   9 advertisement   10 economic   11 earn
12 work / jobs / tasks   13 money   14 work   15 retirement

4.1

ɜː	ɑː	ɔː
bird	park	ball
earn	clerk	floor
first	market	force
nurse	target	law
perk		poor
purse		walk
work		

Test practice
General Training Writing Task 1
Model answer

Dear Mr Smith

It is now three years since I joined this company and while I find my current position of administrative assistant very rewarding, I feel I am ready to take on a more challenging role. I would therefore like to apply for the position of office supervisor.

I am an enthusiastic and energetic employee and I feel that I am well qualified for this role as I have qualifications in business management and I have over ten years' experience working in this industry. I have also recently taken a course in team leadership.

During my time here, I have been responsible for instigating several new systems. As you are aware, many of the operating systems we currently use are outdated and are inadequate for dealing with the large number of customers we now have. If I were given the opportunity to manage this area, then I would plan to gradually update these systems so that the office can run more smoothly.

I would be very grateful if you could consider me for this position.

Yours sincerely   [175 words]

Academic Writing Task 2
Model answer

Practical skills are valuable, and it could be argued that they are now as important as academic qualifications when it comes to getting a job. Nevertheless, it is a mistake to say that qualifications do not matter at all.

In some types of work, qualifications are less important. With manual jobs, such as cleaning and labouring, there is very little theoretical knowledge required. Thus, employers are more likely to seek people with a good working knowledge of the job and what it entails. However, even in these jobs it is important for people to have a minimum level of education, especially if they want to rise above the lowest working level. How can a person without good writing and mathematical skills balance a budget, or deal with legal or safety issues? Therefore, qualifications matter even in more practical types of work.

Nevertheless, it is important to acknowledge that qualifications alone are not sufficient. Students entering the job market with a degree in management, for example, will not be ready to take on a managerial role until they have had proven experience in their field. Furthermore, none of us would want a doctor with only theoretical knowledge to perform an essential operation on us. Having said this, we would also expect doctors and nurses to have a thorough grasp of medical theory, which is essential before any practical training can begin. Therefore, for all disciplines, both practical and theoretical skills are important.

In conclusion, it is true that students who graduate with the highest possible academic qualification but with limited or no practical skills, may struggle to find a job. However, I completely disagree that this makes qualifications redundant. Theoretical knowledge forms an important basis for practical skills, and both are clearly essential.   [255 words]

Unit 18

1.1
Crimes: arson, burglary, fraud, kidnapping, murder, smuggling.
Petty crimes: pickpocketing, vandalism.
Swearing is offensive but is not a crime.
Dumping toxic waste is not considered a crime in all areas.

1.2
2 False (*actions that are offensive to an individual or group of people, but do not violate laws are not crimes*)
3 False (they must enforce the law; *violate the law* means the same as *break the law*)
4 True (*Being guilty of a criminal act usually involves some form of conscious evil intent – conscious* = aware)
5 True (*the reasons behind crime remain elusive – elusive* = difficult to find)
6 True (*crime is influenced by the degree to which others guard over neighborhoods and other people – guard* = protect)
7 True (*research also shows that income inequality correlates to property crime – correlates* = is linked)

1.3

Noun	Verb	Adjective
crime	commit a crime	criminal
deterrent	deter	deterrent
enforcement	enforce	enforceable
offence	offend	offensive
prevention	prevent	preventable
prison, imprisonment, prisoner	imprison	imprisoned
punishment	punish	punishable

1.4
1 criminal   2 enforcement   3 commit
4 criminal / punishable, deter, prevent   5 prevented

2.1
commit a crime; convict a criminal; impose a fine; pass a law

2.2
2 F   3 D   4 A   5 E   6 B

2.3

	Crime	Law
Adjectives	serious, non-violent, drug-related, petty, victimless, random	strict, harsh, tough, existing
Verbs	commit, combat, solve, be involved in a, be tough on	obey, break, enforce, pass, abolish, abide by, introduce

NB *break* (the law) *be tough on* (crime) and *commit* (a crime) are not in the recording.

2.5
1 abiding   2 strict / severe   3 against   4 fine
5 combat   6 prevention   7 above   8 abolished

3.1
1 commit   2 actions   3 punishment   4 petty
5 fine   6 offences   7 imprison   8 committed
9 property / belongings   10 pass   11 deterrent
12 criminals

Test practice
General Training Writing Task 2
Model answer
The way that we deal with crime is important. At the moment, in many places, people who commit crimes are arrested and sent to prison; as crime increases, the prisons become more and

more crowded. I completely disagree that building more prisons would solve these issues.

Adding more prisons would have some benefits. Firstly, it would address the current overcrowding issue. However, if crime is increasing, then surely these extra prisons would soon be filled to capacity? Some people argue that prisons deter would-be criminals, but the rising crime figures seem to suggest that this is not the case. For these reasons, it seems clear that simply building more prisons will not fix either problem for very long.

To find a more effective solution, we need to consider the causes of the problem. Logically, overcrowding in prisons is linked to a rise in criminal activity. However, if the current punishment system is not deterring criminals, then we need to find other ways to approach the issue. As many criminals are forced by their circumstances to break the law, perhaps addressing these needs would help. A further problem is a lack of education, which can prevent people from earning an honest living. So increasing educational programmes would also go some way to help. Thus, it may help to see these criminals as ordinary citizens first.

In conclusion, building more prisons is a short-term and rather ineffective solution and, in my view, is neither the only nor the best way to solve these issues. Prisons only deal with the result of crime; it is far better to find ways to stop it from happening in the first place.   [284 words]

Unit 19

1.2
2 False – they focused on (significant) current affairs stories
3 False – he believes they want to entertain people
4 True
5 False – it is because celebrity stories occupy the front pages

1.3
1 free press   2 broadcast   3 reported   4 networks
5 the media   6 censorship   7 tabloid   8 headlines

1.4
1 press   2 publications   3 sources   4 safeguards
5 controversial   6 front page   7 biased   8 exposés

1.5
1 the press   2 mainstream media (MSM)
3 i) the stories are not always checked by an editor (*editor verification*) and ii) sources can be unreliable.
4 investigative reporting   5 they focus on entertainment (*there is an emphasis on entertainment*) because this is what the public / buyers want (*consumer demand*)

2.2
2 verify   3 investigation   4 publicity   5 exploited
6 unbiased

3.1

Positive	Negative
factual, informative, realistic, unbiased	artificial, attention-grabbing, biased, distorted, intrusive, invasive, pervasive, sensationalist, superficial

3.3
1 tabloids   2 paparazzi   3 intrusive   4 privacy
5 superficial   6 artificial   7 influence   8 celebrity
9 affect   10 distorted   11 stories

4.1

artificial	ʃ	exposed	z	invasion	ʒ
attention	ʃ	exposure	ʒ	invasive	s
biased	s	intrusive	s	publication	ʃ
censor	s	intrusion	ʒ	superficial	ʃ

Test practice
General Training Writing Task 1
Model answer

Dear Rehan

I was reading my weekend copy of The Guardian the other day and came across an article that I thought you'd be really interested in. It's an interview with a young doctor who came over to the UK to work last year. He gives a lot of details about how he coped living and working in a completely new culture, and he also offers some good practical advice about applying for jobs and finding a place to live.

I know you're thinking of applying to come here once you've finished your studies, so I thought you'd find it interesting, especially as he comes from a similar background to you and is working in paediatrics as well. I'm sure his tips and advice will come in handy too!

The article isn't available online because you'd got to have a paid subscription to read the Guardian now, so I've cut it out to and I'll send it with this letter. I hope you find it Useful!

Keep in touch.
All the best

Academic Writing Task 2
Model answer

More and more people now get their news for free online instead of in print. Although this trend may seem positive, it has repercussions both for society and for the publishing industry.

On the surface, access to free news sources seems beneficial. Free resources means we can all remain informed about what is going on in the world. Furthermore, we can access it immediately, instead of waiting for a newspaper or magazine to hit the shops. However, if we are not paying directly for this, then we cannot expect quality reporting. In reality, without skilled editors, writers and reporters, such news stories are often repetitive and error-filled. Added to this is the annoying adverts tracking us all over the internet. Therefore, there are several hidden costs to free news.

Nevertheless, this trend is more than an annoyance. Not only are we presented with poorly edited writing, we are also fed stories that are not factually correct. Consequently, dangerous conspiracy theories circulate far more widely now than in the past, when we relied on mainstream media. For example, there has been a worrying increase in measles outbreaks in some parts of the world, due to false stories about vaccinations. Furthermore, as fewer people now buy newspapers and magazines, many have recently been forced to close. This is particularly concerning for local community news, which those chasing advertising revenue are not interested in promoting. Thus, far from educating us, these free resources will keep us ill-informed.

In conclusion, I believe this trend has had a devastating effect, not only on the publishing industry, but also on society as a whole. What is more, given the forced closure of so many newspapers and magazines, and the lack of regulation of the internet, this is only likely to get worse before it gets better.

Unit 20

1.1
1 abstract art / painting, an artist   2 ballet (dancing), ballet dancers or ballerinas   3 a portrait, an artist
4 a play / the theatre, actors and actresses   5 opera, an opera singer   6 classical music, an orchestra / (classical) musicians   7 a sculpture, a sculptor

1.4
2 No (universal impulse)
3 Yes (reflection)
4 Yes (mundane)
5 Yes (choreographed)
6 Yes (conception)
7 No (burgeoning)
8 No (transcending)

2.1
1 Writers'   2 Literary   3 fair   4 Activities   5 theme
6 Visual   7 exhibition   8 creative   9 galleries
10 crafts   11 Festival   12 interactive   13 Musical
14 concerts

2.2
1 aesthetics   2 festivals   3 accomplished   4 works
5 depict   6 carvings   7 interactive   8 audience
9 participate   10 concerts

2.3

Noun	Verb	Adjective
creation	create	creative
culture		cultural / cultured
influence	influence	influential
inspiration	inspire	inspirational
imagination	imagine	imaginative
participant / participation	participate	participatory
richness / enrichment	enrich	rich

3.2
1 eclectic   2 style   3 popular   4 classical   5 plays
6 role   7 set   8 mood   9 stimulating   10 relaxing
11 inspire   12 distracting   13 headphones   14 escape
15 atmosphere   16 concert   17 electric   18 venues
19 audiences   20 intimacy   21 enriches
22 magical experience   23 the arts

4
atmosphere   classical   edition   festival
fundamental   imagination   literary   monotonous
musical   performance   popular   visual

Test practice
Academic Reading
1 G (*According to Carruthers, memoria was the reason why literature, in a fundamental sense, existed in medieval Europe.*)
2 E (*As Gerald Edelman puts it: 'With that ability come the abilities to model the world, ... through such comparisons comes the possibility of reorganizing plans.'*)
3 B (*In other words, creating narratives is our way of connecting and interacting with our environment (Mink, 1978).*)
4 F (*Instead, our memory prefers creating the past from the perspective of how relevant it is to our present situation.*)
5 A (*Paul Hernadi points out that storytelling and narratives are such widespread phenomena that they could justifiably be included in the list of human universals (Hernadi, 2001).*)

6 D (*The archaeologist* <u>Steven Mithen</u> *has suggested that* <u>this</u>
<u>creativity can be explained by the emergence of a 'cognitively</u>
<u>fluid' mentality – in other words,</u> <u>an ability to link together</u>
<u>information from different areas of our life.</u>)

7 H (*'something is not secure enough by hearing, but it is made*
firm by seeing' (<u>Albertus</u> *l.1. ll. 6–7).*)

8 C (*Our bodies and minds not only adapt to the surrounding*
world, but we actively shape and construct our environment
to better suit our needs (<u>Plotkin</u>*, 1993).*)

9 D (*The second, and more popular, strategy ... was by rote*
learning ... achieved by the <u>frequent repetition</u> *... breaking*
longer texts into numbered segments)

10 F (*The older of these strategies, attributed to Aristotle, relied*
on the concept of <u>'mental images'.</u>)

11 E (*The ... followers of [rote learning] criticised the use of visual*
imagery because of its <u>inaccuracy.</u>)

12 B (*while* <u>in ordinary circumstances</u> *the accuracy of visual*
imagery could not be trusted, this problem would disappear
if the visual imagery was strong enough to make a person
emotionally engaged with the text)

13 H (*According to Carruthers, memoria was the reason*
why <u>literature</u>*, in a fundamental sense, existed in*
medieval Europe.)

Test Four

(*Unit numbers in brackets show the unit where the vocabulary*
tested can be found.)

1 B (Unit 16)	11 A (Unit 17)	21 D (Unit 19)
2 A (Unit 16)	12 A (Unit 17)	22 A (Unit 19)
3 B (Unit 16)	13 B (Unit 18)	23 C (Unit 19)
4 B (Unit 16)	14 A (Unit 18)	24 D (Unit 19)
5 C (Unit 16)	15 D (Unit 18)	25 A (Unit 20)
6 C (Unit 16)	16 C (Unit 18)	26 A (Unit 20)
7 D (Unit 17)	17 A (Unit 18)	27 D (Unit 20)
8 C (Unit 17)	18 D (Unit 18)	28 B (Unit 20)
9 B (Unit 17)	19 A (Unit 19)	29 D (Unit 20)
10 D (Unit 17)	20 B (Unit 19)	30 C (unit 20)

Unit 21

1.2
2 F 3 A 4 C 5 H 6 D 7 E 8 G

1.4
1 *develop* is transitive; *develop*, *vanish*, *exist* and *swerve* are
intransitive
2 *develop*
3 *develop* can have an object, the others cannot
4 A swerve   B exist   C vanish   D develop
5 A *curve*

1.5
2 conj = conjunction: because
3 vi = intransitive verb: differ
4 U = Uncountable: traffic
5 adv = adverb: well
6 prep = preposition: of

1.6
minute = sixty seconds / very small
outlook = view / future situation
material = information / cloth
NB *Minute* has two different pronunciations.

1.7
Phonetic symbols

iː	uː	ɜː	ɑː	ɔː	e
th<u>e</u>se	ch<u>oo</u>se	w<u>or</u>d	h<u>ar</u>d	b<u>all</u>	g<u>ue</u>st
ɒ	ʌ	æ	ə	ʊ	ɪ
wh<u>a</u>t	s<u>o</u>me	att<u>a</u>ck	<u>a</u>bout	p<u>u</u>t	<u>i</u>n

2.1

-ment	-tion	-able	mis-	re-	un-
assessment	assumption	approachable	misinterpret	recreation /	unapproachable
establishment	creation	assessable	misrepresent /	recreate	unassessable
	definition	definable	misrepresentation	redefine	unidentified /
	distribution	identifiable		redistribute	unidentifiable
	identification	variable		reinterpret	
	interpretation			reassess	
	representation			reestablish	
	variation				

2.2

Prefixes: anti-, dis-
Suffixes: -ment, -arian, -ism
2 E   3 A   4 B   5 C

2.3

Possible examples: antibiotic, disagree / disabled, punishment / argument, vegetarian, Marxism / socialism

Unit 22

1.2

A occur   B create   C consistent   D analysis
E significant   F period   G benefit   H theory   I define
J environment

1.3

1 Nouns: analysis, benefit, environment, period, theory
  Verbs: benefit, create, define, occur
  Adjectives: consistent, significant
2 benefit
3 inconsistent, recreate, redefine, recur, insignificant

1.4

	Noun	Verb	Adjective
1	analysis	analyse	analytical
2	benefit	benefit	beneficial
3	consistency	consist	consistent
4	creation / creator / creativity	create	creative
5	definition	define	definable definitive definite
6	environment / environmentalist		environmental
7	occurrence	occur	
8	period / periodical		periodical periodic
9	significance	signify	significant
10	theory	theorise	theoretical

1.5

2&3 B beneficial (adj)   C significance (noun)
D creative (adj)   E define (verb)   F theory (noun)
G consists (verb)   H periodically (adverb)   I analysed (past simple verb)   J occurred (past simple verb)

1.6

2 beneficial   3 consistent   4 recreation   5 defined
6 environment   7 occurred   8 periodically
9 significant   10 theoretical

1.7

2 Environmentalists   3 benefits   4 significant
5 defined   6 consists   7 theory   8 analysis
9 recreate   10 recurrence

1.8

2 environmentalists / environment   3 consists / consist
4 periodically / period   5 beneficial / benefit   6 theory
7 analysed / analysis   8 significance / significant
9 define   10 creative / create

1.9

1
B truly   C advancement   D happiest   E worried
F worrying   G unplugged   H stopped   I sloped
J changeable
2
B inappropriate   C dissimilar   D unnoticed
E disinterested / uninterested   F impatient
G disability / inability   H disorganised / unorganised
I impolite   J unemployment
(NB A *disinterested* person is someone who will gain no advantage by being involved in an activity: *We need a disinterested party to referee the match. Uninterested* means *not interested*. A *disability* is an injury or condition that prevents someone from doing something: *My grandmother is blind but she doesn't let her disability stop her from enjoying life. Inability* is not being able to do something through lack of skill or knowledge: *Your inability to drive a car means that we can't offer you the job.* If someone is *disorganised* then this is seen as a criticism and a general pattern of behaviour. *Unorganised* may be a temporary state.)

2.1

1 analysis of
2 of benefit to
3 consistent with
4 create a new design
5 definition of
6 environmentally friendly

2.2

1 on   2 on   3 for   4 to, in   5 with   6 about, of
7 of   8 for

2.3

2 have   3 take   4 give   5 tell   6 control

2.4

2 likely   3 utterly   4 extremely   5 bitterly
6 absolutely   7 big   8 absolutely

Unit 23

1.1

1 C   2 F   3 A   4 E   5 D   6 B

1.3

A Sentence 4 gives a good overview of the whole graph
B Sentence 1 is a minor detail and you must select and report the main features.
C Sentence 2 is inaccurate – it levelled out until 2000; Sentence 5 is inaccurate – i) this applies to plastic, not glass ii) it should say 10 million tonnes, not 10 tonnes

1.4

↘	↗	→	↘↗↘↗
fall, drop, plunge, downward trend, sharp, steep, significant, reach a low, steadily, rapidly	rise, upward trend, sharp, steep, significant, reach a high, steadily, rapidly, peak	unchanged, remain steady, constant, plateau, fixed, static	fluctuate, unpredictable, wildly

1.5

2 ~~in~~ between   3 ~~from~~ by   4 ~~by~~ from

Unit 24

1.2

Writing is an important skill and <u>young children</u> spend a lot of time <u>practising</u> it.
I completely disagree that <u>they</u> learn <u>everything</u> about writing at <u>this stage</u>. Kids is too informal for IELTS writing. The other words do not fit grammatically.

1.6

1 The number of birds increased significantly in 1994.
2 There was a considerable fall in the number of people attending in 2002.
3 There was a dramatic rise in the percentage of female students in 1990.
4 The temperatures dropped noticeably between 1880 and 1885.
5 There was a constant change in the figures between 2001 and 2006.
6 The temperatures increased slightly in 1909.

1.7

1 overall   2 steady   3 rose   4 doubled   5 of
6 significantly   7 rate   8 consistently   9 peak   10 until
11 dropped   12 trend   13 plateaued   14 in

2.1

1 The diagram shows how chewing gum is made or the process for making chewing gum.
2 There are 7 stages in the process
3 It requires heavy machinery
4 The synthetic pieces, dough-like mixture, and rollers are labelled

2.2

Introduction and <u>overview statement</u>: The diagram shows how chewing gum is made from a synthetic material. <u>This process has seven different stages and requires the use of heavy machinery</u>.

1 First   3 pieces   4 container   5 melted   6 then
7 liquid   8 Next / Then   9 placed   10 container
11 added   12 mixture   13 ingredients   14 passes / travels
15 machine   16 Next / Then   17 shapes / pieces
18 pieces   19 Finally   20 travels / passes

2.1

Sequencing ideas	Adding supporting ideas	Introducing a contrasting idea	Giving examples	Giving an alternative	Giving an explanation	Drawing a conclusion
firstly, now, secondly, finally	in addition, indeed, and, not only … but … also, furthermore, also	nonetheless, however, although, despite, while, whereas, but, on the other hand	such as, to illustrate this, for example	similarly, alternatively, or	that is, in other words, because	as a result, to summarise, consequently, because of, therefore, in conclusion

2.2

2 For example   3 or   4 such as   5 although
6 as a result of

2.3

1 However / Nevertheless
2 Firstly
3 as well as
4 such as
5 Furthermore / In addition
6 but also
7 Thus / Therefore / As a result
8 Nevertheless / However
9 In other words
10 as a result
11 In addition / Furthermore
12 Therefore / Thus

3.1

2 E   3 A/B   4 A/B   5 C   6 F/G   7 F/G

3.2

2 Fortunately, / Thankfully,   3 justifiably
4 Unfortunately,   5 Clearly, / Obviously,

4.1

Recent research at an English university suggests that it doesn't matter what order the letters in a word are, the only important thing is that the first and last letters are in the right place. Even though the middle letters might be mixed up, people don't have a problem reading the words. This is because we read the word as a whole rather than every letter by itself.

4.2

1 though / although
2 people
3 children
4 going to
5 writing
6 plenty / a great deal
7 Personally
8 believe
9 to
10 too (3, 4 and 6 are register problems).

Unit 25

1.1

Acceptance	Application	Apology	Complaint	Enquiry	Recommendation	Thanks
would be delighted, attend, invitation, confirm	be considered, interview, applicant	sorry, excuse, forgive, apologise	dissatisfied, complain, unhappy	wonder, ask, help	suggest, propose	grateful, appreciate

1.2

2 complain   3 forgive   4 grateful   5 attend   6 ask

1.3

2 –   3 with   4 about   5 for   6 –   7 –   8 –
9 for   10 to

1.4

I would be grateful if you could; I look forward to; I have enclosed my CV; Best wishes; Kind regards; Yours faithfully; Yours sincerely

1.5

1 Dear (first name only) ... Best wishes
2 Dear Mr / Ms (family name) ... Kind regards
3 Dear Sir or Madam ... Yours faithfully
4 Dear Mr / Ms (family name) ... Yours sincerely

2.2

Writing is an important skill and <u>*young children*</u> *spend a lot of time* <u>*practising*</u> *it.*
I completely disagree that <u>*they*</u> *learn* <u>*everything*</u> *about writing at* <u>*this stage*</u>. Kids is too informal for IELTS writing. The other words do not fit grammatically.

3.1

Sequencing ideas	Adding supporting ideas	Introducing a contrasting idea	Giving examples	Giving an alternative	Giving an explanation	Drawing a conclusion
first, now, secondly, finally	in addition, and, not only ... but ...also furthermore, also	nonetheless, however, although, despite, while, whereas, but, on the other hand	such as, for example	similarly, alternatively, or	that is, in other words, because	as a result, to summarise, consequently, because of, therefore, in conclusion

3.2

2 For example   3 or   4 such as   5 although
6 as a result of

3.3

1 However / Nevertheless
2 Firstly
3 as well as
4 such as
5 Furthermore / In addition
6 but also
7 Thus / Therefore
8 Nevertheless / However
9 In other words
10 as a result
11 In addition / Furthermore
12 Therefore / Thus

4.1

2 E   3 A/B   4 A/B   5 C   6 F/G   7 F/G

4.2

2 Fortunately / Thankfully   3 justifiably
4 Unfortunately   5 Clearly / Obviously

5

1 though / although
2 people
3 children
4 going to
5 writing
6 plenty / a great deal
7 Personally
8 believe
9 to
10 too (3, 4 and 6 are register problems).

Test Five

(Unit numbers in brackets show the unit where the vocabulary tested can be found.)

1 D (Unit 21)	11 A (Unit 22)	21 C (Unit 24&25)
2 C (Unit 21)	12 C (Unit 22)	22 D (Unit 24&25)
3 C (Unit 21)	13 C (Unit 22)	23 B (Unit 24&25)
4 B (Unit 21)	14 B (Unit 23)	24 B (Unit 23)
5 A (Unit 21)	15 B (Unit 23)	25 D (Unit 24&25)
6 D (Unit 21)	16 A (Unit 23)	26 B (Unit 25)
7 C (Unit 22)	17 B (Unit 23)	27 C (Unit 25)
8 D (Unit 25)	18 A (Unit 22)	28 B (Unit 25)
9 A (Unit 22)	19 D (Unit 24&25)	29 D (Unit 25)
10 B (Unit 22)	20 B (Unit 24&25)	30 A (Unit 25)

Recording scripts

Recording 1a

Speaker A: On Mondays at school a group of us always talk about whatever movies we saw at the weekend. On Saturdays I often get together with my classmates and we see all the latest releases together. I can't remember the last time I saw a film with my parents – we just don't have much in common any more.

Speaker B: My parents are both teachers so you'd imagine I'd have no trouble at all academically. When I was little it was great because we had a really great relationship. But nowadays all we seem to do is argue and that causes a lot of conflict between us, so I don't really feel I can go to them for help. My friends aren't much help either as they've all got the same problem. Thank goodness I get on really well with my tutor at university. She's very approachable and, if I'm struggling with an assignment, I find her advice really helps me.

Speaker C: My parents are quite old so I feel as though they're out of touch with the modern world. They don't seem to have any idea of what things cost. I'm hoping to get a car in the next few months but I'll be taking my older brother along to help. We used to fight a lot when we were growing up but there's a really close bond between us now. He's already had a few cars so I'm sure he'll be a great help.

Speaker D: I play the violin and the piano and my grandad is a great cello player. A lot of my friends at school listen to all the popular bands and singers, but my tastes are totally different. I prefer classical music and they just don't understand it at all. Luckily Grandad shares my taste, so we often buy CDs and talk about them together.

Recording 1b

Teacher: Tell me about your family.

Student: Well, my immediate family is relatively small, just my parents, my two brothers and me. But both of my parents come from very large families so my extended family is very large – I have 25 cousins! Our family gatherings are pretty chaotic, but fun. We're a very close-knit family. Even though we don't live together any more, the family ties are still very strong. When we were little there wasn't very much sibling rivalry between us. I think it's because we had a very stable upbringing. Both of my parents played a very active role in our school life, and our home life, and they taught us to resolve our conflicts in a very fair way. I consider myself very lucky.

Teacher: Who are you most similar to in your family?

Student: Well, you can see a very clear family resemblance between my brothers and me, but everyone tells me that the physical resemblance between me and my maternal grandmother is very striking. Sadly, I never got to meet her because she died before I was born. But I've seen photographs of her at my age and we're quite alike. Other than that, I think I have my father's temperament – we're both very stubborn! But, thankfully, I also inherited his mathematical brain!

Teacher: And what do you think it takes to be a good parent?

Student: Well, I don't think just anyone can be a good parent. Not everyone has the right instincts. I think I have a very strong maternal instinct, because I love taking care of small children. So I hope to become a mother one day. I think it takes a great deal of patience and love.

Recording 1c

Narrator: Listening Part 1. You will hear the director of a child-care centre talking to the parent of a new child. Before you listen, you will have a chance to look at questions 1 – 10.

(25 seconds pause)

Now listen and answer questions 1 to 10.

Director: Good morning, my name is Bob Ferguson and I'm the director of Ascot Child-Care Centre.

Mother: Good morning, I'm Sallyanne Cullen. I made an appointment to enrol my daughter.

Director: That's right, I've got the application form right here. Now, first I need some personal details. So the family name is Cullen, is that right?

Mother: That's right.

Director: Now, what about your daughter? What does she like to be called?

Mother: Oh, her name is Alexandra, but we all just call her Alex, A-L-E-X.

Director: Great. As you know, we organise the children into different age groups. There's the babies' group, the toddlers, aged two to three, and the pre-schoolers – they're aged four to five. How old is your daughter?

Mother: Well, she'd go into the toddler group – she's just turned three.

Director: And we always like to make a note of our children's birthdays so we can celebrate it all together if they are at the centre on that day. When was she born?

Mother: Oh, erm, the eighth of November.

Director: Fine. And we also find it's a great help to know about siblings – sometimes, a problem at the centre can be related to problems with a sibling. Does she have any brothers or sisters?

Mother: Yes, a brother, Fraser. He's two years older.

Director: So that would make him five, is that right?

Mother: Yes, that's right.

Director: Fine. Now, we also need a contact address. Where do you live?

Mother: It's 108 Park Road, that's P-A-R-K, Maidstone.

Director: Good. Now, last of all, we need a telephone number we can call if there are any problems.

Mother: Oh, well, I'll be at work and so will my husband, so the best number to call is 34678890.

Director: Right, and is that a close relative?

Mother: Yes, it's my mother-in-law's number.

Director: We prefer to make a note of how the person is related to the child, so I'll write down 'grandmother'.

Mother: Yes, that does make more sense!

Director: Now, that's all of the personal details. We also like to try and get a picture of your child's personal development. Can you tell me if there are any specific problems she's having? For example, does she get on well with other children? Is sleeping a problem?

Mother: Oh, she gets on well with others, I think, but she does have trouble sleeping. We gave up her daytime nap a long time ago!

Director: That's good to know; I'll make a note of that. She can just have some quiet time while the others are resting if she likes.

Mother: That should be fine. She enjoys drawing quietly.

Director: Right. Now what about other skills? We occasionally take the children swimming, fully supervised of course, and we only go in a paddling pool as we don't expect them to swim by themselves yet. Does your daughter need a lot of help getting changed?

Mother: No, not at all. In fact she's been able to get dressed in the mornings for over a year now, so no problems there!

Director: That must be a big help for you! Now, what about the child-care arrangements? Are there any specific days you require?

Mother: Well, I work Monday to Wednesday, but my mother-in-law has agreed to look after her on Wednesdays.

Director: So does that mean that you'll just need Monday and Tuesday for now?

Mother: That's right.

Director: And what about the pick-up time? We offer extended hours for parents who work a great distance away.

Mother: Hmm … I work until 3 o'clock, but it takes me about half an hour to drive home, so ideally I'd like to pick her up at four if that's OK.

Director: That will be fine. Now is there any other information you'd like to …

Recording 2a

In the first years of a child's life many important milestones are reached. By the end of the first year a baby will have already acquired some social skills. He will enjoy imitating people and will also test parental responses to his behaviour. For example, what do my parents do if I refuse food? In terms of movement, an infant will be able to reach a sitting position unassisted and pull himself up to stand. He may be able to walk momentarily without support. As far as communication is concerned, he will be able to use simple gestures such as shaking his head for 'no', and say 'mama' and 'dada' and he will try to imitate words. When it comes to cognitive development, he will be able to find hidden objects easily and use objects correctly such as drinking from a cup.

By the age of two or three, the infant has reached the toddler stage. In terms of social skills, this means, he is becoming more independent, which may result in the occasional tantrum. However, he has learned to take turns in games and spontaneously expresses affection. His physical development will also have increased significantly as he can now move around a lot faster and even run. He can also climb up stairs or onto relatively low obstacles, and even ride a small tricycle. However, he will still be rather unsteady on his feet at times. When it comes to language and communication he can now understand most sentences and uses four- and five-word sentences. In terms of cognitive development; he's learned to play make-believe games and uses his imagination more. He has also mastered the skill of sorting objects according to their shape and colour.

Between the ages of six and twelve, a child reaches what is termed 'middle childhood' and they will stay in this phase until they reach adolescence. In middle childhood, children's development is more affected by the outside world and the child's world expands to include friends, teachers, sports trainers and so on. Children develop at various rates and while some children in middle childhood seem very mature in terms of their emotional and social skills, others seem very immature. As far as physical milestones are concerned, during this stage growth is steady but less rapid than during the pre-school years. There are some major changes occurring at this stage as baby teeth will come out and permanent adult teeth will grow. As the mouth is not yet fully developed this may cause overcrowding. Eyes will

reach maturity in both size and function. In terms of their cognitive ability, children at this stage master the skills of sequencing and ordering, which are essential for maths. By the end of this period children should have acquired effective reading and writing skills.

Recording 2b

Teacher: What do you remember about your early childhood?

Student: Oh, I remember being very happy! I have a lot of great memories of my childhood. In fact, my sisters and I often reminisce about it. Perhaps when you look back everything seems better, but our summer holidays seemed to go on forever and the sun always seemed to be shining. Nowadays, if we ever have a hot summer day, it always reminds me of my childhood holidays.

Teacher: Do you think you have a good memory or a poor memory?

Student: Well, when I was younger I think I used to have a very good memory. I used to be able to memorise long lists of dates without any trouble. But I find it harder and harder to remember things these days, so now I'd say my memory is quite poor. When I'm studying I find I have to think up strategies to help me, like visualising something associated with a particular word. I even forget important things sometimes, so I have to write myself little notes as a reminder.

Recording 3a

Narrator: Part 1

The heart is considered to be a muscle and, just like any other muscle in your body, your diet has a direct impact on the way that it works. The food you eat every day can affect the way that blood flows through your heart and arteries. A diet that is high in fat can gradually cause a build-up in your arteries that slows down the blood flow and can even block small arteries. If an artery that carries blood to the heart becomes blocked, the heart muscle can die. This is known as a heart attack and sufferers must receive treatment quickly. If the blockage occurs in an artery that carries blood to the brain, part of the brain can die. This is known as a stroke. The effects of a stroke can be debilitating and there is no known cure. The correct diet can help you control your weight and keep your arteries clear, thereby reducing the risk of heart problems and stroke.

Recording 3b

Narrator: Part 2

So, what can you do to lose weight? Well, exercise is by far the best way. Burning calories and working off the fat will help you look and feel better. Regular exercise helps you burn calories faster, even when you are sitting still. But what is the best type of exercise for your heart? Well, studies have shown that aerobic exercise causes you to breathe more deeply and makes your heart work harder to pump blood. Aerobic exercise also raises your heart rate and thus burns calories. Common examples of aerobic exercise include walking briskly, jogging, running, swimming and cycling.

People are often unsure just how much exercise they need. Again, recent studies can help. These have shown that it's best to begin slowly and gradually work up to thirty minutes of exercise, four to six times a week. However, your doctor may make a different recommendation based on your health. For example, it may be best to start with only a couple of minutes of exercise or begin at a fairly slow pace. If you are not used to exercise, be sure to pay careful attention to your body. One sure sign that you may be overdoing it is if you can't carry on a conversation while you exercise. To give your body the chance to recover, it's also best to alternate exercise days with rest days.

Recording 3c

bath, bathe, birth, breath, breathe, death, growth, health, mouth (v), mouth (n), teeth, teethe, writhe

Recording 3d

1 I took a deep breath before diving into the water.
2 The baby's crying because he's teething. He got two new teeth only yesterday.
3 Old people should take care of their health.
4 He's been so happy since the birth of his son.
5 The pain was so bad she was writhing in agony.
6 He can't breathe. You need to get him to hospital.

Recording 4a

Interviewer: Do you think people work too much nowadays?
Speaker 1: Not really. I think people have always worked hard for a living. I mean it's never been easy for anyone, has it? You have to work hard if you want to achieve anything in your life – that's just the way it is and there isn't a lot you can do about it. Life has its ups and downs and I think the best thing to do is accept that and get on with it.
Interviewer: What do you like to do to relax?
Speaker 2: For me there is only one way to relax and that's through sport. I like to live life on the edge, so I do a lot of extreme sports like paragliding and deep sea diving. When you're in a dangerous situation, that's when you really feel alive. I think your attitude has a big impact on your quality of life.
Interviewer: What's your idea of a perfect day?
Speaker 3: I don't think there's any such thing as the perfect day – something always seems to happen to spoil it. Some people say I have a negative attitude, but if I plan a picnic with friends then either it rains or my friends decide not to come along. I think it's a waste of time making plans like that. Life can be full of disappointments.
Interviewer: How would you describe your attitude to life?
Speaker 4: I have a very positive outlook on life. I think it's important to treat every day as special and live life to the full. Some people approach everything as if their glass is half empty. If you do that then it will colour every experience you have. I think if you want to lead a happy life then you need to have a positive approach to everything.

Recording 4b

Narrator: Listening Part 2. You will hear a radio broadcast about activities for children in the school holidays. As you listen, answer questions 1 to 10.
Host: Hello, listeners! Now, the school holidays are fast approaching, so I'd like to welcome Julie Roberts, who's a former teacher, and she's got some great advice about how to keep your children occupied! Welcome to the show, Julie!
Julie: Thanks, Michael.
Host: So, what should parents keep in mind as the holidays get going?
Julie: Well, the first few days of the holidays are often wasted and, if you are not careful, time just flies by, relaxing with friends, and suddenly it's all over and you're rushing to pull everything together for the new term. Therefore, those initial few days are actually a great opportunity to make lists and stock up on school supplies for the following term and so on, while everything is still fresh in your children's minds.
Host: Good idea, and what about days out?

Julie: Well, it's great to have *some* day trips, like going to the zoo, but you have to remember that everyone else has probably had the same idea too, and it can be really disappointing to get there only to stand for hours in the enormous queue outside, which can happen even if you get there before the gates open! So, always book ahead and get your tickets online. That way, when you get to the zoo, it's just a matter of picking up a map and wandering around at your leisure. But remember, not all trips have to be expensive ones. These days, public libraries have some great holiday activities. They *do* usually only change once a week, so it's best not to go more often than that, but it's great to see our libraries so well-used now. They are definitely no longer just a place for the more studious kids or for borrowing books – in fact, you're more likely to see people crowded round the computers than the bookshelves!
Host: That's true, and I believe you have a website with other suggested activities to do at home.
Julie: Yes, I'll tell you about some of them now. The first one is called 'Crafty kids'. Craft is great for everyone from nursery upwards, and the idea here is to put together a kit with things like coloured paper, glue, and so on. Then any time you find your kids are getting restless, you pull out the kit and one of our easy projects, and then just leave them to it! For me, that is the real benefit, especially as I work from home! Next is the Lava lamp project. Now, I know this may sound tricky, but all you need are some basic household items that most people would have in their cupboard. Again, everyone can get involved, though the little ones will need adult supervision. Lava lamps are *great* fun to make and the kids will even learn a bit about chemical reactions, which is a nice added bonus, and at the end, they have a decorative lamp for their bedroom!

There is also the Treasure hunt. Again, this will appeal to all ages, and I find the older ones love helping the young ones out if they start to run out of patience! Now, you *do* need to spend several hours hiding the clues and making the treasure map, but it really *is* worth the effort, and my children always put this one at the top of their list.

Story time might *sound* like it's not much fun, but this activity is not just sitting in a corner reading a book; instead, we get the kids to make up their *own* stories and they'll be telling them through *film*, so you do need access to a digital camera, but that's about all. And again, we've done all the hard work – there is even an instructional video on the website.

Another popular activity is Kitchen time, but don't worry about your little ones because our ideas don't involve any cooking or baking. With just a little help, they can roll up their sleeves and get stuck into making things like play dough and silly putty. The only thing parents will need to think about is cleaning up afterwards, because this is one activity that does tend to get them very excited, and you may find they get a bit carried away with the flour!

If your children are very energetic, why not follow our suggestions for a sport and fitness day? Now, not everyone can participate, and I'd caution against getting the under-5s involved as they're likely to get hurt if the older ones get too competitive, but it can be a great way to burn off energy if you have teens who've been glued to their mobile phones or computer screens for days on end.

And, finally, there's gardening. Obviously, planting seeds won't entertain anyone for long, plus it'd be months before you see anything grow! So our suggestions are for other things like making an interesting pathway, or how to attract more wildlife into your garden. There *is* some building involved, so if you're not handy in that way yourself, you may need to find a friend or relative who *is*. So, that's just some of the ideas on the webs

Recording 5a

Teacher: Can you tell me about your early education?

Student: Well, I went to kindergarten from the age of four and I remember that I didn't enjoy it very much at all. My primary school was a little better, especially because my mum was a teacher in the school. She taught in the junior school and she was actually my teacher in first grade but when I went up to the senior school I didn't see very much of her. After that I was lucky enough to receive a scholarship for a very good high school. My parents couldn't have afforded to send me to a private school so it was a really great opportunity for me. It was a single-sex school so there were no boys. I'm glad I didn't go to a mixed school because I think there are fewer distractions so everyone can just concentrate on their studies.

Recording 5b

So you have graduated from university and decided to continue studying towards a Master's or PhD. At some stage during the next few years will need to consider your thesis. One of the greatest difficulties faced by postgraduate students is choosing a topic to base their dissertation on. Writing a thesis can be very daunting, but the task is much more straightforward if the topic you select is appropriate for you. So, what can you do to solve this problem?

Well there are several things to keep in mind. Firstly you need to do your research so that you are very familiar with all the current literature. On top of this, you also need to be sure that you have a broad knowledge of your area of specialisation. If you do this, it will help you with the next important point in choosing a good subject for your research, which is to ascertain what is relevant in your research area. This will be crucial in helping you to narrow your choices down. From the very beginning, it really is vital to set clear limits and to have a very fixed plan in terms of the scope of your research.

It can be even more helpful to analyse existing research and ask yourself if there are any controversies. Perhaps there is a theory that you may want to challenge and this could be the focus of your study. A further and very important factor to take into account is your own financial resources. If these are limited then you need to avoid choosing a study that will involve costly equipment or surveys. However, if this is the case, you needn't despair or abandon your ideas altogether. Instead, make enquiries into funding from external agencies such as your local government. You may even find that local industries are willing to support your research by providing a grant. It's always worth looking around to see just what is possible. And finally, be sure to make good use of your tutor, especially when it comes to making sure that your findings are accurate.

Recording 5c

academic, assignment, consideration, concentrate, controversy, controversy (both are possible), conduct, distraction, dissertation, economist, educational, educated, research (n), thesis, theory, theoretical

Recording 6a

I'm a French teacher, but I remember when I first started to learn the language I really struggled with it. I didn't really have a problem with the pronunciation like the other kids in my class; I was just overwhelmed by all of the vocabulary. But I persevered and soon I was scoring ten out of ten in all of the tests. By the time I got to university I could produce essays and translate eighteenth century texts without much difficulty and I actually enjoyed learning the grammar rules. Then, as part of my university course I had to go and live in France for a year. That's when I learned that communication was more important than accuracy. As soon as I arrived I realised I didn't know how to order the type of coffee I liked, and trying to find accommodation was a nightmare. I called people about ads in the paper, but I had to keep putting the phone down because I couldn't understand a word they were saying – they all spoke so quickly! There was a very real language barrier. I could see then that there's no point in just knowing words if you can't hold a conversation with a native speaker. Fluency is what helps you to function properly – it's what helps you get a job, hold a conversation or just buy the things you need.

Recording 6b

Teacher: What do you think you need to do to be a good language learner?

Student: Well, you need to be able to put down your textbooks from time to time and forget about accuracy. That's the only way to become more fluent in a language. You also need to speak to native speakers of the language as much as you can.

Teacher: What do you think makes a good language teacher?

Student: I think the best language teachers are those who can speak another language themselves. Teachers also need to be able to explain things clearly and in a way that is easy to follow.

Teacher: What problems do people experience when learning your language?

Student: My first language is very difficult to learn because of the pronunciation. The individual sounds are very strange to other nationalities and often difficult for them to pronounce.

Recording 7a

Speaker 1: I live in a quaint little village about 300 kilometres from the nearest big city. Although it's a long way, the drive from the city is well worth the effort because the surrounding countryside is very scenic. I like living here because it's so peaceful and the air is really fresh, so it's much nicer than in the city. It's a pretty sleepy village, but on Sundays there's a huge market and people come from all the neighbouring villages to buy and sell their local produce.

Speaker 2: The most popular part of my hometown is the beach. We have long stretches of white sand and the water is crystal clear. The sea can be very calm at times but the surf can also be spectacular. Visitors who enjoy water sports are really well catered for as you can go snorkelling, scuba diving and deep-sea fishing. Soon we're going to get our own airport but for now people can only get here by ferry.

Speaker 3: My city is famous for its skyscrapers, statues and fountains – but most of all for its shopping! You can buy anything you want here and we have over fifty large shopping malls. We get a lot of overseas visitors, so our airport is one of the busiest in the world. It's a very exciting and cosmopolitan place to live. Most people don't drive because there are always traffic jams, but the public transport is really well organised. We have some great attractions nearby for visitors, as well as a huge sports stadium and fantastic theme parks. I suppose the only downside is that the air can get a little polluted at times.

Speaker 4: My village is 200 metres above sea level and we overlook the villages and lakes down in the valley below. It's very picturesque up here so we get a lot of visitors, especially artists who want to paint the landscape. They also like our traditional houses. The air is very crisp up here as well, so a lot of people come up here to escape the heat in the city. The roads are pretty treacherous because they're very steep and winding, so most people arrive by train. The scenery on the way up here really is breathtaking.

Recording 7b

boundary, bought, cough, course, country, double, doubt, drought, enough, journal, journey, nought, rough, south, southern, tourism, tourist, trouble, trough

Recording 8a

Speaker 1: I must say I'm never on time. In fact, I was late for meetings three days in a row last week. Everyone's always angry with me because I do tend to keep people waiting a lot. Work is my problem – I get so engrossed that I lose all track of time. I try to get everything else ready before I start, which saves a bit of time, but before I know it a few hours have passed and I'm already late.

Speaker 2: I can't say I'm very punctual. I do my best not to be late because I hate being kept waiting myself, but I do sometimes spend too much time getting ready. If I'm going out somewhere I like to plait my hair, which is very thick, so this can be very time-consuming and I often have to rush through everything else I need to do. I once went to a wedding and I took so long doing my hair that I only just arrived in time to hear the bride say 'I do'.

Speaker 3: I could tell the time at a very early age and I've been obsessed with punctuality ever since! I own about 12 watches and clocks, but none of them shows the right time. I can't stand to be late for work or in a hurry, so I make sure they're all ten minutes fast – and I always carry a spare watch in case one of them stops! That way I always arrive at meetings in plenty of time and I can take my time getting my paperwork ready.

Recording 8b

Narrator: Listening part 4. You will hear a lecturer talking about the history of dentistry. As you listen, answer questions 1 to 10.

Speaker: Welcome to today's lecture looking at the history of dentistry through the ages. Now, dental problems are by no means a new phenomenon. We know that 25,000 years ago, the Cro-Magnon people suffered from both tooth loss and tooth decay. So, these are issues that have plagued humans since time began.

The earliest evidence of people tackling dental issues dates back to 7000 BC, in the Indus Valley Civilisation – the area we now know as Pakistan. While examining remains from that time, researchers found holes that had been deliberately made in several teeth, and they speculate that these were created using a drill, probably by local craftsmen, in a bid to treat tooth decay, and the procedure appears to have been surprisingly effective!

Now, it isn't until 5000 BC that we find any written texts related to dentistry, and a reference to the causes of tooth decay. The first known text was produced by the ancient Sumerians, and it refers to what they called 'tooth worms', which they believed were responsible for dental decay. Interestingly, this idea was not proven false until the 1700s!

Without access to modern medication in ancient times, people were reliant on natural treatments and remedies. A lot of our knowledge about this comes from a famous Ancient Egyptian text from 1500 BC, called the Ebers Papyrus. It's among the oldest medical records known to exist. The papyrus lists around 700 medical treatments, including for dealing with

complications resulting from bad teeth. Now, while today we would use antibiotics to treat this sort of thing, Ancient Egyptian medics would reach for the olive oil, which is commonly accepted to have therapeutic qualities. Another traditional remedy that they would use was based on onions, again, an age-old therapeutic ingredient recognised as having antibiotic properties. In other parts of the world, there's mention of garlic being used. Now you might assume that this was placed in the mouth, against the damaged tooth, but you'd be wrong! The common practice was actually to place it inside the ear! We don't know how this originated but I doubt it was very effective in stopping toothache!

And what about cleaning the teeth? Well, evidence shows that from very early on people were trying to protect their teeth by cleaning them. Tools for doing this again date back to Ancient times, when the Babylonians and the Egyptians would use what I suppose we'd think of as an early sort of toothbrush, although the use of a brushing motion wouldn't come until much later. Instead, they'd fray the end of a twig or a stick and chew on it. The Ancient Chinese also used these "chewing sticks", which they made from aromatic tree twigs to freshen the breath.

When it comes to the practice of dentistry, an important milestone occurred in the fifth century, again in Egypt. Around the world, while a large proportion of early dentistry was practised as part and parcel of general medicine, in Egypt, relatively early on, physicians were treating distinct areas of the body, becoming specialists in one particular field, including for dental problems.

If we jump to Europe and the Middle Ages, dentistry was made available to the wealthier classes thanks to physicians who would visit people in their own home. But, for poorer people, treatment was mainly limited to the removal of rotten teeth and this took place among the food stalls in the market.

Things didn't change very much for several hundred years. Until a Frenchman called Pierre Fauchard. He's thought of as the father of modern dentistry, thanks to his book, The Surgeon Dentist, which was published in 1728. Fauchard began his surgical training at the very young age of 15, when he was in the French navy, and he gained most of his knowledge while treating his fellow sailors, who often suffered from dental problems while at sea. Fauchard was very much ahead of his time. His book described methods for removing decay, and restoring missing teeth, but perhaps most notably, it was Fauchard who first asserted that it was the acids from sugar that led to tooth decay and proposed ways to address this.

Well. That's all we have time for today. Next week, I'll be looking at … (fade)

Recording 9a

The meerkat is found exclusively on the semi-arid plains of southern Africa. In terms of its natural environment, the meerkat avoids woodland and dense vegetation. At night, the meerkat retires to a network of burrows, which it digs with its powerful forelegs. If rocky ground makes this impossible, the meerkat will make its den in the crevices between the rocks.

Meerkats feed mainly on insects, spiders and snails, but their diet occasionally includes small rodents, lizards and the roots of certain plants. They will even tackle dangerous prey such as scorpions and snakes. Relying on its keen sense of smell, the meerkat is a successful forager.

Recording 9b

adapt, agriculture, catastrophe, chemical, climate, disastrous, endangered, genetically, human, natural, vulnerable

Recording 10a

Many people believe that one day we will form a colony on another planet. Today we're going to look at some other planets and consider why it will never be feasible for humans to live on them.

Let's start with Venus. Now, Venus is unusual because it rotates in a different direction from the other planets orbiting the sun. In terms of its physical features it's similar in size to Earth. However, unlike Earth, it doesn't have any oceans. It's also extremely hot, thanks to the thick covering of cloud, which keeps the heat at 484 degrees Celsius. This cloud also reflects sunlight, which is why Venus appears so bright from Earth. A further problem is the continual thunderstorms, which could make life there rather unpleasant. The surface of Venus also has many craters as a result of asteroid collisions.

Next is Mercury, which is a third of the size of our planet. In fact, it's smaller than all the other planets. Life would be difficult there because it's close to the sun and has almost no atmosphere. On Mercury the temperature varies more than on any other planet in the solar system and, as it has no water, it is unable to sustain life.

Let's consider Saturn next. We know a lot more about Saturn nowadays, thanks to the Voyager space probe, which taught us a lot about the rings around Saturn. We also know that Saturn has a large number of moons. Saturn has barely any solid surface, as its composition is mostly gas. It is also extremely hot, making life for humans impossible.

Recording 10b

astronaut, atmosphere, commercial, explorer, exploration, galaxy, horizon, horizontal, outer, satellite, solar system, sustain, universal

Recording 10c

Narrator: Listening Part 3. You will hear two science lecturers called John and Susan discussing space travel and exploration. As you listen, answer questions 1 – 10.

Susan: Hey, John. How was your conference on space exploration?

John: Hi, Susan. Great! There were some fascinating speakers, especially one person, who was an expert on Mars.

Susan: I've never understood the fascination with Mars.

John: Well, I can't see it myself, but he seems to think we might end up living there in the near future, if Earth becomes uninhabitable.

Susan: Well, if we spent the billions of dollars that go into space research looking after our own planet, then perhaps we wouldn't need to worry about colonising another one!

John: Come on, there are so many important things that space exploration can teach us, especially about the history of our own planet and its atmosphere. Plus it gives us knowledge that could help solve some of our problems, like how to manage our resources better.

Susan: Still, I don't really see why they have to send people into space, why can't they just send robots?

John: Well, robotics is a lot more advanced now and, in the long term, it'd probably be cheaper than using a manned spaceship, but don't forget that robots have to be programmed for every possible eventuality.

Susan: Yes, I suppose you're right. Robots can't just react to situations independently the way that people do – they need to be told what to do.

John: That's right. And batteries and so on may have come a long way, but they have to be sure everything will function well when it's up in orbit – they tend not to take risks with new and untested technology. What if it lets you down?

Susan: Yes, I read somewhere that right up until the 2000s, on the space missions, they were still using a lot of technology from the 1960s and 1970s

rather than anything state of the art, simply because they knew it worked and was reliable. I guess they can't afford to just pop up there and fix the odd printer or laptop if it's playing up like more modern tech tends to do.

John: Yeah. I had an interesting chat with a female astronaut at the conference. She's been working on plans for a mission into deep space.

Susan: Oh? What sort of issues are they anticipating?

John: She said the main concerns are all around communication.

Susan: I'd imagine the conditions wouldn't help with that. I mean, with external temperatures as low as minus 455 degrees, that must interfere with signals and equipment.

John: Well, apparently those issues can be dealt with. The real concern is simply how far away the craft will be – there can be long delays before receiving messages, like what to do if there's a sudden power failure or something.

Susan: Hmm, I can see that would be very concerning!

Narrator: You now have some time to look at questions 5 to 10. *(20 second pause)*

Susan: So, tell me, do you really think we should even be contemplating a mission to Mars right now? Shouldn't we wait until we have the technology?

John: Not at all. Think about the humans in Ancient times, the civilisations that built the pyramids or that began building enormous cathedrals that took hundreds of years to complete. Those projects must have seemed just as impossible to people of that time. Sometimes you have to start a project even if you're not going to see it finished. I think we should take the same approach with Mars, even if there's no real progress for ten or more years. It's never too soon to start, in my view.

Susan: I take your point, though I'm still not convinced. But surely you don't actually foresee a time when humans will be living on Mars? How would they deal with the conditions there?

John: I actually think it is feasible.

Susan: But even the dirt on the ground could kill us.

John: True, but there's ways to deal with that. We can easily build shelters well below ground that are self-contained. That way people wouldn't even need to go outside.

Susan: Mm, and I suppose the ground *would* likely contain a lot of resources, so extracting metals, for example, would be possible.

John: Yes, a lot of building materials could be sourced *there*, which opens up a lot more possibilities. But I'll admit, there *are* still a lot of risks involved.

Susan: Yes, but it isn't just the obvious dangers. There are other issues to contend with if you're going to Mars. It's hard to imagine what that would be like.

John: There're definitely social issues to consider. For me, the worst would be trying to keep myself occupied.

Susan: Yes, I mean, we worry now about tedious long-haul flights – with Mars you're talking about years of watching the same movies on some little screen!

John: Ha, true! Well, maybe when the time comes the spaceship will be like a luxurious cruise liner! But even then I'd go crazy looking at the same things day in day out.

Susan: I just can't even contemplate it, to be honest. I need nature and open spaces, and even when they get there, it would be years before they see any of that.

John: Yeah, I agree, that would have a big impact on me too. I guess the first priority on getting there would be managing air and water supplies; they won't be able to let anything go to waste on things like planting trees. But you have to accept that it is within the realms of possibility that *one* day there'll be a space station on Mars.

Susan: Well, I have every faith in science but I can't ever see people living there, I'm afraid.

Recording 11a

Speaker A: I live in a cottage. It's a single-storey building so the rooms are all on the same level. It's about a hundred years old and it's a very traditional design, so there's no concrete or steel to be found. Just about all the buildings in this area were built from timber and stone from the local quarry. It's got a lot of character. What I like best about it are the ceilings. They're quite ornate as they have lots of pretty details on them. Although some people think it's small, I prefer to think of it as cosy.

Speaker B: My flat is in a new high-rise building in the city centre. The design is ultra-modern, so there's a lot of glass and concrete and steel – and not a lot of wood to be seen. Everything is controlled through a state-of-the-art computer system. It's a very functional apartment and there's a space to suit every purpose, but I do find the bedrooms a bit cramped. My favourite spot is the balcony – my building towers over everything else, so I can see for miles.

Speaker C: I live in a two-storey house. It's a very conventional brick building and it's typical of the area where I live. I love the downstairs rooms as they're very spacious. I spend a lot of time in the living room because it's so light and airy. But my favourite feature is definitely the staircase. It curves around at the bottom and just seems to invite you to climb it.

Recording 11b

design, please, device, devise, residence, housing, fasten, destruction, use (n), use (v)

Recording 12a

Man: I need a new phone but I can't decide between the new Nixon 10 and the Optima. Which one do you think is better?

Assistant: Personally, I prefer the Nixon because it's so compact. I find the Optima a bit too big – I like to be able to put my phone in my pocket, especially when I'm going for a run. And my Nixon has a great fitness tracker, so I can keep track of my progress. But the smaller screen means it isn't as good as the Optima when you're watching videos or reading, so it really depends on what you want to use it for.

Man: Well, I have to travel a lot for work and my phone is really important for that. I need something user-friendly and reliable, but also with a great camera – in case I have to make video calls.

Assistant: Have you thought about the latest LTC phone?

Man: No, I haven't. I heard their touch screens weren't great.

Assistant: Yeah, scrolling used to be an issue at times but they seem to have sorted that now. And it's got the best camera on the market at the moment.

Man: Hmm, I think I'd still prefer the Optima – it has some really useful business apps already installed on it, doesn't it?

Assistant: Yes, and the audio quality is great.

Man: That sounds good. With my last phone I had to constantly update it and, on phone calls, I couldn't hear very well and people couldn't always hear me!

Assistant: Yes, a lot of people really only use them for text messaging and social media nowadays. The LTC has more memory though, so you can store a lot more data. If you take a lot of photos, that can be useful. And one downside of the Optima is that the battery doesn't last very long, so you'll have to charge it more often.

Man: I don't mind that. I always carry a charger with me anyway, so …
(*fade*)

Recording 12b

Speaker A: I wash and dry my hair every morning, so this is definitely the electrical appliance I use the most.

Speaker B: Mum! My teacher says I need something to open cans with for my school camping trip tomorrow.

Speaker C: One kitchen gadget I'd really like is a machine to blend up food so I can make my own healthy drinks.

Speaker D: I'm terrible at adding up big numbers, or doing complex sums, so I can't imagine what it was like before these existed.

Speaker E: My mother still washes all her dishes by hand and it takes her a long time. I'd like to get a machine that can do the job for her.

Speaker F: This software is the reason why a computer is much more than just a typewriter. It processes the words instead of just typing them.

Recording 13a

Bill: Just look at this – they're putting one of those cheap restaurant chains in where that nice tea-shop used to be. They're owned by some multinational company. At this rate our culture will disappear altogether and we'll all end up eating the same bland food.

Amy: Well, a lot of people are worried about globalisation and the impact it could have on the local people. But actually I'm beginning to think it works the other way around.

Bill: You can't be serious.

Amy: Yes, I'm reading a book about it actually and the author makes some very valid points.

Bill: He probably works for one of the big multinationals himself!

Amy: Actually, no. I'm pretty sure he's a journalist.

Bill: So, what does he say then?

Amy: Well, he points out that there are far more ethnic restaurants in England than people realise – for example, there are seven Indian restaurants for every one McDonald's in the UK.

Bill: Really? I didn't realise that.

Amy: Yes, and globally, pizzas are actually more popular than burgers. I think globalisation could mean that we end up living a more interesting and multicultural life.

Bill: Yes, but you've got to admit that, worldwide, the soft drinks market is totally dominated by just one or two big companies.

Amy: Well, according to this author, there's a new energy drink taking over the market and it's a joint venture between Thailand and Austria. Without globalisation, international companies just wouldn't merge like that.

Bill: Well I think that globalisation just pushes popular culture to the masses and spreads it even further. When people go travelling to far flung places, they want to see something exotic, not the same icons they see all around them at home!

Amy: Yes, but I doubt the local people there feel they're losing their national identity just because a fast food outlet has opened up. And anyway, the nice thing about it is that, in many places, these chains have to change the food they sell to suit the local culture. So there is a lot of give and take going on and you still get cultural diversity to some extent.

Bill: I suppose so. I suppose so. I guess no one big multinational has a monopoly over the fashion market either, does it?

Amy: That's right, the big fashion labels are spread over a lot of different countries.

Recording 13b

global, globalis**a**tion, implic**a**tion, isol**a**tion, **cu**lture, dom**e**stic, inter**nati**onal, **lo**cal, **sce**ptical, modernis**a**tion, **nati**onal, multicultural, proj**ec**tion, **i**con, multi**nati**onal, popul**a**tion

Recording 14a

Mary: Hi, Jean. You look worried. Is everything OK?

Jean: Hi, Mary. Actually I'm facing a few problems at work and I'm not really sure how to deal with them.

Mary: What sort of problems?

Jean: Well, we've just got a new boss and he's expecting us to start work at 8 o'clock in the morning. Of course that's causing problems for me at home because it means my husband has to take the children to school every morning, which is making him late for work.

Mary: Oh dear. I know how you feel. I had to deal with a similar problem last year.

Jean: How did you tackle it?

Mary: Well, I didn't at first and that created an even worse situation. The traffic is so bad nowadays that I was leaving the house at 6:30 every morning to get there in time. Eventually I realised I would have to address the problem sooner or later, so I raised the issue with my boss.

Jean: Did you manage to resolve it?

Mary: Yes, he was terrific. He said he hadn't realised that the early start would present a problem and he agreed to let me start half an hour later.

Jean: That's great, I'm sure my boss has no idea how much trouble he's caused. Perhaps I should deal with it the same way.

Mary: Well, they say that identifying the problem is the hardest part. Tackling it should be the easy part.

Jean: You haven't met my new boss!

Recording 14b

accepted, crowded, developed, excluded, included, isolated, overpriced, overworked, resolved, stressed, solved

Recording 15a

Narrator: Statement 1

Speaker A: I think it could be beneficial to educate the public this way. Anything we do to raise awareness of these issues is very worthwhile. The more educated people are, the more advantageous it is for the environment.

Speaker B: I honestly think it would be pointless. People just don't read leaflets, so handing them out would be futile. Not only would it be a fruitless exercise, but it would also create more litter!

Narrator: Statement 2

Speaker A: I think this is an unattainable goal. I think it would prove impracticable even to think about trying to achieve this. Our environmental problems are so great now that it's unfeasible to imagine that we could solve all our pollution problems so quickly.

Speaker B: Look, I think everyone in my country is so aware of the impact we're having on the environment that I think it is conceivable that we'll have solved the problem soon. It's quite feasible that we'll all be driving electric cars. They're a viable alternative to petrol-driven cars, so getting rid of pollution is definitely achievable.

Narrator: Statement 3

Speaker A: I think it's improbable that everyone will abandon the chemicals we're using now. So many people have been using them

for years and it's questionable whether they will be able to convince everyone to stop. Yeah, I'd say this one is very doubtful.

Speaker B: There are a lot of great cleaning products now that are eco-friendly and I think governments are liable to start putting pressure on manufacturers to produce more products like these. I think it's quite probable that within ten years everyone will have made the switch.

Recording 15b

1 I refuse to go.
2 Disposing of refuse is a growing problem.
3 There is a conflict here.
4 The two reports conflict with each other.
5 We all need to be present at the meeting.
6 This issue presents an enormous problem.
7 We are making a lot of progress.
8 We need to progress at a faster rate.
9 There has been an increase in carbon emissions.
10 Temperatures are expected to increase.

Recording 16

Let's find out just how environmentally aware you are.

Question one. How many trees do you think it would take to offset the CO_2 emissions from a long distance flight? Well, it's estimated that for each mile or 1.6 km that a jet flies, half a kilo of CO_2 is added to the atmosphere. So a round trip of 10,000 miles would emit about one and a half tonnes of CO_2 per passenger. The amount of CO_2 a tree can absorb depends on factors such as its type, location and age. The company Future Forests says that, on average, it would take 2 trees 99 years to counter the effect of this trip, so the answer here is C.

Question two. What is the most environmentally friendly way to wash your clothes? Well, the solvents used by most dry cleaners are damaging to the environment. In a washing machine, the vast majority of the energy – about 90 per cent of it – goes into heating up the water, not running through the cycle. Washing clothes in hot water, even by hand, uses a lot of energy to heat the water. Keeping washing temperatures low and always washing a full load is the best policy. So the correct answer is C.

Question three. Do you need to always turn off your electric lights to save energy? It is a common myth that flicking the lights on and off uses more energy than leaving them on. In fact an ordinary bulb only has to be turned off for three seconds to outweigh the cost of turning it back on. For energy efficient and other fluorescent bulbs, this rises to five minutes. Energy efficient light bulbs use 75 per cent less energy than ordinary ones – so if you have those, but leave them on as you tidy – you'll probably still use less energy than if you switch your standard bulbs on and off. So the correct answer is B.

Question four. What is the most energy-efficient way of cooking a baked potato? A microwave uses just a third of the electricity required to operate an electric oven, and of course the potato will take much less time to cook, so the correct answer is B.

Question five. What is the best way to help reduce your CO_2 emissions throughout the year? Well, it's estimated that one person taking the train for a year, rather than driving a car, would reduce their CO_2 emission total by 2.9 tonnes. Hanging out your washing rather than using a tumble dryer would cut CO_2 by 0.9 tonnes and working from home one day a week would cut 0.88 tonnes. So the correct answer is A.

Recording 17a

Speaker 1: I'm a student so I only work part-time. I managed to get a job as a shelf stacker in the local supermarket. It's unskilled work and very monotonous, but the pay is quite good. Every week when I get my wages I put them straight into the bank. I'm saving up for a new computer. I've nearly got enough, which is just as well because my prospects aren't good – I think they're going to make me redundant next month!

Speaker 2: My occupation is receptionist at a five-star hotel. I got the job while I was studying. We had to complete part of our course in the workplace, and this is where I was placed. It's a very demanding job and I have to do shift work, which I find exhausting. The perks are great though. I get to stay in luxurious hotels around the world for next to nothing and I get on really well with all the other staff. My father worked in this industry all his life. He retired the same year that I started.

Speaker 3: I work as a labourer on a construction site. It's manual work, so it's very physical, which keeps me nice and fit. My wages aren't great, but I often get to do a lot of overtime, so I can earn more money that way.

Speaker 4: I've always wanted a career in marketing, so I studied as a graphic designer and when I graduated I got a job with a marketing company. I had to compete against some very good candidates to get the job, so I was really pleased. I've recently been promoted and now I'm in charge of several advertising campaigns. I find the job really rewarding, and that's not just because of the great salary. I get to use the skills I learned at college. I also get on very well with my colleagues. Job satisfaction is really important to me.

Recording 17b

bird, earn, first, nurse, perk, purse, work
park, clerk, market, target
ball, floor, law, poor, walk, force

Recording 18

In spite of the large number of prisons we have, crime figures have risen again this year with the number of drug-related crimes in particular increasing. Many law-abiding citizens believe that our existing laws are just not tough enough and do not act as enough of a deterrent against crime. In recent years there has been a move to abolish laws which were deemed to be too harsh or strict and to reduce the punishment for non-violent crimes, such as those against property. On the other hand, in some countries the police can enforce laws against crossing the street at the wrong place by imposing a fine. Laws like this are passed simply to keep us safe and some see them as an intrusion on our privacy. Focusing on petty crimes in this way can also cause people who generally obey the law to resent the police rather than respect them for what they do. They would rather their time was spent solving more serious crimes. It's difficult to believe that reducing punishments will help to combat crime. It goes without saying that laws against serious crimes should be strictly enforced. However, we also need to focus more attention on crime prevention and educating young people to abide by the law. They need to know that no one is above the law and there are serious consequences if they're involved in criminal activities in any way. Some people believe that non-violent crimes or so-called victimless crimes such as fraud should be punished less. However, there is always a victim somewhere, even if that victim is a company and its owners. And victims often feel the effects of a crime for many years, whether the attack is planned or random. Perhaps it's time to start introducing new laws rather than abolishing them.

Recording 19a

Good morning, my name is Dan Taylor and I'm Professor of Sociology here at Manly University.

Our modern society often prides itself on its free press and, with access to the Internet and cable television, the news is broadcast 24 hours a day. However, we have just completed a study which reveals that the general public is increasingly ill-informed today. For this project we compiled a list of what we considered to be the most significant current affairs stories and then we assessed how these stories were reported by newspapers and radio and television networks. Alarmingly, we found that as many as 25 significant news stories were either under-reported or omitted from the news altogether.

It would seem that the media today seeks to entertain rather than inform the public. I define censorship as anything which interferes with the free flow of information in our society. And this would seem to be what tabloid journalism is doing. They are effectively censoring important news stories on the basis that they may not be interesting or entertaining enough. One example is the widening gap between the rich and the poor. This is a major problem in big cities today and yet you are unlikely to find a reference to it in any news headlines. Instead, you're more likely to find stories about the latest celebrity, with important news content relegated to the back pages.

Recording 19b

Teacher: Would you like to be famous?

Student: I think a lot of people want to be famous nowdays and that's why reality TV is so popular. But I wouldn't like to be famous at all. Being famous nowadays simply means that you're in the tabloids a lot and you're followed by the paparazzi everywhere you go. I'd find that very intrusive. Famous people have no privacy at all in any part of their life. Their life also seems to be very superficial because they spend all of their time going to parties and trying to look glamorous. It all seems very artificial to me – they just don't seem to be part of the real world at all.

Teacher: Hmm. Do you think famous people have a positive or a negative influence on young people?

Student: I think they should have a positive influence on young people, but many of them don't. Some personalities are good role models and use their celebrity status to encourage people to think about important issues, but we often see photos of famous people behaving badly.

Teacher: Nowadays we have access to the news 24 hours a day. What effect does this have?

Student: I think it can affect us in both positive and negative ways. On the one hand, it's very convenient to be able to catch up with what's happening in the world at any time of the day or night, no matter where you are. But on the other hand, this kind of news can give you a distorted view of what's happening, because even minor news stories are given more importance than they perhaps should have.

Recording 19c

artificial, attention, biased, censor, exposed, exposure, intrusive, intrusion, invasion, invasive, publication, superficial

Recording 20a

For those of you who are interested in aesthetics, why not consider a visit to Bethania Island this year? The island will host three arts festivals, each one showcasing different areas of the art world. First, there is Living Writers'

Week. Throughout the week there will be talks by local and international writers and a chance to dine with them at the various literary lunches. You'll also be able to pick up old and new editions at the very large book fair. The little ones haven't been forgotten and so there are plenty of children's activities planned as well. As is the case each year, there will be a theme for the festival and this year it is Island Life.

Later in the year, there will be a celebration of the visual arts. There are some very famous and accomplished painters in residence on the island and their work will be featured in a wonderful exhibition. Works by Alex Green, whose paintings depict the beautiful scenery this island is famous for, will be a prominent feature. Visitors to the festival will get the chance to discuss the creative process with the artists and there will also be opportunities to try out your own artistic skills at the workshops being held at various galleries on the island. To top it all off, there will be a display of crafts created by emerging artists. You'll be amazed at the intricate wooden carvings produced by local craftsmen.

And finally, if you love music then you shouldn't miss the Festival of Voices. You will be able to hear performers from around the world. What makes this even more interesting is that some of this year's performances are going to be interactive so members of the audience will be invited to participate as well. One of the stages will be devoted to showcasing musical theatre and the good news is that there will be plenty of free concerts for everyone to enjoy.

Recording 20b

My taste in music is quite eclectic and there isn't really one style of music that I like. I listen to everything from popular music to classical. Music plays a very important role in my life, and I listen to it almost constantly. I find that it helps to set or to change a mood. So I tend to choose my music according to who I'm with or what I'm doing. For example, if I'm driving long distances in my car I prefer to play something stimulating to help keep me awake, but if I'm having a dinner party with friends then I play something more relaxing. I think that music helps to inspire me when I'm working, although my colleagues find it distracting so I tend to listen with headphones on. In that way I can escape into my own little world. When I was younger I would definitely have said that I preferred live music. The atmosphere in a live concert can be electric. Nowadays, though, a lot of popular groups only perform at very large venues in front of audiences of 20,000 or more and I don't really like that. I prefer the intimacy of listening to recorded music, and the sound quality is better as well. Music really enriches our lives – it can turn a boring, monotonous period of time into a magical experience, so I think it's essential to have music and, in fact, all of the arts in your life.

Recording 20c

atmosphere, classical, edition, festival, fundamental, imagination, literary, monotonous, musical, performance, popular, visual

Recording 21

put, these, in, some, ball, choose, word, about, guest, what, attack, hard

Recording 22a

1 analysis, analyse, analytical
2 benefit, benefit, beneficial
3 consistency, consist, consistent
4 creation, creator, creativity, create, creative
5 definition, define, definable, definitive, definite
6 environment, environmentalist, environmental
7 occurrence, occur
8 period, periodical, periodic
9 significance, signify, significant
10 theory, theorise, theoretical

Recording 22b

A Leading environmentalists are concerned about the effects our modern lifestyle is having on global warming.
B Scientists have shown that including fish in our diet may be beneficial in reducing heart disease.
C Satellites have recently sent back important new data from Mars, although it is not yet clear what significance the findings have for future space exploration.
D Young children are often very creative, although many give up art when they begin high school.
E Your essay is good, but you need to define the causes of pollution more clearly.
F I prefer teachers who don't put too much emphasis on learning and studying the theory of chemistry. I'm much more interested in the practical side of things.
G The student council consists of ten undergraduates and four postgraduate students.
H After you've planted your seeds you can't simply leave them to grow, they do need to be checked periodically for weeds and pests.
I We analysed the test results to see whether there really is a link between video games and increased violence.
J The torrential storm last night seems to be part of a pattern – a similar storm occurred two years ago following a severe drought.

Wordlist

UNIT 1

GROWING UP

Nouns

adolescence /ˌædəlˈesəns/
adulthood /ˈædʌlthʊd/
bond /bɒnd/
brotherhood /ˈbrʌðəhʊd/
character /ˈkærəktə/
childhood /ˈtʃaɪldhʊd/
conflict /ˈkɒnflɪkt/
connection /kəˈnekʃən/
fatherhood /ˈfɑːðəhʊd/
friendship /ˈfrendʃɪp/
instinct /ˈɪnstɪŋkt/
interaction /ˌɪntəˈrækʃən/
motherhood /ˈmʌðəhʊd/
nature /ˈneɪtʃə/
parent /ˈpeərənt/
relation /rɪˈleɪʃən/
relationship (between/with)
    /rɪˈleɪʃənʃɪp/
relative /ˈrelətɪv/
resemblance /rɪˈzembləns/
rivalry /ˈraɪvəlri/
sibling /ˈsɪblɪŋ/
teenager /ˈtiːnˌeɪdʒə/
temperament /ˈtempərəmənt/
ties /taɪz/
upbringing /ˈʌpbrɪŋɪŋ/

Compound nouns

active role
extended family
family gathering
immediate family
maternal instinct
sibling rivalry
stable upbringing
striking resemblance

Adjectives

close /kləʊs/
close-knit /ˌkləʊsˈnɪt/
maternal /məˈtɜːnəl/
parental /pəˈrentəl/
rewarding /rɪˈwɔːdɪŋ/
stable /ˈsteɪbl/

Verbs

accommodate /əˈkɒmədeɪt/
adopt /əˈdɒpt/
break down /breɪk daʊn/
develop /dɪˈveləp/
endure /ɪnˈdjʊə/
establish /ɪˈstæblɪʃ/

have sth in common
inherit /ɪnˈherɪt/
interact /ˌɪntəˈrækt/
nurture /ˈnɜːtʃə/
play a role
relate (to) /rɪˈleɪt/

UNIT 2

MENTAL AND PHYSICAL DEVELOPMENT

Nouns

ability /əˈbɪləti/
adolescent /ˌædəlˈesənt/
behaviour /bɪˈheɪvjə/
childhood /ˈtʃaɪldhʊd/
concept /ˈkɒnsept/
consequence /ˈkɒnsɪkwəns/
gesture /ˈdʒestʃə/
growth /grəʊθ/
height /haɪt/
imagination /ɪˌmædʒɪˈneɪʃən/
infancy /ˈɪnfənsi/
infant /ˈɪnfənt/
knowledge /ˈnɒlɪdʒ/
maturity /məˈtʃʊərəti/
memory /ˈmeməri/
milestone /ˈmaɪlstəʊn/
mind /maɪnd/
peers /pɪəz/
period /ˈpɪəriəd/
phase /feɪz/
rate /reɪt/
reminder /rɪˈmaɪndə/
social skills
skill /skɪl/
stage /steɪdʒ/
toddler /ˈtɒdlə/
transition /trænˈzɪʃən/

Adjectives

abstract /ˈæbstrækt/
cognitive /ˈkɒgnətɪv/
clumsy /ˈklʌmzi/
fond /fɒnd/
fully-grown /ˈfʊli grəʊn/
immature /ˌɪməˈtjʊə/
independent /ˌɪndɪˈpendənt/
irresponsible /ˌɪrɪˈspɒnsəbl/
mature /məˈtjʊə/
patient /ˈpeɪʃənt/
rebellious /rɪˈbeliəs/
significant /sɪgˈnɪfɪkənt/
tolerant /ˈtɒlərənt/

Verbs

acquire /əˈkwaɪə/
develop /dɪˈveləp/
gesture /ˈdʒestʃə/
grow /grəʊ/
imitate /ˈɪmɪteɪt/
look back
master /ˈmɑːstə/
mature /məˈtjʊə/
remember /rɪˈmembə/
remind /rɪˈmaɪnd/
reminisce /ˌremɪˈnɪs/
throw a tantrum
visualise /ˈvɪʒuəlaɪz/

Adverbs

typically /ˈtɪpɪkli/

Phrases with *mind*

bear in mind
broaden the mind
have something in mind
have something on your mind
it slipped my mind
keep an open mind
my mind went blank
put your mind at ease

UNIT 3

KEEPING FIT

Nouns

allergy /ˈælədʒi/
anxiety /æŋˈzaɪəti/
appetite /ˈæpɪtaɪt/
artery /ˈɑːtəri/
asset /ˈæset/
benefit /ˈbenɪfɪt/
cravings /ˈkreɪvɪŋz/
depression /dɪˈpreʃən/
diagnosis /ˌdaɪəgˈnəʊsɪs/
diet /ˈdaɪət/
dietician /ˌdaɪəˈtɪʃən/
disease /dɪˈziːz/
(eating) disorder /dɪˈsɔːdə/
exercise /ˈeksəsaɪz/
factor /ˈfæktə/
fast food /fɑːst fuːd/
fat /fæt/
harm /hɑːm/
health /helθ/
heart attack /hɑːt əˈtæk/
infection /ɪnˈfekʃən/
ingredients /ɪnˈgriːdiənts/
insomnia /ɪnˈsɒmniə/

intake /ˈɪnteɪk/
junk food /dʒʌŋk fuːd/
muscle /ˈmʌsəl/
nutrient /ˈnjuːtriənt/
nutrition /njuːˈtrɪʃən/
obesity /əʊˈbiːsəti/
onset /ˈɒnset/
portion /ˈpɔːʃən/
risk /rɪsk/
serving /ˈsɜːvɪŋ/
stress /stres/
stroke /strəʊk/
treatment /ˈtriːtmənt/
therapy /ˈθerəpi/
variety /vəˈraɪəti/
weight /weɪt/

Adjectives

acute /əˈkjuːt/
allergic /əˈlɜːdʒɪk/
alternate /ɒlˈtɜːnət/
brisk /brɪsk/
chronic /ˈkrɒnɪk/
harmful /ˈhɑːmfəl/
healthy /ˈhelθi/
infectious /ɪnˈfekʃəs/
moderate /ˈmɒdərət/
obese /əʊˈbiːs/
overweight /ˈəʊvəweɪt/
persistent /pəˈsɪstənt/
regular /ˈregjʊlə/
vital /ˈvaɪtəl/

Verbs

avoid /əˈvɔɪd/
counteract /ˌkaʊntərˈækt/
curb /kɜːb/
cure /kjʊə/
diminish /dɪˈmɪnɪʃ/
disrupt /dɪsˈrʌpt/
eliminate /ɪˈlɪmɪneɪt/
maintain /meɪnˈteɪn/
overdo /əʊvəˈduː/
overeat /ˌəʊvərˈiːt/
prevent /prɪˈvent/
recommend /ˌrekəˈmend/
recover /rɪˈkʌvə/
reduce /rɪˈdjuːs/
skip /skɪp/
stimulate /ˈstɪmjəleɪt/
trigger /ˈtrɪgə/

UNIT 4

LIFESTYLES

Nouns

activity /æk'tɪvəti/
aspect /'æspekt/
attitude /'ætɪtjuːd/
(achieve a) balance /'bæləns/
competition /ˌkɒmpə'tɪʃən/
creativity /ˌkriːeɪ'tɪvəti/
daily routine
desire /dɪ'zaɪə/
disappointment
   /ˌdɪsə'pɔɪntmənt/
experience /ɪk'spɪəriəns/
fulfillment /fʊl'fɪlmənt/
goal /gəʊl/
hobby /'hɒbi/
insight /'ɪnsaɪt/
leisure /'leʒə/
lifestyle /'laɪfstaɪl/
optimist /'ɒptɪmɪst/
outlook /'aʊtlʊk/
opportunity /ˌɒpə'tjuːnəti/
personality /ˌpɜːsən'æləti/
pessimist /'pesɪmɪst/
priority /praɪ'ɒrəti/
pressure /'preʃə/
realist /'rɪəlɪst/
risk-taker /rɪsk 'teɪkə/
self-expression /self ɪk'spreʃən/
sense /sens/

Adjectives

active /'æktɪv/
bored /bɔːd/
confused /kən'fjuːzd/
dissatisfied /dɪs'sætɪsfaɪd/
intense /ɪn'tens/
materialistic /məˌtɪəriə'lɪstɪk/
negative /'negətɪv/
outdoor /ˌaʊt'dɔː/
positive /'pɒzətɪv/
recreational /ˌrekri'eɪʃənəl/
successful /sək'sesfəl/

Verbs

achieve (a goal) /ə'tʃiːv/
appeal /ə'piːl/
attract /ə'trækt/
choose /tʃuːz/
express /ɪk'spres/
enjoy /ɪn'dʒɔɪ/
fulfil /fʊl'fɪl/
improve /ɪm'pruːv/
motivate /'məʊtɪveɪt/
participate /pɑː'tɪsɪpeɪt/
regret /rɪ'gret/
relax /rɪ'læks/
satisfy /'sætɪsfaɪ/

Verb phrases

lead a happy life
live life on the edge
live life to the full

make a choice
make a decision
make a living
meet a need
miss an opportunity
play a role
put pressure on
set a goal
take part (in)
work hard for a living

Phrases with *life* or *living*

all walks of life
cost of living
lifelong ambition
living expenses
once in a lifetime opportunity
standard of living
way of life

UNIT 5

STUDENT LIFE

Nouns

assignment /ə'saɪnmənt/
college /'kɒlɪdʒ/
controversy /'kɒntrəvɜːsi/
curriculum /kə'rɪkjələm/
dissertation /ˌdɪsə'teɪʃən/
education /ˌedʒʊ'keɪʃən/
exam /ɪg'zæm/
field (of study) /'fiːld/
findings /'faɪndɪŋz/
funding /'fʌndɪŋ/
grade /greɪd/
graduation /ˌgrædʒu'eɪʃən/
grant /grɑːnt/
high school /haɪ skuːl/
homework /'həʊmwɜːk/
junior school /'dʒuːniə skuːl/
kindergarten /'kɪndəˌgɑːtən/
learning disorder
lecturer /'lektʃərə/
library /'laɪbrəri/
limits /'lɪmɪts/
Master's /'mɑːstəz/
nursery /'nɜːsri/
PhD /ˌpiːeɪtʃ'diː/
primary school /'praɪməri skuːl/
program /'prəʊgræm/
project /'prɒdʒekt/
research /rɪ'sɜːtʃ/
resources /rɪ'zɔːsɪz/
results /rɪ'zʌlts/
scholarship /'skɒləʃɪp/
scope /skəʊp/
secondary school /'sekəndri
   skuːl/
sources /'sɔːsɪz/
syllabus /'sɪləbəs/
task /tɑːsk/
theory /'θɪəri/
thesis /'θiːsɪs/

tutor /'tjuːtə/
topic /'tɒpɪk/
university /ˌjuːnɪ'vɜːsəti/

Adjectives

academic /ˌækə'demɪk/
eligible /'elɪdʒəbl/
mixed /'mɪkst/
postgraduate /ˌpəʊs'tgrædʒuət/
relevant /'reləvənt/
senior /'siːniə/
single-sex /ˌsɪŋgl'seks/
studious /'stjuːdiəs/
work-related /wɜːk rɪ'leɪtɪd/

Verbs

adopt (an approach) /ə'dɒpt/
analyse /'ænəlaɪz/
conduct /'kɒndʌkt/
concentrate /'kɒnsəntreɪt/
consider /kən'sɪdə/
find out /faɪnd aʊt/
graduate /'grædʒuət/
learn (about) /lɜːn/
organise /'ɔːgənaɪz/
overcome /ˌəʊvə'kʌm/
review /rɪ'vjuː/
revise /rɪ'vaɪz/
struggle /'strʌgəl/
take (a course) /teɪk/

Adverbs

relatively /'relətɪvli/

UNIT 6

EFFECTIVE COMMUNICATION

Nouns

accuracy /'ækjərəsi/
communication
   /kəˌmjuːnɪ'keɪʃən/
concept /'kɒnsept/
conjecture /kən'dʒektʃə/
dialect /'daɪəlekt/
fluency /'fluːənsi/
gesture /'dʒestʃə/
hesitation /ˌhezɪ'teɪʃən/
language /'læŋgwɪdʒ/
language barrier
linguist /'lɪŋgwɪst/
linguistics /lɪŋ'gwɪstɪks/
means of communication
mother tongue
native speaker
pronunciation /prəˌnʌnsi'eɪʃən/
sign language /saɪn 'læŋgwɪdʒ/
vocabulary /və'kæbjələri/

Adjectives

incoherent /ˌɪnkəʊ'hɪərənt/
inherent /ɪn'herənt/
sophisticated /sə'fɪstɪkeɪtɪd/
spontaneous /spɒn'teɪniəs/

Verbs

clarify /'klærɪfaɪ/
communicate /kə'mjuːnɪkeɪt/
comprehend /ˌkɒmprɪ'hend/
conclude /kən'kluːd/
confirm /kən'fɜːm/
converse /kɒn'vɜːs/
define /dɪ'faɪn/
demonstrate /'demənstreɪt/
distinguish /dɪ'stɪŋgwɪʃ/
emerge /ɪ'mɜːdʒ/
evolve /ɪ'vɒlv/
explain /ɪk'spleɪn/
express /ɪk'spres/
gesture /'dʒestʃə/
illustrate /'ɪləstreɪt/
imply /ɪm'plaɪ/
indicate /'ɪndɪkeɪt/
pronounce /prə'naʊns/
recall /rɪ'kɔːl/
refer (to) /rɪ'fɜː/
signify /'sɪgnɪfaɪ/
state /steɪt/
stutter /'stʌtə/
suggest /sə'dʒest/
translate /trænz'leɪt/

Idioms

have a say
having said that
needless to say
that is to say
there is something to be said for
to say the least
when all is said and done
you can say that again!

UNIT 7

ON THE MOVE

Nouns

accommodation /əˌkɒmə'deɪʃən/
attraction /ə'trækʃən/
community /kə'mjuːnəti/
countryside /'kʌntrɪsaɪd/
destination /ˌdestɪ'neɪʃən/
eco-tourism /'iːkəʊˌtʊərɪzəm/
effect /ɪ'fekt/
facilities /fə'sɪlətiz/
identification
   /aɪˌdentɪfɪ'keɪʃən/
inhabitant /ɪn'hæbɪtənt/
itinerary /aɪ'tɪnərəri/
journey /'dʒɜːni/
landscape /'lændskeɪp/
luggage /'lʌgɪdʒ/
peak /piːk/
tourism /'tʊərɪzəm/
tourist /'tʊərɪst/
transport /'trænspɔːt/
travel /'trævəl/
travelling /'trævəlɪŋ/
trend /trend/

trip /trɪp/
village /'vɪlɪdʒ/

Adjectives

adventurous /əd'ventʃərəs/
budget /'bʌdʒɪt/
breathtaking /'breθ,teɪkɪŋ/
coastal /'kəʊstəl/
cosmopolitan /ˌkɒzmə'pɒlɪtən/
diverse /daɪ'vɜːs/
flexible /'fleksɪbl/
foreign /'fɒrɪn/
local /'ləʊkəl/
luxurious /lʌɡ'ʒʊəriəs/
mountainous /'maʊntɪnəs/
peaceful /'piːsfəl/
picturesque /ˌpɪktʃər'esk/
polluted /pə'luːtɪd/
quaint /kweɪnt/
remote /rɪ'məʊt/
rough /rʌf/
rural /'rʊərəl/
scenic /'siːnɪk/
stunning /'stʌnɪŋ/
tough /tʌf/
traditional /trə'dɪʃənəl/
unspoilt /ʌn'spɔɪlt/
urban /'ɜːbən/

Verbs

affect /ə'fekt/
fluctuate /'flʌktʃʊeɪt/

UNIT 8

THROUGH THE AGES

Nouns

age /eɪdʒ/
archaeologist /ˌɑːki'ɒlədʒɪst/
century /'sentʃəri/
decade /'dekeɪd/
era /'ɪərə/
evidence /'evɪdəns/
excavation /ˌekskə'veɪʃən/
generation /ˌdʒenə'reɪʃən/
the Middle Ages
millennia /mɪ'leniə/
period /'pɪəriəd/
phase /feɪz/
pioneer /ˌpaɪə'nɪə/
timeline /'taɪmlaɪn/

Adjectives

ancient /'eɪnʃənt/
chronological /ˌkrɒnə'lɒdʒɪkəl/
consecutive /kən'sekjʊtɪv/
historical /hɪ'stɒrɪkəl/
imminent /'ɪmɪnənt/
middle-aged /ˌmɪdəl'eɪdʒd/
nostalgic /nɒs'tældʒɪk/
prehistoric /ˌpriːhɪ'stɒrɪk/
prior (to) /praɪə/
punctual /'pʌŋktjuəl/
time-consuming
  /'taɪmkən,sjuːmɪŋ/

Verbs

erode /ɪ'rəʊd/
infer /ɪn'fɜː/
predate /ˌpriː'deɪt/
span /spæn/

Phrases with *time*

in time
lose track of time
on time
save time
spend time
take so long / much time
the right time

Adverbs

chronologically
  /ˌkrɒnə'lɒdʒɪkəli/
formerly /'fɔːməli/
previously /'priːviəsli/
subsequently /'sʌbsɪkwəntli/

UNIT 9

THE NATURAL WORLD

Nouns

agriculture /'æɡrɪkʌltʃə/
animal kingdom
burrow /'bʌrəʊ/
climate /'klaɪmət/
crop(s) /krɒp/
decline /dɪ'klaɪn/
den /den/
disaster /dɪ'zɑːstə/
ecological balance
ecology /iː'kɒlədʒi/
evolution /ˌiːvə'luːʃən/
extinction /ɪk'stɪŋkʃən/
fauna /'fɔːnə/
flora /'flɔːrə/
genetics /dʒə'netɪks/
habitat /'hæbɪtæt/
human nature
insect /'ɪnsekt/
Mother Nature
pesticides /'pestɪsaɪdz/
predator /'predətə/
prey /preɪ/
repercussions /ˌriːpə'kʌʃənz/
scent /sent/
species /'spiːʃiːz/
soil /sɔɪl/
vegetation /ˌvedʒɪ'teɪʃən/
vermin /'vɜːmɪn/
weed /wiːd/

Adjectives

arid /'ærɪd/
catastrophic /ˌkætə'strɒfɪk/
disastrous /dɪ'zɑːstrəs/
domesticated /də'mestɪkeɪtɪd/
endangered /ɪn'deɪndʒəd/
extinct /ɪk'stɪŋkt/
genetically modified

introduced /ˌɪntrə'djuːst/
native /'neɪtɪv/
natural /'nætʃərəl/
resistant /rɪ'zɪstənt/
semi-arid /'semi ˌærɪd/
tropical /'trɒpɪkəl/
vulnerable /'vʌlnərəbəl/
wild /waɪld/

Verbs

adapt /ə'dæpt/
combat /'kɒmbæt/
cultivate /'kʌltɪveɪt/
eradicate /ɪ'rædɪkeɪt/
evolve /ɪ'vɒlv/
hibernate /'haɪbəneɪt/
tolerate /'tɒləreɪt/

UNIT 10

REACHING FOR THE SKIES

Nouns

asteroid /'æstərɔɪd/
astronaut /'æstrənɔːt/
atmosphere /'ætməsfɪə/
cosmos /'kɒzmɒs/
crater /'kreɪtə/
debris /'deɪbriː/
Earth /ɜːθ/
exploration /ˌeksplə'reɪʃən/
explorer /ɪk'splɔːrə/
galaxy /'ɡæləksi/
gas /ɡæs/
gravity /'ɡrævəti/
horizon /hə'raɪzən/
launch /lɔːnʃ/
meteor /'miːtiə/
moon /muːn/
ocean /'əʊʃən/
orbit /'ɔːbɪt/
outer space /'aʊtə speɪs/
planet /'plænɪt/
radiation /ˌreɪdi'eɪʃən/
rocket /'rɒkɪt/
satellite /'sætəlaɪt/
simulator /'sɪmjəleɪtə/
solar system /'səʊlə 'sɪstəm/
space /speɪs/
spacecraft /'speɪskrɑːft/
space shuttle /speɪs 'ʃʌtəl/
space station /speɪs 'steɪʃən/
surface /'sɜːfɪs/
universe /'juːnɪvɜːs/
weightlessness /'weɪtləsnəs/

Adjectives

commercial /kə'mɜːʃəl/
cosmic /'kɒzmɪk/
extreme /ɪk'striːm/
gravitational /ˌɡrævɪ'teɪʃənəl/
horizontal /ˌhɒrɪ'zɒntəl/
inevitable /ɪ'nevɪtəbl/
lunar /'luːnə/
meteoric /ˌmiːti'ɒrɪk/

outer /'aʊtə/
solar /'səʊlə/
terrestrial /tə'restriəl/
toxic /'tɒksɪk/
uninhabitable /ˌʌnɪn'hæbɪtəbl/
universal /ˌjuːnɪ'vɜːsəl/
unmanned /ʌn'mænd/

Verbs

acclimatise /ə'klaɪmətaɪz/
colonise /'kɒlənaɪz/
explore /ɪk'splɔː/
float /fləʊt/
orbit /'ɔːbɪt/
propel /prə'pel/
rotate /rə'teɪt/
sustain /sə'steɪn/
simulate /'sɪmjəleɪt/
undergo /ˌʌndə'ɡəʊ/

UNIT 11

DESIGN AND INNOVATION

Nouns

access /'ækses/
approach /ə'prəʊtʃ/
balcony /'bælkəni/
brick /brɪk/
building /'bɪldɪŋ/
ceiling /'siːlɪŋ/
condition /kən'dɪʃ(ə)n/
concrete /'kɒŋkriːt/
construction /kən'strʌkʃən/
cottage /'kɒtɪdʒ/
design /dɪ'zaɪn/
device /dɪ'vaɪs/
engineering /ˌendʒɪ'nɪərɪŋ/
flooding /'flʌdɪŋ/
housing /'haʊzɪŋ/
innovation /ˌɪnə'veɪʃən/
invention /ɪn'venʃən/
lift shaft /lɪft ʃɑːft/
occupant /'ɒkjəpənt/
operation /ˌɒpə'reɪʃ(ə)n/
pump /pʌmp/
quarry /'kwɒri/
residence /'rezɪdəns/
scheme /skiːm/
skyscraper /'skaɪˌskreɪpə/
staircase /'steəkeɪs/
steel /stiːl/
structure /'strʌktʃə/
tension /'tenʃən/
timber /'tɪmbə/
tunnel /'tʌn(ə)l/

Adjectives

Adjectives
airy /'eəri/
congested /kən'dʒestɪd/
conventional /kən'venʃənəl/
cosy /'kəʊzi/
cramped /kræmpt/

curved /kɜːvd/
disposable /dɪˈspəʊzəbl/
domestic /dəˈmestɪk/
emerging /ɪˈmɜː(r)dʒɪŋ/
expanding /ɪkˈspænd/
feasible /ˈfiːzəb(ə)l/
functional /ˈfʌŋkʃənəl/
futuristic /ˌfjuːtʃəˈrɪstɪk/
high-rise /ˌhaɪˈraɪz/
ingenious /ɪnˈdʒiːniəs/
innovative /ˈɪnəvətɪv/
impassable /ɪmˈpɑːsəb(ə)l/
mass-produced /ˌmæsprəˈdjuːst/
modern /ˈmɒdən/
multi-storey /ˌmʌltiˈstɔːri/
old-fashioned /ˌəʊldˈfæʃənd/
ornate /ɔːˈneɪt/
prefabricated /ˌpriːˈfæbrɪkeɪtɪd/
prosperous /ˈprɒsp(ə)rəs/
single-storey /ˈsɪŋɡəlˈstɔːri/
spacious /ˈspeɪʃəs/
state-of-the-art
traditional /trəˈdɪʃənəl/
tricky /ˈtrɪki/
two-storey /tuːˈstɔːri/
typical /ˈtɪpɪkəl/
ultra-modern /ˌʌltrəˈmɒdən/
underground /ˈʌndə(r)ˌɡraʊnd/
unstable /ʌnˈsteɪb(ə)l/

Verbs
abandon /əˈbændən/
activate /ˈæktɪveɪt/
automate /ˈɔːtəmeɪt/
break down /ˈbreɪkˌdaʊn/
build /bɪld/
collapse /kəˈlæps/
condemn /kənˈdem/
connect /kəˈnekt/
construct /ˈkənstrʌkt/
decorate /ˈdekəreɪt/
demolish /dɪˈmɒlɪʃ/
design /dɪˈzaɪn/
develop /dɪˈveləp/
devise /dɪˈvaɪz/
dig /dɪɡ/
halt /hɔːlt/
invent /ɪnˈvent/
maintain /meɪnˈteɪn/
occupy /ˈɒkjəpaɪ/
reconstruct /ˌriːkənˈstrʌkt/
renovate /ˈrenəveɪt/
struggle /ˈstrʌɡ(ə)l/
support /səˈpɔːt/
triple /ˈtrɪp(ə)l/

UNIT 12

INFORMATION TECHNOLOGY

Nouns
appliance /əˈplaɪəns/
artificial intelligence

automatic pilot
computerisation
  /kəmˌpjuːtəraɪˈzeɪʃən/
broadband /ˈbrɔːdˌbænd/
connection /kəˈnekʃən/
chip /tʃɪp/
cyberattack
data /ˈdeɪtə/
device /dɪˈvaɪs/
function /ˈfʌŋkʃən/
gadget /ˈɡædʒɪt/
platform /ˈplætˌfɔː(r)m/
privacy /ˈpraɪvəsi/
security /sɪˈkjʊərəti/
Smartphone /ˈsmɑː(r)tˌfəʊn/
social media /ˌsəʊʃəlˈmiːdiə/
the Internet
the latest
memory /ˈmeməri/
monitor /ˈmɒnɪtə/
program /ˈprəʊɡræm/
remote control /rɪˈməʊt
  kənˈtrəʊl/
technology /tekˈnɒlədʒi/
telecommunications
  /ˌtelɪkəˌmjuːnɪˈkeɪʃənz/
text message
virtual reality
Wifi /ˈwaɪˌfaɪ/

Adjectives
adequate /ˈædɪkwət/
basic /ˈbeɪsɪk/
compact /ˈkɒmpækt/
cyber /ˈsaɪbə/
dated /ˈdeɪtɪd/
digital /ˈdɪdʒɪtəl/
efficient /ɪˈfɪʃ(ə)nt/
portable /ˈpɔːtəbl/
state-of-the-art
up-to-date /ˌʌptəˈdeɪt/
user-friendly /ˌjuːzəˈfrendli/
virtual /ˈvɜːtʃuəl/
wireless /ˈwaɪə(r)ləs/

Verbs
access /ˈækses/
connect /kəˈnekt/
detect /dɪˈtekt/
disable /dɪsˈeɪb(ə)l/
display /dɪˈspleɪ/
hack /hæk/
monitor /ˈmɒnɪtə(r)/
operate /ˈɒpəreɪt/
scroll /skrəʊl/
store /stɔː/
surpass /səˈpɑːs/
switch off
switch on
track /træk/

Adverbs
remotely /rɪˈməʊtli/

Idioms
stay in touch with

UNIT 13

THE MODERN WORLD

Nouns
attitude /ˈætɪtjuːd/
brand /brænd/
culture /ˈkʌltʃə/
cycle /ˈsaɪkəl/
demographics
  /ˌdeməʊˈɡræfɪks/
development /dɪˈveləpmənt/
diversity /daɪˈvɜːsəti/
globalisation /ˌɡləʊbəlaɪˈzeɪʃən/
hindsight /ˈhaɪndsaɪt/
icon /ˈaɪkɒn/
identity /aɪˈdentəti/
impact /ˈɪmpækt/
implication /ˌɪmplɪˈkeɪʃən/
increase /ˈɪnkriːs/
influence /ˈɪnfluəns/
industry /ˈɪndəstri/
isolation /ˌaɪsəˈleɪʃən/
joint venture
market /ˈmɑːkɪt/
modernisation
  /ˌmɒdənaɪˈzeɪʃən/
(have a) monopoly /məˈnɒpəli/
multiculturalism
  /ˌmʌltiˈkʌltʃərəlɪzəm/
percentage /pəˈsentɪdʒ/
population /ˌpɒpjʊˈleɪʃən/
prediction /prɪˈdɪkʃən/
projection /prəˈdʒekʃən/
proportion /prəˈpɔːʃən/
rate /reɪt/
statistics /stəˈtɪstɪks/
trend /trend/

Adjectives
ageing /ˈeɪdʒɪŋ/
current /ˈkʌrənt/
demographic /ˌdeməˈɡræfɪk/
elderly /ˈeldəli/
ethnic /ˈeθnɪk/
exotic /ɪɡˈzɒtɪk/
global /ˈɡləʊbəl/
local /ˈləʊkəl/
long-term /ˌlɒŋˈtɜːm/
mid-term /ˌmɪdˈtɜːm/
multicultural /ˌmʌltiˈkʌltʃərəl/
productive /prəˈdʌktɪv/
sceptical /ˈskeptɪkəl/
short-term /ˌʃɔːtˈtɜːm/
subsequent /ˈsʌbsɪkwənt/
wealthy /ˈwelθi/
worldwide /ˌwɜːldˈwaɪd/

Verbs
compound /ˈkʌmpaʊnd/
contribute /kənˈtrɪbjuːt/
decline /dɪˈklaɪn/
diminish /dɪˈmɪnɪʃ/
dominate /ˈdɒmɪneɪt/
dwindle /ˈdwɪndəl/

factor /ˈfæktə/
indicate /ˈɪndɪkeɪt/
merge /mɜːdʒ/
migrate /maɪˈɡreɪt/

UNIT 14

URBANISATION

Nouns
benefit /ˈbenɪfɪt/
challenge /ˈtʃælɪndʒ/
compromise /ˈkɒmprəmaɪz/
difficulty /ˈdɪfɪkəlti/
dilemma /dɪˈlemə/
inhabitant /ɪnˈhæbɪtənt/
infrastructure /ˈɪnfrəˌstrʌktʃə/
isolation /ˌaɪsəˈleɪʃən/
issue /ˈɪʃuː/
megacity /ˈmeɡəsɪti/
migrant /ˈmaɪɡrənt/
obstacle /ˈɒbstəkəl/
overpopulation
  /ˌəʊvəˌpɒpjʊˈleɪʃən/
population /ˌpɒpjʊˈleɪʃən/
poverty /ˈpɒvəti/
resolution /ˌrezəˈluːʃən/
setback /ˈsetbæk/
slum /slʌm/
solution /səˈluːʃən/
tolerance /ˈtɒlərəns/
traffic /ˈtræfɪk/
urbanisation /ɜːbənaɪˈzeɪʃən/

Adjectives
adequate /ˈædɪkwət/
basic /ˈbeɪsɪk/
booming /ˈbuːmɪŋ/
catastrophic /ˌkætəˈstrɒfɪk/
crowded /ˈkraʊdɪd/
decent /ˈdiːsənt/
developing /dɪˈveləpɪŋ/
double-edged /ˌdʌblˈedʒd/
isolated /ˈaɪsəleɪtɪd/
one-sided /ˌwʌnˈsaɪdɪd/
long-sighted /lɒŋˈsaɪtɪd/
long-term /ˌlɒŋˈtɜːm/
overpriced /ˌəʊvəˈpraɪst/
overworked /ˌəʊvəˈwɜːkt/
pressing /ˈpresɪŋ/
rural /ˈrʊərəl/
short-sighted /ʃɔːtˈsaɪtɪd/
short-term /ˌʃɔːtˈtɜːm/
staggering /ˈstæɡərɪŋ/
tolerant /ˈtɒlərənt/

Verbs
address /əˈdres/
adjust /əˈdʒʌst/
aggravate /ˈæɡrəveɪt/
cause /kɔːz/
compete /kəmˈpiːt/
compound /ˈkʌmpaʊnd/
deal with

deteriorate /dɪˈtɪəriəreɪt/
enhance /ɪnˈhɑːns/
exacerbate /ɪgˈzæsəbeɪt/
exclude /ɪksˈkluːd/
face /feɪs/
flourish /ˈflʌrɪʃ/
identify /aɪˈdentɪfaɪ/
improve /ɪmˈpruːv/
include /ɪnˈkluːd/
linger /ˈlɪŋgə/
modify /ˈmɒdɪfaɪ/
overcome /ˌəʊvəˈkʌm/
present /ˈprezˈənt/
raise /reɪz/
reform /rɪˈfɔːm/
regulate /ˈregjəleɪt/
remedy /ˈremədi/
resolve /rɪˈzɒlv/
tackle /ˈtækəl/
tolerate /ˈtɒləreɪt/
transform /trænsˈfɔːm/
worsen /ˈwɜːsən/

Verb phrases
find a solution
overcome a difficulty
reach/find a compromise
remedy a situation
resolve an issue

UNIT 15

THE GREEN REVOLUTION

Nouns
acid rain /ˈæsɪd reɪn/
biodiversity /ˌbaɪəʊdaɪˈvɜːsəti/
climate change
contamination
  /kənˌtæmɪˈneɪʃən/
deforestation /diːˌfɒrɪˈsteɪʃən/
disposal /dɪˈspəʊzəl/
drought /draʊt/
ecosystem /ˈiːkəʊˌsɪstəm/
emission /ɪˈmɪʃən/
the environment
erosion /ɪˈrəʊʒən/
exhaust (fumes) /ɪgˈzɔːst/
fertiliser /ˈfɜːtɪlaɪzə/
flood /flʌd/
food chain /fuːd tʃeɪn/
fumes /fjuːmz/
greenhouse gases
impact /ˈɪmpækt/
pollutant /pəˈluːtənt/
pollution /pəˈluːʃən/
process /ˈprəʊses/
refuse /ˈrefjuːs/
strain /streɪn/
threat /θret/
waste /weɪst/

Adjectives
achievable /əˈtʃiːvəbl/
advantageous /ˌædvənˈteɪdʒəs/

at risk /æt rɪsk/
beneficial /ˌbenɪˈfɪʃəl/
chronic /ˈkrɒnɪk/
conceivable /kənˈsiːvəbl/
contaminated /kənˈtæmɪneɪtɪd/
devastating /ˈdevəsteɪtɪŋ/
doubtful /ˈdaʊtfəl/
environmental
  /ɪnˌvaɪrənˈmentəl/
environmentally friendly
feasible /ˈfiːzəbl/
fruitless /ˈfruːtləs/
futile /ˈfjuːtaɪl/
immune /ɪˈmjuːn/
impracticable /ɪmˈpræktɪkəbl/
improbable /ɪmˈprɒbəbl/
in danger (of)
insoluble /ɪnˈsɒljəbl/
irreparable /ɪˈrepərəbl/
irreplaceable /ˌɪrɪˈpleɪsəbl/
irreversible /ˌɪrɪˈvɜːsəbl/
liable /ˈlaɪəbl/
life-threatening /ˈlaɪfˌθretənɪŋ/
pervasive /pəˈveɪsɪv/
pointless /ˈpɔɪntləs/
pristine /ˈprɪstiːn/
questionable /ˈkwestʃənəbl/
recyclable /ˌriːˈsaɪkləbl/
sustainable /səˈsteɪnəbl/
taxing /ˈtæksɪŋ/
unattainable /ˌʌnəˈteɪnəbl/
unlikely /ʌnˈlaɪkli/
unprecedented /ʌnˈpresɪdəntɪd/
useless /ˈjuːsləs/
viable /ˈvaɪəbl/
vital /ˈvaɪtəl/
worthwhile /ˌwɜːθˈwaɪl/

Verbs
confront /kənˈfrʌnt/
contaminate /kənˈtæmɪneɪt/
dispose of
dump /dʌmp/
threaten /ˈθretən/

Adverbs
inexorably /ɪˈneksərəbli/
inevitably /ɪˈnevɪtəbli/

UNIT 16

THE ENERGY CRISIS

Nouns
atmosphere /ˈætməsfɪə/
balance /ˈbæləns/
biofuel /ˈbaɪəʊfjuəl/
carbon /ˈkɑːbən/
carbon dioxide /ˈkɑːbən
  daɪˈɒksaɪd/
crisis /ˈkraɪsɪs/
electricity /ˌɪlekˈtrɪsɪti/
emissions /ɪˈmɪʃənz/
exhaust /ɪgˈzɔːst/
fossil fuel /ˈfɒsəl ˈfjuːəl/

fuel /ˈfjuːəl/
fumes /fjuːmz/
gas /gæs/
greenhouse gas /ˈgriːnhaʊs gæs/
hybrid /ˈhaɪbrɪd/
hydrogen /ˈhaɪdrədʒən/
petrol /ˈpetrəl/
resources /rɪˈzɔːsɪz/
turbine /ˈtɜːbaɪn/
vehicle /ˈvɪəkəl/

Adjectives
alternative /ɒlˈtɜːnətɪv/
critical /ˈkrɪtɪkəl/
disposable /dɪˈspəʊzəbl/
drastic /ˈdræstɪk/
eco-friendly /ˈiːkəʊˌfrendli/
effective /ɪˈfektɪv/
efficient /ɪˈfɪʃənt/
environmentally friendly
nuclear /ˈnjuːkliə/
rechargeable /riːˈtʃɑːdʒəbl/
renewable /rɪˈnjuːəbl/
solar /ˈsəʊlə/
unleaded (petrol) /ʌnˈledɪd/

Verbs
absorb /əbˈzɔːb/
conserve /kənˈsɜːv/
consume /kənˈsjuːm/
convert /kʌnˈvɜːt/
counter /ˈkaʊntə/
deplete /dɪˈpliːt/
diminish /dɪˈmɪnɪʃ/
discharge /dɪsˈtʃɑːdʒ/
dwindle /ˈdwɪndəl/
emit /ɪˈmɪt/
expend /ɪkˈspend/
limit /ˈlɪmɪt/
maintain /meɪnˈteɪn/
outweigh /ˌaʊtˈweɪ/
preserve /prɪˈzɜːv/
retain /rɪˈteɪn/
waste /weɪst/

UNIT 17

TALKING BUSINESS

Nouns
advertisement /ədˈvɜːtɪsmənt/
advertising /ˈædvətaɪzɪŋ/
boss /bɒs/
campaign /kæmˈpeɪn/
candidate /ˈkændɪdət/
career /kəˈrɪə/
clerk /klɑːk/
client /ˈklaɪənt/
colleague /ˈkɒliːg/
company /ˈkʌmpəni/
consumer /kənˈsjuːmə/
credibility /ˌkredəˈbɪləti/
customer /ˈkʌstəmə/
earnings /ˈɜːnɪŋz/
employee /ɪmˈplɔɪiː/

employer /ɪmˈplɔɪə/
employment /ɪmˈplɔɪmənt/
experience /ɪkˈspɪəriəns/
goods /gʊdz/
income /ˈɪnkʌm/
industry /ˈɪndəstri/
interview /ˈɪntəvjuː/
job /dʒɒb/
job satisfaction
labourer /ˈleɪbərə/
management /ˈmænɪdʒmənt/
manual work /ˈmænjuəl wɜːk/
market /ˈmɑːkɪt/
marketing /ˈmɑːkɪtɪŋ/
meeting /ˈmiːtɪŋ/
money /ˈmʌni/
niche /niːʃ/
occupation /ˌɒkjəˈpeɪʃən/
office /ˈɒfɪs/
overtime /ˈəʊvətaɪm/
packaging /ˈpækɪdʒɪŋ/
pay /peɪ/
perk /pɜːk/
product /ˈprɒdʌkt/
profession /prəˈfeʃən/
prospects /ˈprɒspekts/
qualifications /ˌkwɒlɪfɪˈkeɪʃənz/
retirement /rɪˈtaɪəmənt/
salary /ˈsæləri/
shares /ʃeəz/
shift work /ʃɪft wɜːk/
skills /skɪlz/
staff /stɑːf/
supervisor /ˈsuːpəvaɪzə/
takeover /ˈteɪkˌəʊvə/
target /ˈtɑːgɪt/
trade /treɪd/
trend /trend/
unemployment /ˌʌnɪmˈplɔɪmənt/
wages /ˈweɪdʒɪz/
workforce /ˈwɜːkfɔːs/
workplace /ˈwɜːkpleɪs/

Adjectives
casual /ˈkæʒuəl/
demanding /dɪˈmɑːndɪŋ/
economic /ˌiːkəˈnɒmɪk/
economical /ˌiːkəˈnɒmɪkəl/
exhausting /ɪgˈzɔːstɪŋ/
hospitality /ˌhɒspɪˈtæləti/
monotonous /məˈnɒtənəs/
part-time /ˌpɑːtˈtaɪm/
retail /ˈriːteɪl/
redundant /rɪˈdʌndənt/
rewarding /rɪˈwɔːdɪŋ/
unemployed /ˌʌnɪmˈplɔɪd/
unskilled /ʌnˈskɪld/

Verbs
apply /əˈplaɪ/
compete /kəmˈpiːt/
earn /ɜːn/
endorse /ɪnˈdɔːs/
invest (in) /ɪnˈvest/
persuade /pəˈsweɪd/

to be promoted
request /rɪˈkwest/
retire /rɪˈtaɪə/

UNIT 18

THE LAW

Nouns

actions /ˈækʃənz/
arson /ˈɑːsən/
authority /ɔːˈθɒrəti/
burglary /ˈbɜːgləri/
consequences /ˈkɒnsɪkwənsɪz/
convict /ˈkɒnvɪkt/
crime /kraɪm/
crime rate /kraɪm reɪt/
criminal /ˈkrɪmɪnəl/
deterrent /dɪˈterənt/
evidence /ˈevɪdəns/
fine /faɪn/
fraud /frɔːd/
imprisonment /ɪmˈprɪzənmənt/
inequality /ˌɪnɪˈkwɒləti/
intent /ɪnˈtent/
intrusion /ɪnˈtruːʒən/
judge /dʒʌdʒ/
jury /ˈdʒʊəri/
kidnapping /ˈkɪdnæpɪŋ/
lawyer /ˈlɔɪə/
motive /ˈməʊtɪv/
murder /ˈmɜːdə/
offence /əˈfens/
pickpocketing /ˈpɪkpɒkɪtɪŋ/
prevention /prɪˈvenʃən/
prison /ˈprɪzən/
prisoner /ˈprɪzənə/
property crime /ˈprɒpəti kraɪm/
prosecutor /ˈprɒsɪkjuːtə/
protection /prəˈtekʃən/
punishment /ˈpʌnɪʃmənt/
recklessness /ˈrekləsnəs/
smuggling /ˈsmʌglɪŋ/
social system /ˈsəʊʃəl ˈsɪstəm/
swearing /ˈsweərɪŋ/
the accused
toxic waste /ˈtɒksɪk weɪst/
vandalism /ˈvændəlɪzəm/
victim /ˈvɪktɪm/
violation /ˌvaɪəˈleɪʃən/

Adjectives

criminal /ˈkrɪmɪnəl/
drug-related /drʌg rɪˈleɪtɪd/
evil /ˈiːvəl/
guilty /ˈgɪlti/
harsh /hɑːʃ/
innocent /ˈɪnəsənt/
intentional /ɪnˈtenʃənəl/
law-abiding /ˈlɔːəˌbaɪdɪŋ/
non-violent /ˌnɒnˈvaɪələnt/
offensive /əˈfensɪv/
on trial /ɒn traɪəl/

petty (crime) /ˈpeti/
punishable /ˈpʌnɪʃəbl/
random /ˈrændəm/
strict /strɪkt/
unintentional /ˌʌnɪnˈtenʃənəl/
victimless /ˈvɪktɪmləs/

Verbs

abide (by) /əˈbaɪd/
abolish /əˈbɒlɪʃ/
combat /ˈkɒmbæt/
deter /dɪˈtɜː/
enforce /ɪnˈfɔːs/
imprison /ɪmˈprɪzən/
monitor /ˈmɒnɪtə/
obey /əˈbeɪ/
offend /əˈfend/
perpetrate /ˈpɜːpɪtreɪt/
prevent /prɪˈvent/
protect /prəˈtekt/
prove /pruːv/
punish /ˈpʌnɪʃ/
resent /rɪˈzent/
respect /rɪˈspekt/
violate /ˈvaɪəleɪt/

Verb phrases

accept the consequences
commit a crime
convict a criminal
impose a fine
pass a law
solve a crime

UNIT 19

THE MEDIA

Nouns

access /ˈækses/
attitude /ˈætɪtjuːd/
author /ˈɔːθə/
bias /ˈbaɪəs/
censorship /ˈsensəʃɪp/
challenge /ˈtʃælɪndʒ/
credibility /ˌkredəˈbɪləti/
current affairs /ˈkʌrənt əˈfeəz/
editor /ˈedɪtə/
exposé /ekˈspəʊzeɪ/
exposure /ɪkˈspəʊʒə/
fame /feɪm/
free press /friː pres/
ideology /ˌaɪdiˈɒlədʒi/
influence /ˈɪnfluəns/
the internet
investigation /ɪnˌvestɪˈgeɪʃən/
issue /ˈɪʃuː/
journal /ˈdʒɜːnəl/
journalism /ˈdʒɜːnəlɪzəm/
mainstream media
mass media /mæs ˈmiːdiə/
media /ˈmiːdiə/
network /ˈnetwɜːk/
the news
newspaper /ˈnjuːsˌpeɪpə/

newsstand /ˈnjuːzstænd/
opinion /əˈpɪnjən/
paparazzi /ˌpæpəˈrætsi/
press /pres/
privacy /ˈprɪvəsi/
publication /ˌpʌblɪˈkeɪʃən/
publicity /pʌbˈlɪsəti/
publisher /ˈpʌblɪʃə/
relevance /ˈreləvəns/
safeguard /ˈseɪfgɑːd/
source /sɔːs/
speculation /ˌspekjəˈleɪʃən/
tabloid /ˈtæblɔɪd/

Adjectives

alternative /ɒlˈtɜːnətɪv/
artificial /ˌɑːtɪˈfɪʃəl/
attention-grabbing /əˈtenʃən
ˈgræbɪŋ/
biased /ˈbaɪəst/
celebrity /səˈlebrəti/
controversial /ˌkɒntrəˈvɜːʃəl/
distorted /dɪˈstɔːtɪd/
entertaining /ˌentəˈteɪnɪŋ/
factual /ˈfæktʃuəl/
informative /ɪnˈfɔːmətɪv/
intrusive /ɪnˈtruːsɪv/
investigative /ɪnˈvestɪgətɪv/
mainstream /ˈmeɪnstriːm/
online /ˈɒnlaɪn/
pervasive /pəˈveɪsɪv/
realistic /ˌrɪəˈlɪstɪk/
sensationalist /senˈseɪʃənəlɪst/
superficial /ˌsuːpəˈfɪʃəl/
unbiased /ʌnˈbaɪəst/
up-to-date
well-informed /ˌwelɪnˈfɔːmd/

Verbs

affect /əˈfekt/
broadcast /ˈbrɔːdkɑːst/
censor /ˈsensə/
control /kənˈtrəʊl/
exploit /eksˈplɔɪt/
expose /ɪkˈspəʊz/
inform /ɪnˈfɔːm/
intrude /ɪnˈtruːd/
invade /ɪnˈveɪd/
investigate /ɪnˈvestɪgeɪt/
publicise /ˈpʌblɪsaɪz/
publish /ˈpʌblɪʃ/
report /rɪˈpɔːt/
review /rɪˈvjuː/
verify /ˈverɪfaɪ/

UNIT 20

THE ARTS

Nouns

actor /ˈæktə/
actress /ˈæktrəs/
aesthetics /iːsˈθetɪks/
appreciation /əˌpriːʃiˈeɪʃən/

artist /ˈɑːtɪst/
atmosphere /ˈætməsfɪə/
attention /əˈtenʃ(ə)n/
audience /ˈɔːdiəns/
awe /ɔː/
ballerina /ˌbæləˈriːnə/
ballet /ˈbæleɪ/
carving /ˈkɑːvɪŋ/
concert /ˈkɒnsət/
crafts /krɑːfts/
creation /kriˈeɪʃən/
culture /ˈkʌltʃə/
emotion /ɪˈməʊʃən/
exhibition /ˌeksɪˈbɪʃən/
expression /ɪkˈspreʃən/
festival /ˈfestɪvəl/
gallery /ˈgæləri/
image /ˈɪmɪdʒ/
imagination /ɪˌmædʒɪˈneɪʃən/
influence /ˈɪnfluəns/
inspiration /ˌɪnspɪˈreɪʃən/
intimacy /ˈɪntɪməsi/
literature /ˈlɪtrətʃə/
mood /muːd/
musician /mjuːˈzɪʃən/
opera /ˈɒpərə/
orchestra /ˈɔːkɪstrə/
painting /ˈpeɪntɪŋ/
performance /pəˈfɔːməns/
the performing arts
play /pleɪ/
portrait /ˈpɔːtreɪt/
proportion /prəˈpɔːʃən/
response /rɪˈspɒns/
sculptor /ˈskʌlptə/
sculpture /ˈskʌlptʃə/
sensation /senˈseɪʃ(ə)n/
sense /sens/
stimulus /ˈstɪmjələs/
style /staɪl/
taste /teɪst/
theatre /ˈθɪətə/
theme /θiːm/
venue /ˈvenjuː/
version /ˈvɜː(r)ʃ(ə)n/
works /wɜːks/
writer /ˈraɪtə/

Adjectives

abstract /ˈæbstrækt/
accomplished /əˈkʌmplɪʃt/
aesthetic /iːsˈθetɪk/
awe-inspiring
brightly coloured
classical /ˈklæsɪkəl/
creative /kriˈeɪtɪv/
cultural /ˈkʌltʃərəl/
distracting /dɪˈstræktɪŋ/
eclectic /ekˈlektɪk/
electric /ɪˈlektrɪk/
emotional /ɪˈməʊʃənəl/
fundamental /ˌfʌndəˈmentəl/
imaginative /ɪˈmædʒɪnətɪv/
influential /ˌɪnfluˈenʃəl/

inspirational /ˌɪnspɪˈreɪʃənəl/
interactive /ˌɪntəˈæktɪv/
literary /ˈlɪtərəri/
live /laɪv/
magical /ˈmædʒɪkəl/
monotonous /məˈnɒtənəs/
novel /ˈnɒv(ə)l/
passionate /ˈpæʃənət/
popular /ˈpɒpjələ/
prominent /ˈprɒmɪnənt/
relaxing /rɪˈlæksɪŋ/
traditional /trəˈdɪʃ(ə)nəl/
stimulating /ˈstɪmjəleɪtɪŋ/
viral /ˈvaɪrəl/
visual /ˈvɪʒuəl/
vivid /ˈvɪvɪd/

Verbs
appreciate /əˈpriːʃiˌeɪt/
artistic /ɑː(r)ˈtɪstɪk/
attract /əˈtrækt/
create /kriˈeɪt/
decorate /ˈdekəreɪt/
depict /dɪˈpɪkt/
enrich /ɪnˈrɪtʃ/
escape /ɪˈskeɪp/
imagine /ɪˈmædʒɪn/
imitate /ˈɪmɪteɪt/
influence /ˈɪnfluəns/
inspire /ɪnˈspaɪə/
participate /pɑːˈtɪsɪpeɪt/
perform /pəˈfɔːm/
provoke /prəˈvəʊk/

Acknowledgements

The author and publishers are grateful to the following reviewers for their valuable insights and suggestions:

Sean Choi, Anthony Cosgrove; Maria Heron; Julie King; David Larbalestier, Simon Raw, Bruce Williams; Judith Wilson; Carole Allsop; Susan Kingsley.

The authors and publishers acknowledge the following sources of copyright material and are grateful for the permissions granted. While every effort has been made, it has not always been possible to identify the sources of all the material used, or to trace all copyright holders. If any omissions are brought to our notice, we will be happy to include the appropriate acknowledgements on reprinting and in the next update to the digital edition, as applicable.

Key: U = Unit.

Text

U4: Text adapted from 'UF researcher leisure activities defy simple classifications' by Cathy Keen, from Science Daily, www.sciencedaily.com. Copyright © Science Daily LLC. Reproduced with permission; **U6**: Text adapted from 'Signs of Success' 19 February 2004. Copyright © The Economist Newspaper Limited. Reproduced with permission; Text adapted from 'First words: let's stick together' by Richard Fullagar, Nature Australia, Autumn 2004. Copyright © Australian Museum 2006. Reproduced with permission; **U11:** Text adapted from 'The home of the future, then and now' by Sheryl N Hamilton, Canadian Home Economics Journal, March 2003. Copyright © 2007 CNET Networks Inc. Reproduced with permission; **U14**: Text adapted from 'Rags, bones and recycling bins' by Tim Cooper, History Today, February 2006. Copyright © History Today. Reproduced with permission; **U18**: Text adapted from 'Crime' from The World of Sociology, Thomson Learning. Copyright © 2002 The Gale Group. Reproduced with permission; **U20**: Text adapted from 'Brain of the beholder' by David Sokol, Cosmos Magazine, February/March 2007. Copyright © Luna Media Pty Ltd, all rights reserved. Reproduced with permission; Text adapted from 'Storytelling – Narratives of the mind' by Dr Tom Sjöblom, University of Helsinki; **U21**: Text extracts from the word 'choice' from Cambridge Advanced Learner's Dictionary, 2005, Cambridge University Press; **U23**: US Environmental Protection Agency for the graph, 'National Recycling Rates, 1960 – 2005', www.epa.gov.

Photography

The following images have been sourced from Getty Images.

U4: gbh007/iStock/Getty Images Plus; Prakasit Khuansuwan/EyeEm; **U7**: Tony Burns; **U8**: Nicholas Eveleig/DigitalVision; Jason Hawke/Corbis NX / Getty Images Plus; **U9**: GlobalP/iStock/Getty Images Plus; bradleyblackburn/iStock/Getty Images Plus; phototropic/E+; levkr/iStock/Getty Images Plus; Zoya2222/iStock/Getty Images Plus; goldhafen/E+; Rosemary Calvert/Stone; Francisco Grande/500px; © Jackie Bale/Moment Open; **U10**: Leonello Calvetti/Stocktrek Images/Stocktrek Images; **U12**: thawornnurak/iStock/Getty Images Plus; **U14**: Levi Bianco/Moment; Sascha Kilmer/Moment; **U19**: vm/Slovenia; **U20**: dimapf/iStock/Getty Images Plus; EmirMemedovski/E+; ZU_09/DigitalVision Vectors; Hill Street Studios/DigitalVision; Juanmonino/iStock/Getty Images Plus; Hill Street Studios/DigitalVision; Gilmanshin/iStock/Getty Images Plus.

Illustration

Robert Calow, Mark Duffin, Karen Donnelly, Dylan Gibson, Julian Mosedale, Roger Penwill.

Audio

Audio production by Dan Strauss.

Typesetting

Typeset by QBS Learning.

tracklist